THE ORIGINAL ATHEISTS

Also by S. T. JOSHI

The Unbelievers

The Agnostic Reader

God's Defenders

Atheism: A Reader

THE ORIGINAL ATHEISTS

FIRST THOUGHTS ON NONBELIEF

Edited By S. T. JOSHI

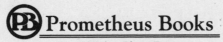 **Prometheus Books**

59 John Glenn Drive
Amherst, New York 14228

Published 2014 by Prometheus Books

Cover design by Nicole Sommer-Lecht

Inquiries should be addressed to
Prometheus Books
59 John Glenn Drive
Amherst, New York 14228
VOICE: 716–691–0133
FAX: 716–691–0137
WWW.PROMETHEUSBOOKS.COM

18 17 16 15 14   5 4 3 2 1

Library of Congress Cataloging-in-Publication Data

The original atheists : first thoughts on nonbelief / edited by S.T. Joshi.
    pages cm
  Includes bibliographical references and index.
  ISBN 978-1-61614-841-6 (pbk.)
  ISBN 978-1-61614-842-3 (ebook)
  1. Atheism. 2. Atheists. I. Joshi, S. T., 1958- editor of compilation.

BL2747.3.O57 2014
211'.80922--dc23

                                     2013031770

Printed in the United States of America

CONTENTS

INTRODUCTION

The first atheist of whom we know is one Diagoras, who lived in the late fifth century BCE. It is typical that nothing of his works aside from random fragments survives and that he was forced to flee Athens because he declared that there were no gods. Even in the ages preceding Christianity, the enunciation of explicitly atheistic, or even agnostic, views carried with it the threat of both legal punishment and social obloquy. It is therefore unsurprising that, once Christianity gained ascendancy in the Roman Empire (in the early fourth century CE), avowed atheists were few and far between. All that changed with the dawn of the eighteenth century in Europe, and the following question must be asked: Why? More pertinently, Why now?

The answers are multitudinous and complex but can be boiled down to two important developments that had occurred over the preceding several centuries. The Renaissance that began in the late fourteenth and early fifteenth centuries generated two discrete but parallel intellectual movements—the advance of science and the rediscovery of classical learning. The former is perhaps the better known, but it is still worth underscoring. There is scarcely any question that the revolutionary findings of such thinkers as Copernicus, Kepler, and Galileo had the effect of knocking the earth and its occupants from both physical and moral centrality in the universe. If our planet was only a tiny atom in the midst of a virtually boundless array of stars, galaxies, and nebulae, then it became harder to believe that a god had specifically designed the earth for a chosen species called human beings. Complementary developments in other sciences had the effect of replacing *supernatural causation* with *natural causation*: increasingly, God was no longer required to explain the workings of the universe or the creation and development of natural organisms. All this work culminated in the discoveries of Sir Isaac Newton (1642–1727), who became a kind of intellectual icon who was thought to have explained the workings of the universe once and for all. It was the deist Alexander Pope who deliberately evoked (and, indeed, gently parodied) religious imagery in describing Newton's achievements:

Nature and Nature's Laws lay hid in Night:
God said, *Let Newton be!* and all was Light.[1]

The second development—the resuscitation of classical learning—had a somewhat more indirect role in the growing secularism of the age, but it was ultimately no less significant. In the medieval era, only Plato and Aristotle were read and studied—chiefly, in Plato's case, for the fancied similarities of his ethical views to those of Christianity, and, in Aristotle's, for purportedly supplying the logical foundation for Christian metaphysical thought. The great majority of "pagan" writers from the Greco-Roman period were shunned as benighted figures who had failed to benefit from Christian teaching. Dante may have fetishized Virgil as his spiritual leader in the *Divine Comedy*, but less superficially Christian writers were under the ban. The Renaissance, however, had rediscovered the thought of such thinkers as the pre-Socratics (including Leucippus and Democritus, the founders of atomism), the Stoics (also in some regards considered forerunners of Christian moral belief), and in particular Epicurus and his Roman disciple Lucretius. The Epicurean belief that the gods lived in the spaces between the stars and, in their perfection, had no concern or involvement with a flawed humanity, was an intriguing hypothesis; it was not surprising that, even in antiquity, the Epicureans were considered closet atheists. It didn't hurt that Lucretius had expounded Epicureanism with extraordinary panache in his long poem *De Rerum Natura* (first century BCE), with lengthy sections on the utter extinction of consciousness upon the death of the body, the natural origin of human and other life on earth, and other topics that would become the cornerstones of atheistic, agnostic, and deist thought in the centuries to come. His pungent line *"Tantum religio potuit suadere malorum"* (1.101: "How many evils can religion engender!") was not overlooked.

While there were skeptics and agnostics prior to the eighteenth century, they remained solitary and isolated figures: Michel de Montaigne (1533–1592) was perhaps the most noteworthy, his pregnant utterance *"Que scais-je?"* ("What do I know?") becoming the epitome of skepticism. Let us recall that Michael Servetus (1509?–1553), Giordano Bruno (1548–1600), and any number of other figures were executed for expressing heterodox views: any open declaration of atheism would have been a one-way ticket to the stake.

The seventeenth century laid the groundwork for the secularism to come. Galileo's humiliation by the Inquisition in 1633—he was forced to declare that the sun revolved around the earth, even though he knew better—generated outrage at such an infringement of intellectual freedom. At about the same time, Sir Francis Bacon was laying down the outlines of philosophical empiricism with such works as *The Advancement of Learning* (1605) and *Novum Organum* (1620). Thomas Hobbes, in *Leviathan* (1651) and other works, proclaimed a resolute materialism that saw even God and the human soul as material entities; as a result, he was frequently branded an atheist, even though he rejected the accusation. In France, Descartes and his followers championed deductive reasoning in their Cartesian philosophy; nominally, Descartes claimed that this methodology allowed for a proof of the existence of God on rationalist grounds, but his searching inquiry into the grounds for belief of any proposition, however self-evident, had broader ramifications than he himself realized. It was at this time that the tormented Christian Blaise Pascal expressed, in his *Pensées* (1669), a searing doubt about the truths of the Christian revelation that no doubt echoed that of many of his contemporaries.

In the late seventeenth century, Pierre Bayle (1647–1706) was a pioneer of skepticism. His multivolume *Dictionnaire historique et critique* (1695–97) not only revealed a prodigious learning in science, history, and religion, but also expressed severe doubts about the role of religion in political and social life and frankly advocated religious toleration. The work was manifestly a precursor, from many perspectives, to the *Encyclopédie* (1751–72) of Diderot and d'Alembert.

And yet, in a real sense, the French Enlightenment of the eighteenth century, whose intellectual luminaries were so numerous and so vocal, had its origin in England. Bacon was manifestly a revered ancestor of the scientific method, and John Locke's *Essay concerning Human Understanding* (1690) was a grand summation of empiricism in much the same way that Newton's work summed up current thinking on astronomy and physics. Deism, the dominant "religion" of Enlightenment thinkers, also originated in England, with such figures as Charles Blount (*The Oracles of Reason*, 1695), John Toland (*Christianity Not Mysterious*, 1696), Anthony Collins (*A Discourse of Free-Thinking*, 1713), and numerous others. The main thrust of these works was the discounting of the "miracles" of the Bible, which were increasingly seen as implausible and even unworthy of belief: a God who had presumably designed the natural world as a smoothly running machine would, it was believed, never stoop to such legerdemain as stopping the sun in its tracks (as in the tale of Joshua) or even permitting Jesus to walk on water. With Newton and others confirming the unvarying regularity of Nature, God was left as a kind of Epicurean figure who had started the mechanism at the beginning of time and lay back to admire his handiwork without further intervening in human affairs. This line of thought culminated in David Hume's celebrated essay "Of Miracles" (1748), although it was also reflected in Conyers Middleton's influential treatise *A Free Inquiry into the Miraculous Powers* (1749).

With the dawn of the eighteenth century, all these tendencies fused into open or at least veiled expressions of atheism. Even if the renegade ex-priest Jean Meslier (1664–1729) was something of an outlier in the ferocity of his condemnation of Christianity and of religion in general, other thinkers were not slow to declare themselves religious skeptics. Among the thinkers included in this book, Meslier, d'Holbach, Diderot, Hume, and Bentham can, with fair certainty, be called atheists; most of the others were deists, secularists, or doubters. It is also possible that some of these, among many others, resisted any *public* declaration of atheism because of the threat of legal penalties. In many of their writings, these thinkers exhibit an outward respect toward religion in general and Christianity in particular while delivering pungent and fatal blows to its central arguments.

One of the means by which religious doctrine was questioned was by the new field of anthropology, practiced by thinkers in both France and England. A renewed focus on the study of history, reaching back into the earliest stages of primitive human life, suggested that religion and its appurtenances— ritual, divination, and so on—were natural products of a stage of primitive existence whereby human beings were confronted with natural forces whose operation they failed to understand, and which they thereby attributed to the work of superhuman entities. The chapter from Etienne Bonnot de Condillac's *Treatise on Systems* (1749), printed here, is a penetrating investigation of this subject, and it also was utilized in what is without doubt the most exhaustive treatise on atheism written in that century, and perhaps any century—that is, d'Holbach's *System of Nature* (1770). It is true that these thinkers could not draw upon much fieldwork in their anthropological arguments, which accordingly remained largely theoretical; but this work—culminating in David Hume's *Natural History of Religion* (1757)—proved to be remarkably prescient and was substantially confirmed a century or more later when such anthropologists as Edward Burnett Tylor (*Primitive Culture*, 1871) presented very similar arguments.

The study of history damaged respect for religion in other regards, by questioning its role in the course of human affairs. Montesquieu (Charles-Louis de Secondat, Baron de La Brède et de Montesquieu, 1689–1755) praised Christianity lavishly in *The Spirit of Laws* (1748) but condemned the Inquisition. In England, Edward Gibbon's *Decline and Fall of the Roman Empire* (1776–88) saw in Christianity the chief culprit in the fall of the Roman Empire. And Condorcet (Marie Jean Antoine Nicolas de Caritat, marquis de Condorcet, 1743–1794), in *Sketch of an Historical Picture of the Progress of the Human Spirit* (1795), saw an inexorable historical progression from the barbarism of medieval Christianity to the rationalism of his day.

The one significant obstacle toward a fully viable atheistic view of the universe—or, more specifically, of the operation of natural forces on this planet—was the perceived validity of the argument from design. This argument—that the phenomena of earthly life, and in particular those of the human organism, show such a congruence between means and ends that they must have been designed by an intelligent and all-powerful entity—was what largely prevented Voltaire from becoming a full-fledged atheist. The best that other thinkers—such as La Mattrie in *Man a Machine* (1748)—could do was merely to assert that Nature (now virtually personified, especially among deists) could in fact have engendered the human eye, the human hand, and other objects that seem superficially to have required a creator-god. Kant, in the *Critique of Pure Reason* (1781), simply declared that the argument from design was insufficient to establish the existence of a deity, but that is as far as he could go. It required the theory of evolution to destroy the argument once and for all, although it continues to rear its head implausibly and fallaciously in the contemporary "intelligent design" movement.

The relationship between religion and the state was the subject of abundant discussion among Enlightenment thinkers, especially in France. This is because the Catholic Church still occupied a position of unique centrality within the French polity. The clergy was considered the First Estate, and it had immense wealth and power. Voltaire's polemical works on religion (including his satires, such as *La Pucelle* [1755], a bawdy satire on Joan of Arc) were repeatedly condemned by the state and the church and were regularly banned, forcing him to publish many of his works anonymously or pseudonymously.

Once again, the French in particular looked to England as a model for the proper role of religion within the state. England had never engaged in the religious wars that, in the seventeenth century, had ravaged continental Europe and done much to create revulsion in intellectuals who were appalled at the idea of waging war over arcane points of religious doctrine. It is true that England (and more particularly Scotland, under the influence of rigid Presbyterians) had participated to some degree in the witchcraft trials that, in Europe, caused hundreds of thousands of men, women, and children to be executed. But following the Glorious Revolution of 1688, the Anglican Church in England was largely defanged, and French *philosophes* could only look with envy at the relative powerlessness of the established church in England. When, in 1762, the French church engaged in such a spasm of barbarity as the execution of Jean Calas (a Protestant who was accused of murdering his son because he had suspected him of secretly converting to Roman Catholicism), Voltaire immediately responded with the *Treatise on Toleration* (1763). Admittedly, Voltaire placed no particular emphasis on the need to preserve the separation of church and state; nor, like Pierre Bayle, did he defend tolerance on the grounds of individual liberty of conscience. Following contemporary British example, which gradually removed civil disabilities from dissenters but still prohibited individuals who were not members of the Church of England from holding public office or even from practicing their religion openly, Voltaire presented the case for toleration as a means of maintaining social order: an established church is not in itself an evil, so long as it is not fanatical, superstitious, or intolerant.

These and similar arguments undoubtedly had their effect on a core group of American Enlightenment thinkers as they were nurturing the birth of their country. Notwithstanding the tendentious polemics of certain pious historians, past and present, there is little doubt that such figures as Thomas Jefferson and James Madison were thorough skeptics and deists whose understanding of history made it clear to them that the United States must avoid the intertwining of religion and the state, for the benefit of both religion and the state. This is why Madison, in "Memorial and Remonstrance against Religious Assessments" (1784–85), warned that even the minimal infringement of religious liberty that was being proposed by the Virginia state legislature (a small tax to support "teachers of the Christian religion") was an opening wedge that could lead to tyranny. His thoughts on the issue led to the passage of the First Amendment, the strongest guarantee of religious freedom in modern history.

To be sure, not all thinkers in the eighteenth century were atheists or secularists. The most significant exception was perhaps Jean-Jacques Rousseau, a devout Christian who was nonetheless sufficiently heterodox in several of his opinions that some of his works—such as *Émile* (1762), advocating religious toleration—were condemned in both Catholic France and Calvinist Geneva. Many American political figures, such as George Washington and John Adams, were pious in varying degrees, although they too recognized the virtues of separating church from state. But it is undeniable that the freethinkers of the French, German, British, and American Enlightenments— both by their challenging writings and by the courage with which many of them defied persecution by religious bodies that had the power to condemn, exile, and even execute them—laid the intellectual groundwork for the atheists of succeeding centuries. Their work remains vital, not least because of the vigor and fearlessness with which it took on the forces of religion and combated them with a bracing mix of reason, passion, and satire. As such, they set an example that we would do well to follow.

A NOTE ON THIS EDITION

This volume presents substantial selections from leading French, German, English, and American thinkers of the eighteenth and early nineteenth centuries on the subject of religion. In the case of the selections from French and German thinkers, I have generally used translations in the public domain but have substantially revised these translations by consultation with the original texts and in the interests of presenting more up-to-date renditions. In the case of the British and American selections, I have generally preserved archaic usages in order to give readers a sense of the flavor of the original documents, although in a few cases I have modified some typographical usages (such as excessive use of italics) for ease of reading. I have preserved some, but not all, of the footnotes contained in the original texts; these are carefully identified as the work of the authors. All other footnotes not so identified are my own.

In writing the notes, I have sought to clarify historical, philosophical, and other cultural references that may not be familiar to the general reader. I have also supplied headnotes providing background on the authors and their works and a bibliography at the end of the volume providing citations for further reading about the general topic of this book and on the individual authors.

PART 1

THE FRENCH
AND GERMAN
ENLIGHTENMENTS

From *Testament* (1729)

JEAN MESLIER

[Jean Meslier (1664–1729) was a French Catholic priest serving in the town of Étrépigny, in Champagne. Seemingly devout and selfless (he lived in poverty, giving much of his income to the poor), he created a posthumous furor when an immense tract titled *Testament* was found soon after his death. This document not only repudiated Christianity in all its particulars but also religious faith in general, even that of the deists; accordingly, this work has been seen as the first full-length treatise advocating atheism. In 1762, Voltaire published an abstract of the *Testament*, adding material of his own. A volume published in 1772 titled *Le Bon Sens* (*Common Sense*) was attributed to Meslier but is in fact the work of Baron d'Holbach. In the following extract (part of what Voltaire published in 1762), Meslier heaps scorn on the obviously false prophecies of the Old and New Testaments and points out other absurdities in scripture.]

OF THE FALSITY OF THE CHRISTIAN RELIGION

Let us proceed to the pretended visions and divine revelations upon which our Christ-worshippers establish the truth and certainty of their religion.

In order to give a just idea of it, I believe it is best to say in general that they are such that if any one should now dare to boast of similar ones, or wish to make them valued, he would certainly be regarded as a fool or a fanatic.

Here is what the pretended visions and divine revelations are:

God, as these pretended Holy Books claim, having appeared for the first time to Abraham, said to him: "Get thee out of thy country, and from thy kindred, and from thy father's house, unto a land that I will show thee" [Gen. 12:1]. Abraham, having gone there, God, says the Bible, appeared a second time to him, and said, "'Unto thy seed will I give this land,' and there builded he an altar unto the Lord, who appeared unto him" [Gen. 12:7]. After the death of Isaac, his son, Jacob going one day to Mesopotamia to look for a suitable wife, having walked all the day and being tired from the long distance, wanted to rest toward evening. Lying upon the ground, with his head resting upon a few stones, he fell asleep, and during his sleep he saw a ladder set upon the earth, and the top of it reached to Heaven; and beheld the angels of God ascending and descending on it. "And behold, the Lord stood above it, and said: 'I am the Lord, God of Abraham, thy father, and the God of Isaac; the land whereon thou liest, to thee will I give it, and to thy seed. And thy seed shall be as the dust of the earth, and thou shalt spread abroad to the west and to the east, and to the north and to the south: and in thee and in thy seed shall all the nations of the earth be blessed. And behold, I am with thee and will keep thee in all places whither thou goest, and will bring thee again into this land: for I will not leave thee until I have done that which I have spoken to thee of.' And Jacob awaked out of his sleep, and he said, 'Surely the Lord is in this place; and I knew it not.' And he was afraid, and said, 'How dreadful is this place! this is none other than the house of God, and this is the gate of Heaven.' And Jacob rose up early in the morning, and took the stone that he had put for his pillow, and set it up for a pillar, and poured oil upon the top of it" [Gen. 28:13–18], and made at the same time a vow to God, that if he should return safe and sound, he would give Him a tithe of all he might possess.

Here is yet another vision. Watching the flocks of his father-in-law, Laban, who had promised him that all the speckled lambs produced by his sheep should be his recompense, he dreamed one night that he saw all the males leap upon the females, and all the lambs they brought forth were speckled. In this beautiful dream, God appeared to him, and said: "Lift up now thine eyes, and see, all the rams which leap upon the cattle are ring-streaked, speckled, and grizzled; for I have seen all that Laban doeth unto thee. . . . Now arise, get thee out from this land, and return unto the land of thy kindred" [Gen. 31:12–13]. As he was returning with his whole family, and with everything he obtained from his father-in-law, he had, says the Bible, a wrestle with an unknown man during the whole night, until the next morning, and as this man had not been able to subdue him, he asked him who he was. Jacob told him his name; and he said: "Thy name shall be called no more Jacob, but Israel; for as a prince hast thou power with God and with men, and hast prevailed" [Gen. 31:28].

This is a specimen of the first of these pretended visions and divine revelations. We can judge of the others by these. Now, what appearance of Divinity is there in dreams so gross and illusions so vain? As if some foreigners, Germans, for instance, should come into our France and, after seeing all the beautiful provinces of our kingdom, should claim that God had appeared to them in their country, that he had told them to go into France, and that he would give to them and to their posterity all the beautiful lands, domains, and provinces of this kingdom that extend from the rivers Rhine and Rhone, even to the sea; that he would make an everlasting alliance with them, that he would multiply their race, that he would make their posterity as numerous as the stars of Heaven and as the sands of the sea, etc.—who would not laugh at such folly, and consider these strangers insane fools!

Now there is no reason to think otherwise of all that has been said by these pretended Holy Patriarchs, Abraham, Isaac, and Jacob, in regard to the divine revelations they claim to have had. As to the institution of bloody sacrifices, the Holy Scriptures attribute it to God. As it would be too wearisome to go into the disgusting details of these sacrifices, I refer the reader to Exodus.

Were not men insane and blind to believe they were honoring God by tearing into pieces, butchering, and burning his own creatures, under the pretext of offering them as sacrifices to him? And even now, how is it that our Christ-worshippers are so extravagant as to expect to please God the Father by offering up to him the sacrifice of his divine son, in remembrance of his being shamefully nailed to a cross upon which he died? Certainly this can spring only from an obstinate blindness of mind.

In regard to the detail of the sacrifices of animals, it consists only in colored clothing, blood, plucks, livers, birds' crops, kidneys, claws, skins, in the dung, smoke, cakes, certain measures of oil and wine, the whole being offered and infected by dirty ceremonies as filthy and contemptible as the most extravagant performances of magic. What is most horrible in all this is that the law of this detestable Jewish people commanded that even human beings should be offered up as sacrifices. The barbarians, whoever they were, who introduced this horrible law commanded to put to death any man who had been consecrated to the God of the Jews, whom they called Adonai: and it is according to this execrable precept that Jephthah sacrificed his daughter, and that Saul wanted to sacrifice his son.

But here is yet another proof of the falsity of these revelations of which we have spoken. It is the lack of the fulfillment of the great and magnificent promises by which they were accompanied, for it is evident that these promises have never been fulfilled.

The proof of this consists in three principal points:

Firstly. Their posterity was to be more numerous than all the other nations of the world.

Secondly. The people who should spring from their race were to be the happiest, the holiest, and the most victorious of all the people of the earth.

Thirdly. His covenant was to be everlasting, and they should possess forever the country he should give them.

Now it is plain that these promises never were fulfilled.

Firstly. It is certain that the Jewish people, or the people of Israel—which is the only one that can be regarded as having descended from the Patriarchs Abraham, Isaac, and Jacob, and the only ones to whom these promises should have been fulfilled—have never been so numerous that it could be compared with the other nations of the earth, much less with the sands of the sea, etc., for we see that in the very time when it was the most numerous and the most flourishing, it never occupied more than the little sterile provinces of Palestine and its environs, which are almost nothing in comparison with the vast extent of a multitude of flourishing kingdoms that are in all corners of the earth.

Secondly. They have never been fulfilled concerning the great blessings with which they were to be favored; for, although they won a few small victories over some poor nations whom they plundered, this did not prevent them from being conquered and reduced to servitude; their kingdom was destroyed as well as their nation, by the Roman army; and even now the remainder of this unfortunate nation is looked upon as the vilest and most contemptible of all the earth, having no country, no dominion, no superiority.

Finally, these promises have not been fulfilled in respect to this everlasting covenant, which God ought to have fulfilled to them; because we do not see now, and we have never seen, any evidence of this covenant; and, on the contrary, they have been for many centuries excluded from the possession of the small country they pretended God had promised they should enjoy forever. Thus, since these pretended promises were never fulfilled, it is certain evidence of their falsity; which proves, plainly, that the pretended Holy Books that contain them were not of divine inspiration. Therefore it is useless for our Christ-worshippers to pretend to make use of them as infallible testimony to prove the truth of their religion.

THE HOLY SCRIPTURES

(1) The Old Testament

Our Christ-worshippers add to their reasons for belief and to the proofs of the truth of their testimony, the prophecies that are, as they pretend, sure evidences of the truth of the revelations or inspirations of God, there being no one but God who could predict future events so long before they came to pass as those that have been predicted by the prophets.

Let us see, then, who these pretended prophets are, and if we ought to consider them as important as our Christ-worshippers pretend they are. These men were only visionaries and fanatics, who acted and spoke according to the impulsions of their ruling passions, and who imagined that it was the Spirit of God by which they spoke and acted; or they were impostors who pretended to be prophets, and who, in order the more easily to deceive the ignorant and simple-minded, boasted of acting and speaking by the Spirit of God. I would like to know how an Ezekiel would be received who should say that God made him eat for his breakfast a roll of parchment; commanded him to be tied like an insane man and lie three hundred and ninety days upon his right side, and forty days upon his left, and commanded him to eat human dung upon his bread, and afterward, as an accommodation, cow's dung. I ask how such a filthy statement would be received by the most stupid people of our provinces?

What can be yet a greater proof of the falsity of these pretended prophecies than the violence with which these prophets reproach one another for speaking falsely in the name of God, reproaches that they claim to make on behalf of God. They all say, "Beware of false prophets!" as the quacks say, "Beware of counterfeit pills!" How could these insane impostors tell the future? No prophecy in favor of their Jewish nation was ever fulfilled. The number of prophecies that predict the prosperity and the greatness of Jerusalem is almost innumerable; in explanation of this, it will be said that it is very natural that a subdued and captive people should comfort themselves in their real afflictions by imaginary hopes—as a year after King James was deposed, the Irish people of his party forged several prophecies in regard to him.[1]

But if these promises made to the Jews had been really true, the Jewish nation long ago would have been, and would still be, the most numerous, the most powerful, the most blessed, and the most victorious of all nations.

(2) The New Testament

Let us examine the pretended prophecies that are contained in the Gospels.

Firstly. An angel having appeared in a dream to a man named Joseph, father, or at least so reputed, of Jesus, son of Mary, said unto him:

"Joseph, thou son of David, fear not to take unto thee Mary thy wife, for that which is conceived in her is of the Holy Ghost. And she shall bring forth a Son, and thou shalt call His name Jesus; for He shall save His people from their sins" [Matt. 1:20–21].

This angel said also to Mary:

"Fear not, Mary, for thou hast found favor with God. And behold, thou shalt conceive in thy womb and bring forth a son, and shalt call his name Jesus. He shall be great, and shall be called the Son of the Highest: and the Lord God shall give unto Him the throne of his father David. And he shall reign over the house of Jacob for ever; and of his kingdom there shall be no end" [Luke 1:30–33].

Jesus began to preach and to say:

"Repent, for the kingdom of Heaven is at hand. . . . Take no thought for your life, what ye shall eat, or what ye shall drink; nor yet for your body, what ye shall put on. Is not the life more than meat, and the body than raiment? . . . for your heavenly Father knoweth that ye have need of all these things. But seek ye first the kingdom of God and his righteousness, and all these things shall be added unto you" [Matt. 4:17, 6:25, 32–33].

Now, let every man who has not lost common sense examine if this Jesus ever was a king, or if his disciples had abundance of all things. This Jesus promised to deliver the world from sin. Is there any prophecy that is more false? Is not our age a striking proof of it? It is said that Jesus came to save his people. In what way did he save it? It is the greatest number that rules any party. For example, one or two dozen Spaniards or Frenchmen do not constitute the French or Spanish people; and if an army of a hundred and twenty thousand men were taken prisoners of war by an army of enemies that was stronger, and if the chief of this army should redeem only a few men, such as ten or twelve soldiers or officers, by paying their ransom, it could not be claimed that he had delivered or redeemed his army. Then who is this God who has been sacrificed, who died to save the world, and leaves so many nations damned? What a pity! and what horror!

Jesus Christ says that we have but to ask and we shall receive, and to seek and we shall find. He assures us that all we ask of God in his name shall be granted, and that if we have faith as a grain of mustard-seed, we could by one word remove mountains. If this promise is true, nothing appears impossible to our Christ-worshippers who have faith in Jesus. However, the contrary happens. If Mohammed had made the promises to his votaries that Christ made to his, without success, what would not be said about it? They would cry out, "Ah, the cheat! ah, the impostor!" These Christ-worshippers are in the same condition: they have been blind, and have not even yet recovered from their blindness; on the contrary, they are so ingenious in deceiving themselves that they pretend that these promises have been fulfilled from the beginning of Christianity; that at that time it was necessary to have miracles in order to convince the doubters of the truth of religion; but once this religion was sufficiently established, the miracles were no longer necessary. Where, then, is their proof of all this?

Besides, he who made these promises did not limit them to a certain time, or to certain places, or to certain persons; but he made them generally to everybody. The faith of those who believe, says he, shall be followed by these miracles: "In my name shall they cast out devils; they shall speak in new tongues; they shall take up serpents" [Mark 16:17–18], etc.

In regard to the removal of mountains, he positively says that "if ye shall say unto this mountain, *Be thou removed, and be thou cast into the sea; it shall be done*" [Matt. 21:21], provided that he does not doubt in his heart, but believes that all he commands will be done. Are not all these promises given in a general way, without restriction as to time, place, or persons?

It is said that all the sects that are founded on errors and imposture will come to a shameful end. But if Jesus Christ intends to say that he has established a society of followers who will not fall either into vice or error, these words are absolutely false, as there is in Christendom no sect, no society, and no church that is not full of errors and vices, especially the Roman Church, although it claims to be the purest and the holiest of all. It was born into error, or rather it was conceived and formed in error; and even now it is full of delusions that are contrary to the intentions, the sentiments, or the doctrine of its founder, because it has, contrary to his intention, abolished the laws of the Jews, which he approved, and which he came himself, as he said, to fulfill and not to destroy. It has fallen into the errors and idolatry of paganism, as is seen by the idolatrous worship that is offered to its God of dough, to its saints, to their images, and to their relics.

I know well that our Christ-worshippers consider it a lack of intelligence to accept literally the promises and prophecies as they are expressed; they reject the literal and natural sense of the words, to give them a mystical and spiritual sense which they call allegorical and figurative. They claim, for example, that the people of Israel and Judea, to whom these promises were made, were not understood as the Israelites after the body, but the Israelites in spirit: that is to say, the Christians who are the Israel of God, the true chosen people; that by the promise made to this enslaved people, to deliver it from captivity, it is understood to be not the corporal deliverance of a single captive people, but the spiritual deliverance of all men from the servitude of the Devil, which was to be accomplished by their Divine Savior; that by the abundance of riches, and all the temporal blessings promised to this people, is meant the abundance of spiritual graces; and finally, that by the city of Jerusalem is meant not the terrestrial Jerusalem, but the spiritual Jerusalem, which is the Christian Church.

But it is easy to see that these spiritual and allegorical meanings, having only a strange, imaginary sense, being a subterfuge of the interpreters, cannot serve to show the truth or the falsehood of a proposition, or of any promises whatever. It is ridiculous to forge such allegorical meanings, since it is only by the relations of the natural and true sense that we can judge of their truth or falsehood. A proposition, a promise, for example, that is considered true in the proper and natural sense of the terms in which it is expressed will not become false in itself under cover of a strange sense, one that does not belong to it. By the same reasoning, what is manifestly false in its proper and natural sense will not become true in itself, although we give it a strange sense, one foreign to the true.

We can say that the prophecies of the Old Testament, adjusted to the New, would be very absurd and puerile things. For example, Abraham had two wives, of whom the one, who was only a servant, represented the synagogue, and the other one, his lawful wife, represented the Christian Church; and that this Abraham had two sons, of whom the one born of Hagar, the servant, represented the Old Testament, and the other, born of Sarah, the wife, represented the New Testament. Who would not laugh at such a ridiculous doctrine?

Is it not amusing that a piece of red cloth, exhibited by a prostitute as a signal to spies in the Old Testament, is made to represent the blood of Jesus Christ shed in the New? If—according to this manner of interpreting allegorically all that is said, done, and practiced in the ancient law of the Jews—we should interpret in the same allegorical way all the discourses, actions, and adventures of the famous Don Quixote de la Mancha, we would find the same sort of mysteries and ridiculous figures.

It is nevertheless upon this absurd foundation that the whole Christian religion rests. Thus it is that there is scarcely anything in this ancient law that the Christ-worshipping doctors do not try to explain in a mystical way to build up their system. The most false and ridiculous prophecy ever made is that of Jesus, in Luke, where it is pretended that there will be signs in the sun and in the moon, and that the Son of Man will appear in a cloud to judge men; and this is predicted for the generation living at that time. Has it come to pass? *Did* the Son of Man appear in a cloud?

Errors of Doctrine and of Morality

The Christian Apostolical Roman Religion teaches, and compels belief, that there is but one God, and, at the same time, that there are three divine persons, each one being God. This is absurd; for if there are three who are truly God, then there are three Gods. It is false, then, to say that there is but one God; or if this is true, it is false to say that there are really three who are one God, for one and three cannot be claimed to be one and the same number. It is also said that the first of these pretended divine persons, called the Father, has brought forth the second person, which is called the Son, and that these first two persons together have produced the third, which is called the Holy Ghost, and, nevertheless, these three pretended divine persons do not depend the one upon the other, and even that one is not older than the other. This, too, is manifestly absurd; because one thing cannot receive its existence from another thing without some dependence on this other; and a thing must necessarily exist in order to give birth to another. If, then, the second and the third persons of the Divinity have received their existence from the first person, they must necessarily depend for their existence on this first person, who gave them birth, or who begot them, and it is necessary also that the first person of the Divinity, who gave birth to the two other persons, should have existed before them; because what does not exist cannot beget anything. Nevertheless, it is repugnant as well as absurd to claim that anything could be begotten or born without having had a beginning. Now, according to our Christ-worshippers, the second and third persons of the Divinity were begotten and born; then they had a beginning, and the first person had none, not being begotten by another; it therefore follows necessarily that one existed before the other.

Our Christ-worshippers, who feel these absurdities and cannot avoid them by any good reasoning, have no other recourse than to say that we must ignore human reason and humbly adore these sublime mysteries without wishing to understand them; but what they call faith is refuted when they tell us that we must submit; it is telling us that we must blindly believe what we do not believe. Our Christ-worshippers condemn the blindness of the ancient pagans, who worshipped several gods; they deride the genealogy of those gods, their birth, their marriages, and the generating of their children; yet they do not observe that they themselves say things that are much more ridiculous and absurd.

If the pagans believed that there were goddesses as well as gods, that these gods and goddesses married and begat children, they thought of nothing, then, but what is natural; for they did not believe that the gods were without body or feeling; they believed they were similar to men. Why should there not be females as well as males? It is not more reasonable to deny or to recognize the one than the other; and supposing there were gods and goddesses, why should they not beget children in the ordinary way? There would be certainly nothing ridiculous or absurd in this doctrine, if it were true that their gods existed. But in the doctrine of our Christ-worshippers there is something absolutely ridiculous and absurd; for besides claiming that one god forms three, and that these three form but one, they pretend that this triple and unique God has neither body, form, nor face; that the first person of this triple and unique God, whom they call the Father, begot of himself a second person, which they call the Son, and which is the same as his father, being, like him, without body, form, or face. If this is true, why is it that the first one is called father rather than mother, or the second called son rather than daughter? For if the first one is really father instead of mother, and if the second is son instead of daughter, there must be something in both of these two persons that causes the one to be father rather than mother, and the other to be son rather than daughter. Now who can assert that they are males and not females? But how should they be rather males than females, as they have neither body, form, nor face? That is not an imaginable thing, and destroys itself. No matter, they claim that these two persons, without body, form, or face, and, consequently, without difference of sex, are nevertheless father and son, and that they produced by their mutual love a third person, whom they called the Holy Ghost, who has, like the other two, no body, no form, and no face. What abominable nonsense!

As our Christ-worshippers limit the power of God the father to begetting but one son, why do they not desire that this second person, and the third, should have the same power to beget a son like themselves? If this power to beget a son is perfection in the first person, it is, then, a perfection and a power that does not exist in the second and in the third person. Thus these two persons, lacking a perfection and a power that is found in the first one, are consequently not equal with him. If, on the contrary, they say that this power to beget a son is no perfection, they should not attribute it to the first person any more than to the other two; for we should attribute perfections only to an absolutely perfect being. Besides, they would not dare to say that the power to beget a divine person is not a perfection; and if they claim that this first person could have begotten several sons and daughters, but that he desired but this only son, and that the two other persons did not desire to beget any others, we could ask them, *firstly*, whence they know this, for we do not see in their pretended Holy Scriptures that any one of these divine personages reveals any such assertions; how, then, can our Christ-worshippers know anything about it? They speak only according to their ideas and to their hollow imaginations. *Secondly*, we could not avoid saying that if these pretended divine personages had the power of begetting several children and did not wish to make use of it, the consequence would be that this divine power was ineffectual. It would be entirely without effect in the third person, who did not beget or produce any, and would be almost without effect in the two others, because they limited it. Then this power of begetting or producing an unlimited number of children would remain idle and useless; it would be inconsistent to suppose this of divine personages, one of whom had already produced a son.

Our Christ-worshippers blame and condemn the pagans because they attribute divinity to mortal men and worship them as gods after their death; they are right in doing this. But these pagans did only what our Christ-worshippers still do in attributing divinity to their Christ; doing which, they condemn themselves also, because they are in the same error as these pagans, in that they worship a man who was mortal, and so very mortal that he died shamefully upon a cross.

It would be of no use for our Christ-worshippers to say that there was a great difference between their Jesus Christ and the pagan gods, under the pretense that their Christ was, as they claim, really God and man at the same time, while the divinity was incarnated in Him, by means of which the divine nature found itself united personally, as they say, with human nature; these two natures would have made of Jesus Christ a true god and a true man; this is what never happened, they claim, in the pagan gods.

But it is easy to show the weakness of this reply; for, on the one hand, was it not as easy to the pagans as to the Christians to say that the divinity was incarnated in the men whom they worshipped as gods? On the other hand, if the divinity wanted to incarnate and unite in the human nature of their Jesus Christ, how did they know that this divinity would not wish also to incarnate and unite himself personally to the human nature of those great men and those admirable women who, by their virtue, by their good qualities, or by their noble actions, have excelled the generality of people and made themselves worshipped as gods and goddesses? And if our Christ-worshippers do not wish to believe that divinity was ever incarnated in these great personages, why do they wish to persuade us that he was incarnated in their Jesus? Where is the proof? Their faith and their belief; but as the pagans rely on the same proof, we conclude both to be equally in error.

But what is more ridiculous in Christianity than in paganism is that the pagans have generally attributed divinity only to great men, authors of arts and sciences, and those who excelled in virtues useful to their country. But to whom do our God-Christ-worshippers attribute divinity? To a nobody, to a vile and contemptible man, who had neither talent, science, nor ability; born of poor parents, and who, while he figured in the world, passed for a monomaniac and a seditious fool, who was disdained, ridiculed, persecuted, whipped, and, finally, was hanged like most of those who wanted to act the same part, when they had neither the courage nor skill. About that time there were several other impostors who claimed to be the true promised Messiah; among others a certain Judas, a Galilean, a Theodorus, a Barcon, and others who, under this vain pretext, abused the people and tried to excite them, in order to win them, but they all perished.

Let us pass now to his discourses and to some of his actions, which are the most singular of this kind: "Repent," said he to the people, "for the kingdom of Heaven is at hand; believe these good tidings" [Mark 1:15]. And he went all over Galilee preaching this pretended approach of the kingdom of Heaven.

As no one has seen the arrival of this kingdom of Heaven, it is evident that it was but imaginary. But let us see other predictions, the praise, and the description of this beautiful kingdom.

Behold what he said to the people:

The kingdom of Heaven is likened unto a man who sowed good seed in his field. But while he slept, his enemy came and sowed tares among the wheat and went his way. Again, the kingdom of Heaven is like unto treasure hidden in a field, which, when a man has found, he hideth again, and for joy thereof goes and sells all that he has and buys that field. Again, the kingdom of Heaven is like unto a merchantman seeking goodly pearls, who, when he had found one pearl of great price, went and sold all he had, and bought it. Again, the kingdom of Heaven is like unto a net that was cast into the sea and gathered of every kind; which, when it was full, they drew to shore, and sat down and gathered the good into vessels, but cast the bad away. It is like a grain of mustard-seed, which a man took and sowed in his field, which, indeed, is the least of all seeds, but when it is grown it is the greatest among herbs, etc.

Is this a language worthy of a god? We will pass the same judgment upon him if we examine his actions more closely. Because, *firstly*, he is represented as running all over a country preaching the approach of a pretended kingdom; *secondly*, as having been transported by the Devil upon a high mountain, from which he believed he saw all the kingdoms of the world; this could only happen to a visionist; for it is certain, there is no mountain upon the earth from which he could see even one entire kingdom, unless it was the little kingdom of Yvetot, which is in France; thus it was only in imagination that he saw all these kingdoms and was transported upon this mountain, as well as upon the pinnacle of the temple. *Thirdly*, when he cured the deaf-mute, spoken of in St. Mark, it is said that he placed his fingers in the ears, spit, and touched his tongue, then casting his eyes up to Heaven, he sighed deeply, and said unto him: "Ephphatha!" [Mark 7:34]. Finally, let us read all that is related of him, and we can judge whether there is anything in the world more ridiculous.

Having considered some of the silly things attributed to God by our Christ-worshippers, let us look a little further into their mysteries. They worship one God in three persons, or three persons in one God, and they attri-bute to themselves the power of forming gods out of dough, and of making as many as they want. For, according to their principles, they have only to say four words over a certain quantity of wine or over these little images of paste, to make as many gods of them as they desire. What folly! With all the pretended power of their Christ, they would not be able to make the smallest fly, and yet they claim the ability to produce millions of gods. One must be struck by a strange blindness to maintain such pitiable things, and that upon such a vain foundation as the equivocal words of a fanatic. Do not these blind theologians see that it means opening a wide door to all sorts of idolatries, to adore these paste images under the pretext that the priests have the power of consecrating them and changing them into gods? Can't the priests of the idols boast of having a similar ability?

Do they not see, also, that the same reasoning that demonstrates the vanity of the gods or idols of wood, of stone, etc., which the pagans wor-shipped, shows exactly the same vanity of the gods and idols of paste or flour that our Christ-worshippers adore? By what right do they deride the falseness of the pagan gods? Is it not because they are only the work of human hands, mute and insensible images? And what kind of gods are those that we preserve in boxes for fear of mice?

What are these boasted resources of the Christ-worshippers? Their morality? It is the same as in all religions, but their cruel dogmas produced and taught persecution and trouble. Their miracles? But what people has not its own, and what wise men do not disdain these fables? Their prophecies? Have we not shown their falsity? Their morals? Are they not often infamous? The establishment of their religion? But did not fanaticism begin, and has not intrigue visibly sustained this edifice? The doctrine? But is it not the height of absurdity?

From *Man a Machine* (1748)

JULIEN OFFRAY DE LA METTRIE

[Julien Offray de La Mettrie (1709–1751) studied theology in his early years but turned to the study of philosophy, natural science, and medicine. For much of his relatively brief adult life, he practiced medicine and surgery. In 1745 he published *Histoire naturelle de l'âme* (*The Natural History of the Soul*), creating a furor by his adoption of a strictly materialist stance toward the human body and soul. This work and others caused La Mettrie to flee to Prussia, where he elicited further outrage with *Discours de bonheur* (1748; *Discourse on Happiness*), which frankly advocated hedonism. Today La Mettrie's reputation rests largely on *L'Homme machine* (1748; *Man a Machine*), which extended Descartes' argument that animals were mere "machines" without free will; La Mettrie argued that no distinction could be made between animals and human beings in this regard. In the following extract, La Mettrie engages in a brief aside on religion, claiming that the deists' argument from design is not a sufficient refutation against atheism.]

I do not mean to call in question the existence of a supreme being; on the contrary, it seems to me that the greatest degree of probability is in favor of this belief. But since the existence of this being goes no further than that of any other toward proving the need of worship, it is a theoretical truth of very little practical value. Therefore, since we may say, after such long experience, that religion does not imply exact honesty, the same reasons authorize us to think that atheism does not exclude it.

Furthermore, who can be sure that the reason for man's existence is not simply the fact that he exists? Perhaps he was thrown by chance on some spot on the earth's surface, nobody knows how nor why, but simply that he must live and die, like the mushrooms that appear from day to day, or like those flowers that border the ditches and cover the walls.

Let us not lose ourselves in the infinite, for we are not made to have the least idea thereof; it is absolutely impossible for us to get back to the origin of things. Besides, it does not matter for our peace of mind whether matter is eternal or was created, whether there is or is not a god. How foolish to torment ourselves so much about things that we cannot know, and which would not make us any happier even were we to gain knowledge about them!

But, some will say, read all the works of Fénelon, Nieuwentyt, Abbadie, Derham, Retz, and the rest.[1] Well! what will they teach me, or rather what have they taught me? They are only tiresome repetitions of zealots, one of whom adds only verbiage to the other, more likely to strengthen than to undermine the foundations of atheism. The number of evidences drawn from the spectacle of nature does not give these evidences any more force. Either the mere structure of a finger, an ear, an eye, a single observation of Malpighi[2] proves all, and doubtless much better than Descartes and Malebranche[3] proved it, or all the other evidences prove nothing. Deists, and even Christians, should therefore be content to point out that throughout the animal kingdom the same aims are pursued and accomplished by an infinite number of different mechanisms, all of them however exactly geometrical. For what stronger weapons could there be with which to overthrow atheists? It is true that if my reason does not deceive me, man and the whole universe seem to have been designed for this unity of aim. The sun, air, water, the organism, the shape of bodies—everything is brought to a focus in the eye as in a mirror that faithfully presents to the imagination all the objects reflected in it, in accordance with the laws required by the infinite variety of bodies that take part in vision. In ears we find everywhere a striking variety, and yet the difference of structure in men, animals, birds, and fish does not produce different uses. All ears are so mathematically made that they tend equally to one and the same end, namely, hearing. But would Chance, the Deist asks, be a great enough geometrician to vary thus, at her pleasure, the works of which she is supposed to be the author, without being hindered by so great a diversity from gaining the same end? Again, the Deist will bring forward as a difficulty those parts of the animal that are clearly contained in it for future use, the butterfly in the caterpillar, man in the sperm, a whole polyp in each of its parts, the valvule in the oval orifice, the lungs in the fetus, the teeth in their sockets, the bones in the fluid from which they detach themselves and (in an incomprehensible manner) harden. And since the partisans of this theory, far from neglecting anything that would strengthen it, never tire of piling up proof upon proof, they are willing to avail themselves of everything, even of the weakness of the mind in certain cases. Look, they say, at men like Spinoza, Vanini, Desbarreau, and Boindin,[4] apostles who honor Deism more than they harm it. The duration of their health was the measure of their unbelief, and one rarely fails, they add, to renounce atheism when the passions—with their instrument, the body—have grown weak.

That is certainly the most that can be said in favor of the existence of God: although the last argument is frivolous in that these conversions are short, and the mind almost always regains its former opinions and acts accordingly, as soon as it has regained or rather rediscovered its strength in that of the body. That is, at least, much more than was said by the physician Diderot, in his *Pensées Philosophiques*, a sublime work that will not convince a single atheist. What reply can, in truth, be made to a man who says, "We do not know nature; causes hidden in her breast might have produced everything. In your turn, observe the polyp of Trembley:[5] does it not contain in itself the causes that bring about regeneration? Why, then, would it be absurd to think that there are physical causes by reason of which everything has been made, and to which the whole chain of this vast universe is so necessarily bound and held that nothing that happens could have failed to happen—causes of which we are so invincibly ignorant that we have had recourse to a God, who, as some aver, is not even a logical entity? Thus to destroy chance is not to prove the existence of a supreme being, since there may be some other thing that is neither chance nor God—I mean, nature. It follows that the study of nature can make only unbelievers; and the way of thinking of all its more successful investigators proves this."

The weight of the universe, therefore, far from crushing a real atheist, does not even shake him. All these evidences of a creator, repeated thousands and thousands of times, evidences that are placed far above the comprehension of men like us, are self-evident (however far one push the argument) only to the anti-Pyrrhonians,[6] or to those who have enough confidence in their reason to believe themselves capable of judging on the basis of certain phenomena, against which, as you see, the atheists can urge others perhaps equally strong and absolutely opposed. For if we listen to the naturalists again, they will tell us that the very causes that, in a chemist's hands, by a chance combination, made the first mirror, in the hands of nature made the pure water, the mirror of the simple shepherdess; that the motion that keeps the world going could have created it, that each body has taken the place assigned to it by its own nature, that the air must have surrounded the earth, and that iron and the other metals are produced by internal motions of the earth, for one and the same reason; that the sun is as much a natural product as electricity, that it was not made to warm the earth and its inhabitants, whom it sometimes burns, any more than the rain was made to make the seeds grow, which it often spoils; that the mirror and the water were no more made for people to see themselves in, than were all other polished bodies with this same property; that the eye is in truth a kind of glass in which the soul can contemplate the image of objects as they are presented to it by these bodies, but that it is not proved that this organ was really made expressly for this contemplation, nor purposely placed in its socket, and in short that it may well be that Lucretius, the physician Lamy,[7] and all Epicureans both ancient and modern were right when they suggested that the eye sees only because it is formed and placed as it is, and that, given once for all the same rules of motion followed by nature in the generation and development of bodies, this marvelous organ could not have been formed and placed differently.

Such is the pro and the con, and the summary of those fine arguments that will eternally divide the philosophers. I do not take either side.

Non nostrum inter vos tantas componere lites.
[It is not our place to settle such disagreements among you.][8]

This is what I said to one of my friends, a Frenchman, as frank a Pyrronian as I, a man of much merit, and worthy of a better fate. He gave me a very singular answer in regard to the matter. "It is true," he told me, "that the pro and con should not disturb at all the soul of a philosopher, who sees that nothing is proved with sufficient clarity to force his consent, and that the arguments offered on one side are neutralized by those of the other. However," he continued, "the universe will never be happy, unless it is atheistic." Here are this wretch's reasons. If atheism, said he, were generally accepted, all the branches of religion would then be destroyed and cut off at the roots. No more theological wars, no more soldiers of religion—such terrible soldiers! Nature, infected with a sacred poison, would regain its rights and its purity. Deaf to all other voices, tranquil mortals would follow only the spontaneous dictates of their own being, the only commands that can never be despised with impunity and that alone can lead us to happiness through the pleasant paths of virtue.

Such is natural law: whoever rigidly observes it is a good man and deserves the confidence of the entire human race. Whoever fails to follow it scrupulously affects, in vain, the specious exterior of another religion; he is a scamp or a hypocrite whom I distrust.

After this, let a vain people think otherwise; let them dare affirm that even probity is at stake in not believing in revelation; in a word, that another religion than that of nature is necessary, whatever it may be. Such an assertion is wretched and pitiable; and so is the good opinion that each one gives us of the religion he has embraced! We do not seek here the votes of the crowd. Whoever raises in his heart altars to superstition is born to worship idols and not to thrill to virtue.

"On the Origin and Progress of Divination" (1749)

ÉTIENNE BONNOT DE CONDILLAC

[Étienne Bonnot de Condillac (1715–1780) spent most of his career in philosophical speculation, conducting pioneering work in psychology and epistemology. In such works as the *Essai sur l'origine des connaissances humaines* (1746; *Essay on the Origin of Human Knowledge*), the *Traité des systèmes* (1749; *Treatise on Systems*), and the *Traité des sensations* (1754; *Treatise on Sensations*), Condillac built upon the epistemology of John Locke in championing sensation as the ultimate origin of all human knowledge; but he rejected Locke's belief that the senses can provide us with intuitive knowledge. This stance appeared to lead Condillac toward atheism and materialism, but he claimed to reject both, although his religious skepticism is evident throughout his writings. In the following chapter from the *Traité des systèmes*, Condillac uses a rudimentary anthropology to sketch a naturalistic account of the development of divination, astrology, and other quasi-religious methods by which primitive peoples sought to understand the world around them.]

The mind of the people, like that of the philosopher, is systematic, but it is not as easy to identify the principles that lead it astray. Its errors accumulate in such great numbers and are sustained by analogies that are sometimes so subtle that the person himself is unable to recognize his own work in the systems he has formed. The history of divination is a very clear example of this. I will reveal the train of ideas by which so many superstitions have had their birth.

If the life of man had been only uninterrupted sensations of pleasure or of pain, in one case happy without any idea of unhappiness, in the other case unhappy without any idea of happiness, he would have enjoyed his happiness or suffered his unhappiness without searching to discover if some entity looked out for his preservation or worked toward his harm. It is the alternation of the one and the other of these states that has caused him to reflect that he is never so unhappy that his nature does not allow him to be sometimes happy, and also that he is never so happy that he cannot become unhappy. Hence arises the hope of seeing the end of the evils he suffers, and the fear of losing the good things he enjoys. The more he takes note of these alternations, the more he sees that he is not in control of the causes that produce them. Each circumstance teaches him his dependence on everything that surrounds him; and, when he learns how to lead his reflection to trace effects to their true cause, everything will indicate or demonstrate to him the existence of the first being.

Among the evils to which we are exposed, the cause is in some cases evident, and in other cases we do not know to whom to attribute them. These latter evils were one source of conjecture for those minds who believed they were exploring nature, when they were only consulting their own imaginations. This manner of satisfying their curiosity, still common today, was the only one available for those men unenlightened by experience; this, then, was the first effort of intellection. As long as the evils affected only a few, none of these conjectures became so widespread as to become a general opinion. But if they were more common? What of the plague, for example, which ravages the earth? This phenomenon attracts the attention of everyone, and men of imagination do not fail to adopt the systems they have devised. Now to what cause can still-crude minds attribute the evils that assault them if not to entities who gain pleasure in making the human race unhappy?

However, it would have been dreadful to be always afraid. As such, hope was not slow in modifying this system. It imagined more favorable entities, capable of counterbalancing the power of the others. People therefore believed that they were loved by these creatures, just as they were hated by the others.

People multiplied these two kinds of entities according to circumstances. The air was filled with them; there were aerial spirits and genies of all sorts.

Houses were opened to them; they became the household gods. Finally they were scattered in the woods and the water, everywhere, because fear and hope accompanied men everywhere.

But it was not enough to people the earth with friendly or hostile entities. The influence of the sun on all creatures was too obvious not to be remarked upon. Without doubt, this star was at an early date placed among the benevolent stars. Soon the influence of the moon was also assumed, as was, gradually, that of all the stars that could be clearly seen. The imagination then attributed a good or evil character to this influence; and from that time onward the heavens seemed to conduce to the good or ill of humanity. Nothing could occur that was not significant; the stars were studied, and their different positions accorded with different effects. People did not, for example, fail to attribute the greatest events—famines, wars, the death of kings, and so on—to the rarest and most extraordinary phenomena, such as eclipses and comets: the imagination willingly assumed a relation between these things.

If men had been able to consider that everything in the universe is connected, and that what we take to be the action of only one of its parts is the result of the combined actions of all the parts together, from the largest bodies to the smallest atoms, they would never have dreamed of regarding a single planet or constellation as the source of what happened to them; they would have perceived how unreasonable it was, in explaining an event, to take note of only the smallest part of its contributing causes. But fear, the first principle of this prejudice, does not allow them to reflect; it shows them the danger, it magnifies it, and people are only too happy to attribute that danger to some cause or other. It provides a kind of solace to the evils we suffer.

The influence of the stars was therefore recognized, and the only question was to divide among them the dispensation of goods and evils. This is the basis for this division.

Men, familiar with the language of articulate sounds, judged that nothing could be more natural than to give things the names that had been given to them in the beginning. They believed this because these names seemed natural to them: they had no other reason, and this is what led them astray; moreover, this opinion doubtless had a certain basis. In fact, it is certain that, when people wished to name things, they were compelled, in order to make themselves understood, to choose words that had the greatest analogy either with their ideas or with the language of action that presided over the formation of language. But people imagined that these names recalled what these objects were in themselves, and accordingly they assumed that only the gods could have taught them to men. Philosophers, for their part, too biased or vain to suspect the limits of the human mind, were convinced that the first inventors of languages had understood the nature of entities. The study of names must therefore have seemed an entirely proper means of discovering the essence of things; and what confirmed this opinion was that, among these names, people saw many that still clearly indicated the properties or character of the objects. Once this prejudice was generally received, it was not difficult to determine the influence that could be attributed to each planet.

Men who had become famous were placed among the ranks of gods, and after their apotheosis they were assumed to have preserved the same character that they had on earth. Either because, during their lifetime, their names were given to the stars through flattery, or because this was done only after their death, to mark the place destined to receive them, the divinities and the stars had the same names.

Therefore, one only had to refer to the character of each god to guess the influence of each planet. Hence, Jupiter signified dignity, great care, justice, etc.; Mars, strength, courage, vengeance, boldness, etc.; Venus, beauty, grace, sensuality, love of pleasure, etc.; in a word, people judged each planet based on the idea that had been formed of the god whose name it bore. As for the zodiacal signs, they owed their power to the animals after which they had been named.

People did not stop there. If a power had at one time been attributed to the stars, there was no reason for limiting its influence. If this planet produced a given effect, why would it not produce another effect that had some relation to the first? Astrologers' imaginations passed, in this manner, from one analogy to another; it is no longer possible to discover the varying collocations of ideas by which their systems were formed. The same planet must, in the end, produce totally different effects, and the most opposed planets must produce altogether similar ones. Thus everything will be confused by the same manner of reasoning that had at first assigned a particular power to each star.

There was no way to assign this influence indifferently to every part of the heavens. It was natural to believe that those parts with little observable variation had no influence, or that, if they did, they tended to keep things always the same. This is why the astrologers, limiting everything to the revolutions of the zodiac, usually attributed influence only to the dozen signs and the planets that proceed through them.

As each planet in this system had a single power appropriate to it, it was natural to infer that they mutually modified their action, according to the place in the sky they occupied, and the relations existing between them.

People should thereby have concluded that each planet's power changed at each moment; but it was not possible to determine this power, and astrology would have become impracticable.

This was not the account given by astrologers who had a vested interest in preying upon the naïveté of the people, nor that given by those who, acting in good faith, were the first to be deceived. It was therefore established that, in order to judge the influence of the planets, there was no need to observe them in all points of the zodiac; and people restricted themselves to the dozen principal positions of the signs.

Another difficulty was overcome in the same manner. It was not enough to have determined the constellation in which a given star had to be observed; there was a further need to decide if notice should be taken of the place that we occupied on the earth. On what basis could it be supposed that a planet produced similar effects on a Chinese person and on a French person, since the direction of its rays was not the same on the one as on the other? But such precision would have made the calculations too troublesome. Given its distance from the heavens, the earth was considered a point, and it was determined that the different directions of the rays were so insignificant that there was no need to take them into account.

But what could prove particularly embarrassing to the astrologers was that, in their system, the stars had to influence an animal at each moment, that is to say, from the point when it was conceived up to the point when it died: they could not find any reason for suspending this action up to a certain time after conception, nor for entirely stopping it before the moment of death.

Now the planets, passing alternatively from a state where they exercised all their power to a state where they could have none, must therefore have successively cancelled each other out; we would have come upon all the vicissitudes that this combat must necessarily have produced, and the sequence of events would have been pretty much the same for every man. If there had been some difference, it would have been only insofar as the stars whose influence was perceived at the beginning had made impressions so profound that they could never have been entirely effaced. Therefore, in order to determine this difference, there would have been a need to determine the exact moment of conception; there would even have been a need to go back even further: for why would it not have been said that the action of the stars had prepared the seed long before the animal was conceived?

We cannot guess how the astrologers would have surmounted these difficulties if a prejudice had not come to their aid. Happily for them, people were always convinced that we are, through the course of our lives, what we are born. As a result, the astrologers laid down the principle that it was enough to observe the stars in relation to the moment of birth. It is obvious how this maxim put their minds at ease.

Nevertheless, it was still quite difficult to ascertain the exact moment of a man's birth. Even if the most precise astronomer had observed it, one could not be assured that there had not been some error. Now an error of a minute, a second, or something even smaller was enough to change the given influence. But the astrologers had no interest in pursuing such precision, which would have made their art impracticable; and the people who consulted them, curious to learn about their future, were content if anything at all had been predicted. Therefore, astrologers limited themselves to the day and hour of birth, as if events would have been the same for all persons who had been born on the same day and hour. Some prided themselves on greater precision to gain greater belief for their charlatanry.

As this system of astrology took shape, it began making predictions. Among the many, some were confirmed by events and brought credit to the astrologers; others did not strike a blow against astrology at all. People simply rejected those astrologers whom they believed to be ignorant; or, if they were thought to be skilled, they were excused by attributing to some error in calculations what in fact was a flaw in the whole art; still more often, people simply didn't pay attention. Once people give way to superstition, they simply wander from one error to the next. Out of a thousand observations, 999 can save them from error; they make only one, and that is the one they seize upon.

Oftentimes, astrologers successfully used a stratagem—to utter their predictions in an obscure and equivocal manner, and to leave to events the trouble of clarifying them. But they did not always have to be so clever, and sometimes they effected the accomplishment of their prophecies by means of the imaginations of the people concerned. Those prophecies that threatened some evil more generally came to fruition than the others, because fear has much greater power over us than hope. The examples of this are very common.

There was, therefore, a danger for believers in astrology to cast their horoscopes. I will add that there is even some danger for unbelievers. If some disagreeable events are predicted for me that have some relation to the various circumstances that are naturally associated with my way of life, each of these circumstances will remind me of them in spite of myself. These sad images will trouble me more or less in proportion to the vividness with which I remember them. The impression will be strong, especially if during infancy I had believed in astrology: for, even though I am now rational, my imagination will continue to have the influence over me that it had when I was not. In vain will I tell myself that it is madness to be disturbed; philosophical enough to understand how ill-founded my disturbance is, I will not be able to dispel it.

I have read somewhere that a young man, destined by birth and by his talent to have a role in the government of the republic, began to have some favorable position there. To be agreeable, he accompanied two or three of his friends to a prophetess. They in turn urged him to have his horoscope drawn, but to no avail. Convinced as anyone could be of the futility of this art, he spoke to the prophetess only with ridicule. "You may joke," she replied irritably, "but I tell you that you will lose your head on a scaffold." The young man was unaware that the prediction had made the slightest impression on him; he laughed at it and walked away unconcerned. Nevertheless, his imagination had been struck, and he was astonished that the prophetess's prediction recurred to him at every opportunity and tormented him as if he had believed it. He long struggled against this madness; but the slightest disturbance in the republic brought it to the fore and rendered all his efforts futile. Finally he found no other remedy for it but to give up public life and exile himself from his own country, to go and live under a more tranquil government.

One could conclude from this that philosophy consists more in making us sufficiently distrust ourselves to avoid all those occasions where our minds might be deceived, than in flattering ourselves that we will always be able to avoid the disturbances that imagination can cause.

When astrologers could cite a few predictions justified by events, they boasted that a long series of observations testified in their favor.

I will not stop here to destroy a similar pretension; its falsity is manifest. It is indisputable that the precision of the astrologers' observations depends on the knowledge acquired in astronomy. The progress that has recently been made in this latter science shows clearly how over the centuries astrologers have been ignorant of many things needed for their art.

Nevertheless, they were not slow in creating systems. The Chaldeans and the Egyptians each had their principles; the Greeks, who inherited this absurd art from them, made some changes in it, as they did in everything they borrowed from other peoples; the Arabs, in their turn, treated Greek astrology with the same liberty and transmitted to the modern age those systems that each astrologer adds to or subtracts from as he pleases. The astrologers agree only on one point—that there is an art of knowing the future by the study of the stars. As for the laws that ought to be followed, each astrologer prescribes a particular set that he favors and condemns all others.

The people, however, did not see how little intelligence prevailed among the astrologers and believed that all fables told to them were truths that long experience had confirmed. They did not at all doubt, for example, that the planets divided up the days, nights, hours, countries, plants, trees, and minerals, and that each object was under the dominion of some star; the sky was a book where one could read what would happen to empires, kingdoms, states, cities, and individuals. Astrological works allow us to see that this division has no other basis than some imaginary relation between the character that had been given to the stars and the things that people wished to put under each of the stars' protection.

It was a substantial achievement to have provided in this manner for the government of the world, but, in the eyes of astrologers, there still remained a considerable inconvenience: the benevolent stars sometimes encountered obstacles in making us feel the effects of their influence. There was a search for remedies; and, as it was believed that the stars were gods, or that they were at least animated by intelligences who were in charge of taking care of our world, the astrologers imagined that we had only to call upon these spirits and to make them descend to the earth: this was called *evocation*.

It was believed that the stars were happier in those places where they exercised a greater power, and that they had a particular inclination toward those objects that were under their protection. As a result, people invoked the stars in the name of those things; and, in order to pray with more hope, people took a stick and used it to trace the figures of these objects in the air, on the ground, and on walls. Such, I think, is the origin of magic. Since this superstition was probably born at a time when the language of action was very familiar, it was natural that people attached magical power to certain movements.

There was more. It was believed that, if it was important to be able to summon these entities, it was even more important to have on one's person something that would continually assure us of their protection. People reasoned on the same principles as before, and they concluded that it was enough to engrave the same figures that were customarily sketched in order to evoke them and the prayers offered them. No one doubted that this artifice would succeed, provided that one took the precaution of choosing the stone and the metal sympathetic to the planet whose aid one wished to gain, and to engrave upon them the day and hour assigned to the planet, and above all to choose the moment when it was in the celestial position where it exercised all its power. Such is the origin of abracadabra and talismans.

Another cause contributed heavily in maintaining and expanding these prejudices.

The establishment of alphabets had caused the meaning of hieroglyphs to be entirely forgotten, and so it was easy for priests to make these characters pass before people's eyes for sacred objects that concealed the greatest mysteries. The priests attributed to them such power as it pleased them, and people believed them all the more willingly because they did not doubt that the gods were the authors of hieroglyphic science—that is, a science that could include everything precisely because no one knew what it included. As such, all the hieroglyphic characters passed gradually into magic, and this system became all the more fertile.

From this magic, combined with the mysterious science of hieroglyphics, other superstitions were born.

Hieroglyphics included all kinds of features; every line therefore became a sign. Thus the magicians, instead of consulting the heavens, did no more than to examine the hand of a person who had approached them, and they were able to promise either a good or a bad fortune based on the character of the lines that were traced there. But because their principles did not allow anything to happen without the influence of the stars, each line was assigned to one of the planets. This was enough for the magicians to attribute the same portents to it, and this art became all the easier to practice. It was given the name *palmistry*.

On the one hand, in hieroglyphic writing the sun, the moon, and the stars served to represent states, empires, kings, and great men; the eclipse and extinction of these luminaries signaled temporal disasters; fire and flood signified a desolation produced by war or famine; a serpent indicated some ailment; a viper, money; frogs, impostors; partridges, impious persons; a swallow, afflictions or death. In a word, there was no known object that did not serve to foretell the future.

On the other hand, in sleep the human imagination always acts to create different combinations of known objects. It cannot fail to remind people of the same objects that were used in hieroglyphic writing. However, no one yet suspected that dreams were the product of the imagination. When it was a matter of actions that we make with knowledge and reflection, it was said that "they are the effects of our will," and that was thought to explain everything. But involuntary actions seemed to occur without our aid; as a result, to what could these be attributed except to a god? Hence the gods were the authors of both hieroglyphs and dreams; there could be no doubt that, during sleep, they wished to make their will known to us when they used the same language that they had created for writing. Such is the origin of *oneiromancy*, or the interpretation of dreams.

Once this prejudice was accepted—that the gods were the origin of all involuntary actions—we see how men found in themselves reasons for fear and hope. An accidental gesture, a foot inadvertently brought forth in front of the other, a sneeze—everything became a presage for good or ill.

Among hieroglyphic figures, there were birds who flew toward different parts of the world or appeared to be singing. In the beginning, there was a writing that was used to refer to entirely natural things, such as changes in the seasons, winds, and so on. But when hieroglyphs became sacred things, they were endowed with mystery; and it was probably as a result of this prejudice that augurs imagined that they could ascertain the future by the flight and the singing of birds.

The gods, always busy explicating the future to men, must have been even busier during the times of sacrifice: it was even natural to think that they struck the victim and imprinted on his breast the marks of their anger or favor. It could therefore not have been unimportant to note the details of sacrifices, and above all to examine the entrails of animals that had been immolated. Such was the origin of the art of the haruspex.

Although people expressed no doubt of these ways of knowing the future, they were too curious not to have a frequent sense of their inadequacy. They yearned for something more precise, and their wish was granted in the circumstances that led to oracles. Certain words, inadvertently uttered by the person presiding over the sacrifices, were by chance found to have a relation to the reason why the gods were invoked; they were thus taken to be inspired. This success resulted in more than one slip of this sort; and, because the less control a person had over his movements, the more they seemed to come from a god, it was often believed that oracles could only be given by someone in a trance. This is why people built temples only in those places where exhalations from the earth had the property of causing mental disturbance. Elsewhere, people used other means of causing a trance; at last, as they became more and more superstitious, people required fewer precautions, and prophecies made calmly became very common.

All that remained was to make the statues of the gods move and speak. In this, the imposture of priests satisfied people's superstition. The statues became oracles.

Imagination moves fast when it goes astray, because nothing is so fertile as a false principle. There are gods everywhere; they are in charge of everything;

thus, anything can make us aware of our future destiny. By this reasoning, the most common things, as also the rarest, all become, depending on circumstances, auguries for good or ill. The objects that inspired veneration, bearing in this way a relation to the idea of divinity, seemed especially fitting to satisfy human curiosity. It is thus, for example, that a high regard for Homer made people believe that prophecies could be found in his works.

The opinions of philosophers contributed in extending one phase of these prejudices. According to them, our soul is only a portion of the soul of the world. Enveloped in matter, it no longer took part in the divinity of the substance from which it had been separated. But in dreams, in trances, and in all unreflective actions, the soul's intercourse with the body was interrupted: it went back into the divine breast, and the future was revealed to it.

Magicians also knew how to take advantage of the knowledge they had acquired of medicine. They profited from superstition, which always attributed to supernatural causes those phenomena whose workings people failed to understand.

Finally, politics promoted priestly divination; for nothing of consequence was undertaken without consulting augurs, haruspices, and oracles.

In this way everything tended to foster gross errors. These errors were so widespread that the light of religion was unable to prevent their expansion, at least in part among the Jews and the Christians. Among them people were seen to make use of ceremonies to summon the devil and the dead that were quite similar to those of the pagans to summon stars and demons; people were seen searching through scripture for discoveries in physics and everything that could satisfy their curiosity or their greed.

Such is the system of divination of astrologers, magicians, dream-interpreters, augurs, haruspices, etc. If we could follow all the writers who sought to establish these absurdities, we would see that they all take their departure from the same starting point, and that they all go astray depending on where their imaginations lead them. We would even see them go so far astray, and by routes so bizarre, that we would have difficulty ascertaining the initial occasion for their errors. But it is enough to show how natural it was for people to adopt these prejudices, and yet how absurd it was to believe in them.

From *Philosophical Dictionary* (1764)

VOLTAIRE (FRANÇOIS-MARIE AROUET)

[Much of the life of François-Marie Arouet (1694–1778), who adopted the pseudonym Voltaire, was spent in a battle against organized religion. A number of his early poems, including *Epître à Uranie* (*Epistle to Urania*) (1722) and *La Henriade* (*The Henriad*) (1723), attacked religious fanaticism. In 1755, after Louis XV forbade him to enter France, Voltaire settled first in Geneva, then in Ferney, just across the border from Switzerland; his estate there became a magnet for many of the intellectuals of Europe. He wrote a searing poem on the Lisbon earthquake of 1755, wondering how God could have allowed so many people to die (many of them in churches, as the earthquake had occurred on a Sunday). He also expressed his scorn of religion and religiously based philosophy in fiction, including *Candide* (1759). The torture and execution of a Protestant, Jean Calas, led to Voltaire's fiery *Traité sur la tolérance* (1763; *Treatise on Toleration*), arguing for religious tolerance not on the basis of freedom of thought, but on that of preserving social and political order. He wrote numerous and increasingly censorious attacks on Christianity, including *Questions sur les miracles* (1767; *Questions on Miracles*); *Examen important de milord Bolingbroke* (1767; *Lord Bolingbroke's Important Examination*); and *Dieu et les hommes* (1769; *God and Human Beings*). With his health failing, he returned to Paris in early 1778, dying a few months later.

In the following extracts from his celebrated *Dictionnaire philosophique*

(1764f.; *Philosophical Dictionary*), Voltaire addresses many of the absurdities and illogicalities associated with the Christian religion. Although he never espoused overt atheism, and indeed regarded atheists as dangerous libertines, Voltaire was ferociously anticlerical, as his repeated cry "Ecrasez l'infâme!" ("Crush the infamy!"), directed at the Catholic church, attests.]

CHRISTIANITY

God himself came down from heaven and died to redeem mankind and extirpate sin forever from the face of the earth; and yet he left the greater part of mankind a prey to error, crime, and the devil. This, to our weak intellects, appears a fatal contradiction. But it is not for us to question Providence; our duty is to humble ourselves in the dust before it.

Several learned men have testified their surprise at not finding in the historian Flavius Josephus any mention of Jesus Christ; for all men of true learning are now agreed that the short passage relative to him in that history has been interpolated.[1] The father of Flavius Josephus must, however, have been witness to all the miracles of Jesus. Josephus was of the priestly race and related to Herod's wife, Mariamne. He gives us long details of all that prince's actions, yet says not a word of the life or death of Jesus; nor does this historian, who disguises none of Herod's cruelties, say one word of the general massacre of the infants ordered by him on hearing that there was born a king of the Jews. The Greek calendar estimates the number of children murdered on this occasion at 14,000. This is, of all actions of all tyrants, the most horrible. There is no example of it in the history of the whole world.

Yet the best writer the Jews have ever had, the only one esteemed by the Greeks and Romans, makes no mention of an event so singular and so frightful. He says nothing of the appearance of a new star in the east after the birth of our Savior—a brilliant phenomenon that could not escape the knowledge of a historian so enlightened as Josephus. He is also silent regarding the darkness that, on our Savior's death, covered the whole earth for three hours at midday—the great number of graves that opened at that moment, and the multitude of the just that rose again.

The learned are constantly evincing their surprise that no Roman historian speaks of these prodigies, happening in the empire of Tiberius, under the eyes of a Roman governor and a Roman garrison, who must have sent to the emperor and the Senate a detailed account of the most miraculous event that mankind had ever heard of. Rome itself must have been plunged for three hours in impenetrable darkness; such a prodigy would have had a place in the annals of Rome, and in those of every nation. But it was not God's will that these divine things should be written down by their profane hands.

The same persons also find some difficulties in the gospel history. They remark that, in Matthew, Jesus Christ tells the scribes and Pharisees that all the innocent blood that has been shed upon earth, from that of Abel the Just down to that of Zachary, son of Barac, whom they slew between the temple and the altar, shall be upon their heads.

There is not (say they) in the Hebrew history any Zachary slain in the temple before the coming of the Messiah, nor in His time; but in the history of the siege of Jerusalem, by Josephus, there is a Zachary, son of Barac, slain by the faction of the Zelotes. This is in the nineteenth chapter of the fourth book. Hence they suspect that the gospel according to St. Matthew was written after the taking of Jerusalem by Titus. But every doubt, every objection of this kind, vanishes when it is considered how great a difference there must be between books divinely inspired and the books of men. It was God's pleasure to envelop alike in awful obscurity his birth, his life, and his death. His ways are in all things different from ours.

The learned have also been much tormented by the difference between the two genealogies of Jesus Christ. St. Matthew makes Joseph the son of Jacob, Jacob of Matthan, Matthan of Eleazar [Matt. 1:16–17]. St. Luke, on the contrary, says that Joseph was the son of Heli, Heli of Matthat, Matthat of Levi, Levi of Melchi, etc. [Luke 3:24]. They will not reconcile the fifty-six progenitors up to Abraham, given to Jesus by Luke, with the forty-two other forefathers up to the same Abraham, given him by Matthew; and they are quite staggered by Matthew's giving only forty-one generations, while he speaks of forty-two.

They raise other difficulties about Jesus being the son, not of Joseph, but of Mary. They moreover raise some doubts respecting our Savior's miracles, quoting St. Augustine, St. Hilary,[2] and others, who have given to the accounts of these miracles a mystical or allegorical sense; as, for example, to the fig tree cursed and blasted for not having borne figs when it was not the fig season; the devils sent into the bodies of swine in a country where no swine were kept; the water changed into wine at the end of a feast, when the guests were already too much heated. But all these learned critics are confounded by the faith, which is only the purer for their cavils. The sole design of this article is to follow the historical thread and give a precise idea of the facts about which there is no dispute.

First, then, Jesus was born under the Mosaic law; he was circumcised according to that law; he fulfilled all its precepts; he kept all its feasts; he did not reveal the mystery of his incarnation; he never told the Jews he was born of a virgin; he received John's blessing in the waters of the Jordan, a ceremony to which various of the Jews submitted; but he never baptized anyone; he never spoke of the seven sacraments; he instituted no ecclesiastical hierarchy during his life. He concealed from his contemporaries that he was the Son of God, begotten from all eternity, consubstantial with his Father; and that the Holy Ghost proceeded from the Father and the Son. He did not say that his person was composed of two natures and two wills. He left these mysteries to be announced to men in the course of time by those who were to be enlightened by the Holy Ghost. So long as he lived, he departed in nothing from the law of his fathers. In the eyes of men he was no more than a just man, pleasing to God, persecuted by the envious and condemned to death by prejudiced magistrates. He left his holy church, established by him, to do all the rest. [. . .]

Let us consider the state of religion in the Roman Empire at that period. Mysteries and expiations were in credit almost throughout the earth. The emperors, the great, and the philosophers had, it is true, no faith in these mysteries; but the people, who in religious matters give the law to the great, imposed on them the necessity of conforming in appearance to their worship. To succeed in chaining the multitude you must seem to wear the same fetters. Cicero himself was initiated in the Eleusinian mysteries. The knowledge of only one God was the principal tenet inculcated in these mysteries and magnificent festivals. It is undeniable that the prayers and hymns handed down to us as belonging to these mysteries are the most pious and most admirable of the relics of paganism. The Christians, who likewise adored only one God, had thereby greater facility in converting some of the Gentiles. Some of the philosophers of Plato's sect became Christians; hence in the three first centuries the fathers of the church were all Platonists.

DELUGE (UNIVERSAL)

We begin with observing that we are believers in the universal deluge, because it is recorded in the holy Hebrew Scriptures transmitted to Christians. We consider it a miracle:

1. Because all the facts by which God condescends to interfere in the sacred books are so many miracles.

2. Because the sea could not rise fifteen cubits, or twenty-one and a half standard feet, above the highest mountains, without leaving its bed dry and, at the same time, violating all the laws of gravity and the equilibrium of fluids, which would evidently require a miracle.

3. Because, even although it might rise to the height mentioned, the ark could not have contained, according to known physical laws, all the living things of the earth, together with their food, for so long a time; considering that lions, tigers, panthers, leopards, lynxes, rhinoceroses, bears, wolves, hyenas, eagles, hawks, kites, vultures, falcons, and all carnivorous animals, which feed on flesh alone, would have died of hunger, even after having devoured all the other species.

There was printed some time ago, in an appendix to Pascal's "Thoughts," a dissertation of a merchant of Rouen, called Le Peletier, in which he proposes a plan for building a vessel in which all kinds of animals might be included and maintained for the space of a year. It is clear that this merchant never superintended even a poultry-yard. We can only look upon M. Le Peletier, the architect of the ark, as a visionary, who knew nothing about menageries; and upon the deluge as an adorable miracle, fearful, and incomprehensible to the feeble reason of M. Le Peletier, as well as to our own.

4. Because the physical impossibility of a universal deluge, by natural means, can be strictly demonstrated. The demonstration is as follows: All the seas cover half the globe. A common measure of their depths near the

shores, and in the open ocean, is assumed to be five hundred feet. In order that they might cover both hemispheres to the depth of five hundred feet, not only would an ocean of that depth be necessary over all the land, but a new sea would, in addition, be required to envelop the ocean at present existing, without which the laws of hydrostatics would occasion the dispersion of that other new mass of water five hundred feet deep, which should remain covering the land. Thus, then, two new oceans are required to cover the terraqueous globe merely to the depth of five hundred feet.

Supposing the mountains to be only twenty thousand feet high, forty oceans, each five hundred feet in height, would be required to accumulate on each other, merely in order to equal the height of the mountains. Every successive ocean would contain all the others, and the last of them all would have a circumference containing forty times that of the first.

In order to form this mass of water, it would be necessary to create it out of nothing. In order to withdraw it, it would be necessary to annihilate it. The event of the deluge, then, is a double miracle, and the greatest that has ever manifested the power of the eternal Sovereign of all worlds. [. . .]

I do not comprehend how God created a race of men in order to drown them, and then substituted in their place a race still viler than the first.

How seven pairs of all kinds of clean animals should come from the four quarters of the globe, together with two pairs of unclean ones, without the wolves devouring the sheep on the way, or the kites the pigeons, etc.

How eight persons could keep in order, feed, and water such an immense number of inmates, shut up in an ark for nearly two years; for, after the cessation of the deluge, it would be necessary to have food for all these passengers for another year, given that the herbage was so scanty.

I am not like M. Le Peletier. I admire everything and explain nothing.

FAITH

Divine faith, about which so much has been written, is evidently nothing more than incredulity brought under subjection, for we certainly have no other faculty than the understanding by which we can believe; and the objects of faith are not those of the understanding. We can believe only what appears to be true, and nothing can appear true but in one of the three following ways: by intuition or feeling, as I exist, I see the sun; by an accumulation of probability amounting to certainty, as there is a city called Constantinople; or by positive demonstration, as triangles of the same base and height are equal.

Faith, therefore, being nothing at all of this description, can no more be a belief, a persuasion, than it can be yellow or red. It can be nothing but the annihilation of reason, a silence of adoration at the contemplation of things absolutely incomprehensible. Thus, speaking philosophically, no person believes in the Trinity; no person believes that the same body can be in a thousand places at once; and he who says, "I believe these mysteries," will see, beyond the possibility of a doubt, if he reflects for a moment on what passes in his mind, that these words mean no more than, "I respect these mysteries; I submit myself to those who announce them." For they agree with me that my reason, or their own reason, does not believe them; but it is clear that if my *reason* is not persuaded, *I* am not persuaded. I and my reason cannot possibly be two different beings. It is an absolute contradiction that I should receive as true what my understanding rejects as false. Faith, therefore, is nothing but submissive or deferential incredulity.

But why should this submission be exercised when my understanding invincibly recoils? The reason, we well know, is that my understanding has been persuaded that the mysteries of my faith are laid down by God Himself. All, then, that I can do, as a reasonable being, is to be silent and adore. This is what divines call external faith; and this faith neither is, nor can be, anything more than respect for things incomprehensible, because of the reliance I place on those who teach them.

If God Himself were to say to me, "Thought is of an olive color"; "the square of a certain number is bitter"; I should certainly understand nothing at all from these words. I could not adopt them either as true or false. But I will repeat them, if He commands me to do it; and I will make others repeat them at the risk of my life. This is not faith; it is nothing more than obedience.

In order to obtain a foundation then for this obedience, it is merely necessary to examine the books that require it. Our understanding, therefore, should investigate the books of the Old and New Testament, just as it would

Plutarch or Livy; and if it finds in them incontestable and decisive evidences—evidences obvious to all minds, and such as would be admitted by men of all nations—that God Himself is their author, then it is our incumbent duty to subject our understanding to the yoke of faith.

FANATICISM

Fanaticism is the effect of a false conscience, which makes religion subservient to the caprices of the imagination, and the excesses of the passions. [. . .]

It is dreadful to observe how the opinion that the wrath of heaven might be appeased by human massacre spread, after being once started, through almost every religion; and what various reasons have been given for the sacrifice, as though to preclude, if possible, the escape of anyone from extirpation. Sometimes they are enemies who must be immolated to Mars the exterminator. The Scythians slay upon the altars of this deity a hundredth part of their prisoners of war; and from this usage attending victory, we may form some judgment of the justice of war. Accordingly, among other nations it was engaged in solely to supply these human sacrifices, so that, having first been instituted, as it would seem, to expiate the horrors of war, they at length came to serve as a justification of them.

Sometimes a barbarous deity requires victims from among the just and good. The Getae eagerly dispute the honor of personally conveying to Zamolxis the vows and devotions of their country.[3] He whose good fortune has destined him to be the sacrifice is thrown with the greatest violence upon a range of spears, fixed for the purpose. If on falling he receives a mortal wound, it augurs well as to the success of the negotiation and the merit of the envoy; but if he survives the wound, he is a wretch with whom the god would not condescend to hold any communication.

Sometimes children are demanded, and the respective divinities recall the life they had only recently imparted: "Justice," says Montaigne, "thirsting for the blood of innocence!"[4] Sometimes the call is for the dearest and nearest blood: the Carthaginians sacrificed their own sons to Saturn, as if Time did not devour them with sufficient speed. Sometimes the demand was for the blood of the most beautiful. That Amestris, who had buried twelve men alive in order to obtain from Pluto, in return for so revolting an offering, a somewhat longer life—that same Amestris further sacrifices to that insatiable divinity twelve daughters of the highest personages in Persia;[5] as the sacrificing priests have always taught men that they ought to offer on the altar the most valuable of their possessions. It is upon this principle that among some nations the first-born were immolated, and that among others they were redeemed by offerings more valuable to the ministers of sacrifice. This it is, unquestionably, that introduced into Europe the practice prevalent for centuries of devoting children to celibacy at the early age of five years, and shutting up in a cloister the brothers of a hereditary prince, just as in Asia the practice is to murder them.

Sometimes it is the purest blood that is demanded. We read of certain Indians, if I recollect rightly, who hospitably entertain all who visit them and make a merit of killing every sensible and virtuous stranger who enters their country, so that his talents and virtues may remain with them. Sometimes it is the most sacred blood that is required. With the majority of idolaters, priests perform the office of executioner at the altar; and among the Siberians, it is the practice to kill the priests in order to dispatch them to pray in the other world for the fulfillment of the wishes of the people.

But let us turn our attention to other frenzies and other spectacles. All Europe passes into Asia by a road inundated with the blood of Jews, who commit suicide to avoid falling into the hands of their enemies. This epidemic depopulates one-half of the inhabited world: kings, pontiffs, women, the young and the old, all yield to the influence of the holy madness that, for a series of two hundred years, instigated the slaughter of innumerable nations at the tomb of a god of peace. Then were to be seen lying oracles, and military hermits, monarchs in pulpits, and prelates in camps. All the different states constitute one delirious populace; barriers of mountains and seas are surmounted; legitimate possessions are abandoned to enable their owners to fly to conquests that were no longer, in point of fertility, the land of promise; manners become corrupted under foreign skies; princes, after having exhausted their respective kingdoms to redeem a country that had never been theirs, complete the ruin of them for their personal ransom; thousands of soldiers, wandering under the banners of many chieftains, acknowledge the authority of none and hasten their defeat by their desertion; and the disease terminates only to be succeeded by a contagion still more horrible and desolating.

The same spirit of fanaticism cherished the rage for distant conquests: scarcely had Europe repaired its losses when the discovery of a new world hastened the ruin of our own. At that terrible injunction, "Go and conquer," America was desolated and its inhabitants exterminated; Africa and Europe were exhausted in vain to repeople it; the poison of money and of pleasure having enervated the species, the world became nearly a desert and appeared likely every day to advance nearer to desolation by the continual wars that were kindled on our continent, from the ambition of extending its power to foreign lands.

Let us now compute the immense number of slaves that fanaticism has made, whether in Asia, where uncircumcision was a mark of infamy, or in Africa, where the Christian name was a crime, or in America, where the pretext of baptism absolutely extinguished the feelings of humanity. Let us compute the thousands who have been seen to perish either on scaffolds in the ages of persecution, or in civil wars by the hands of their fellow citizens, or by their own hands through excessive austerities, and maceration. Let us survey the surface of the earth and glance at the various standards unfurled and blazing in the name of religion; in Spain against the Moors, in France against the Turks, in Hungary against the Tartars; at the numerous military orders founded for converting infidels by the point of the sword, and slaughtering one another at the foot of the altar they had come to defend. Let us then look down from the appalling tribunal thus raised on the bodies of the innocent and miserable, in order to judge the living, as God, with a balance widely different, will judge the dead.

In a word, let us contemplate the horrors of fifteen centuries, all frequently renewed in the course of a single one: unarmed men slain at the feet of altars; kings destroyed by the dagger or by poison; a large state reduced to half its extent by the fury of its own citizens; the nation at once the most warlike and the most pacific on the face of the globe, divided in fierce hostility against itself; the sword unsheathed between the sons and the father; usurpers, tyrants, executioners, sacrilegious robbers, and bloodstained parricides violating, under the impulse of religion, every convention divine or human—such is the deadly picture of fanaticism.

INQUISITION

The Inquisition is an ecclesiastical jurisdiction established by the See of Rome in Italy, Spain, Portugal, and even in the Indies, for the purpose of searching out and extirpating infidels, Jews, and heretics.

That we may not be suspected of resorting to falsehood in order to render this tribunal odious, we shall in this present article give the abstract of a Latin work on the "Origin and Progress of the Office of the Holy Inquisition," printed by the royal press at Madrid in 1598, by order of Luis de Páramo, inquisitor in the kingdom of Sicily.[6]

Without going back to the origin of the Inquisition, which Páramo thinks he discovers in the manner in which God is said to have proceeded against Adam and Eve, let us abide by the new law of which Jesus Christ, according to him, was the chief inquisitor. He exercised the functions of that office on the thirteenth day after his birth, by announcing to the city of Jerusalem, through the three kings or Magi, his appearance in the world, and afterwards by causing Herod to be devoured alive by worms; by driving the buyers and sellers out of the temple; and finally, by delivering Judaea into the hands of tyrants, who pillaged it in punishment of its unbelief.

After Jesus Christ, St. Peter, St. Paul, and the rest of the apostles exercised the office of inquisitor, which they transmitted to the popes and bishops, and their successors. St. Dominic having arrived in France with the bishop of Osma, of which he was archdeacon, became animated with zeal against the Albigenses and obtained the regard and favor of Simon, Count de Montfort. Having been appointed by the pope inquisitor in Languedoc, he there founded his order, which was approved of and ratified, in 1216, by Honorius III. Under the auspices of St. Madelaine, Count Montfort took the city of Gezer by assault and put all the inhabitants to the sword; and at Laval, four hundred Albigenses were burned at once. "In all the histories of the Inquisition that I ever read," says Páramo, "I never met with an act of faith so eminent, or a spectacle so solemn. At the village of Cazera, sixty were burned; and in another place a hundred and eighty."

The Inquisition was adopted by the count of Toulouse in 1229 and confided to the Dominicans by Pope Gregory IX in 1233; Innocent IV in 1251 established it in the whole of Italy, with the exception of Naples. At first, indeed, heretics were not subjected in the Milanese to the punishment of death, which they nevertheless so richly deserved, because the popes were not sufficiently respected by the emperor Frederick, to whom that state belonged; but a short time afterwards heretics were burned at Milan as well as in the other parts of Italy; and our author remarks that in 1315, after some thousands of heretics had spread themselves through Cremasco, a small territory included in the jurisdiction of the Milanese, the Dominican brothers burned the greater part of them and thus checked the ravages of the theological pestilence by the flames.

As the first canon of the Council of Toulouse enjoined the bishops to appoint in every parish a priest and two or three laymen of reputation, who should be bound by oath to search carefully and frequently for heretics, in houses, caves, and all places wherever they might be able to hide themselves, and to give the speediest information to the bishop, the seigneur of the place, or his bailiff, after having taken all necessary precautions against the escape of any heretics discovered, the inquisitors must have acted at this time in concert with the bishops. The prisons of the bishop and of the Inquisition were frequently the same; and, although in the course of the procedure the inquisitor might act in his own name, he could not, without the intervention of the bishop, apply the torture, pronounce any definitive sentence, or condemn to perpetual imprisonment, etc. The frequent disputes that occurred between the bishops and the inquisitors, on the limits of their authority, on the spoils of the condemned, etc., compelled Pope Sixtus IV, in 1473, to make the inquisitions independent and separate from the tribunals of the bishops. He created for Spain an Inquisitor-general, with full powers to nominate particular inquisitors; and Ferdinand V, in 1478, founded and endowed the Inquisition.

At the solicitation of Turrecremata (or Torquemada), a brother of the Dominican order and grand inquisitor of Spain, the same Ferdinand, surnamed the Catholic, banished from his kingdom all the Jews, allowing them three months from the publication of his edict, after the expiration of which period they were not to be found in any of the Spanish dominions under pain of death. They were permitted, on quitting the kingdom, to take with them the goods and merchandise they had purchased, but forbidden to take out of it any quantities of gold or silver.

The brother Turrecremata followed up and strengthened this edict, in the diocese of Toledo, by prohibiting all Christians, under pain of excommunication, from giving anything whatever to the Jews, even what might be necessary to preserve life itself.

As a result of these decrees, about a million Jews departed from Catalonia, the kingdom of Aragon, that of Valencia, and other countries subject to the dominion of Ferdinand; the greater part of whom perished miserably; so that they compare the calamities they suffered during this period to those they experienced under Titus and Vespasian. This expulsion of the Jews gave incredible joy to all Catholic sovereigns.

Some divines blamed these edicts of the king of Spain; their principal reasons are that unbelievers ought not to be forced to embrace the faith of Jesus Christ, and that these violences are a disgrace to our religion.

But these arguments are very weak, and I contend, says Páramo, that the edict is pious, just, and praiseworthy, as the violence with which the Jews are required to be converted is not an absolute but a conditional violence, since they might avoid it by leaving their country. Besides, they might corrupt those of the Jews who were newly converted, and even Christians themselves; but, as St. Paul says, what communion is there between justice and iniquity, light and darkness, Jesus Christ and Belial? [2 Cor. 6:15].

With respect to the confiscation of their goods, nothing could be more equitable, as they had acquired them only by usury toward Christians, who therefore only received back what was in fact their own.

In short, by the death of our Lord the Jews became slaves, and everything that a slave possesses belongs to his master. We had to suspend our narrative for a moment to make these remarks, in opposition to persons who have thus calumniated the piety, the spotless justice, and the sanctity of the Catholic king.

At Seville, where an example of severity to the Jews was ardently desired, it was the holy will of God, who knows how to draw good out of evil, that a young man who was waiting as a result of an assignation should see through the chinks of a partition an assembly of Jews, and consequently inform against them. A great number of the unhappy wretches were apprehended and punished as they deserved. By virtue of different edicts of the kings of Spain, and of the inquisitors, general and particular, established in that kingdom, there were, in a very short time, about two thousand heretics burned at Seville, and more than four thousand from 1482 to 1520. A vast number of others were condemned to perpetual imprisonment or exposed to inflictions of different descriptions. The emigration from it was so great that five hundred houses were supposed to be left quite empty, and in the whole diocese, three thousand; and altogether more than a hundred thousand heretics were put to death, or punished in some other manner, or went into banishment to avoid severer suffering. Such was the destruction of heretics accomplished by these pious brethren.

The establishment of the Inquisition at Toledo was a fruitful source of revenue to the Catholic Church. In the short space of two years it actually burned at the stake fifty-two obstinate heretics, and two hundred and twenty more were outlawed; whence we may easily conjecture how useful the Inquisition has been from its original establishment, since in so short a period it performed such wonders.

From the beginning of the fifteenth century, Pope Boniface IX attempted in vain to establish the Inquisition in Portugal, where he created the provincial of the Dominicans, Vincent de Lisbon, inquisitor-general. Some years later, Innocent VII named as inquisitor the Minim Didacus de Sylva; King John I wrote to that pope that the establishment of the Inquisition in his kingdom was contrary to the good of his subjects, to his own interests, and perhaps also to the interests of religion.

The pope, affected by the representations of a too mild and easy monarch, revoked all the powers granted to the inquisitors newly established and authorized Mark, bishop of Senigaglia, to absolve the persons accused; which he accordingly did. Those who had been deprived of their dignities and offices were re-established in them, and many were delivered from the fear of the confiscation of their property.

But how admirable, continues Páramo, is the Lord in all his ways! What the sovereign pontiffs had been unable effectually to obtain with all their urgency, King John granted spontaneously to a dexterous impostor, whom God made use of as an instrument for accomplishing the good work. In fact, the wicked are frequently useful instruments in God's hands, and he does not reject the good they bring about. Thus, when John remarks to our Lord Jesus Christ, "Master, we saw one casting out devils in thy name; and we forbade him, because he followeth not us," Jesus answered him, "Forbid him not; for he that is not against us is for us" [Luke 9:49–50].

Páramo relates afterwards that he saw in the library of St. Laurence, at the Escorial, a manuscript in the handwriting of Saavedra, in which that knave details his fabrication of a false bull, and obtaining thereby his *entrée* into Seville as legate, with a train of a hundred and twenty domestics; his defrauding of thirteen thousand ducats the heirs of a rich nobleman in that neighborhood, during his twenty days' residence in the palace of the archbishop, by producing a counterfeit bond for the same sum, which the nobleman acknowledged, in that instrument, to have borrowed of the legate when he visited Rome; and finally, after his arrival at Badajoz, the permission granted him by King John III, to whom he was presented by means of forged letters of the pope, to establish tribunals of the Inquisition in the principal cities of the kingdom.

These tribunals began immediately to exercise their jurisdiction; and a vast number of condemnations and executions of relapsed heretics took place, as also of absolutions of recanting and penitent heretics. Six months had passed in this manner, when the truth was made apparent of that expression in the Gospel, "There is nothing . . . hid, that shall not be known" [Luke 12:2]. The Marquis de Villeneuve de Barcarotta, a Spanish nobleman, assisted by the governor of Mora, had the impostor apprehended and conducted to Madrid. He was there carried before John de Tavera, archbishop of Toledo. That prelate, perfectly astonished at all that now transpired of the knavery and address of the false legate, dispatched all the depositions and documents relative to the case to Pope Paul III; as he did also the acts of the inquisitions that Saavedra had established, and by which it appeared that a great number of heretics had already been judged and condemned, and that the impostor had extorted from his victims more than three hundred thousand ducats.

The pope could not help acknowledging in this the finger of God and a miracle of His providence; he accordingly formed the congregation of the tribunal of the Inquisition, under the denomination of "The Holy Office," in 1545, and Sixtus V confirmed it in 1588. [. . .]

When the Spaniards passed over to America they carried the Inquisition with them; the Portuguese introduced it in the Indies, immediately upon its being established at Lisbon, which led to the observation that Luis de Páramo makes in his preface, that this flourishing and verdant tree had extended its branches and its roots throughout the world and produced the most pleasant fruits.

ORIGINAL SIN

This is a subject on which the Socinians[7] or Unitarians take occasion to exult and triumph. They designate this foundation of Christianity its "original sin." It is an insult to God, they say; it is accusing Him of the most absurd barbarity to have the boldness to assert that He formed all the successive generations of mankind to deliver them over to eternal tortures, under the pretext of their original ancestor having eaten of a particular fruit in a garden. This sacrilegious imputation is so much the more inexcusable among Christians, as there is not a single word respecting this same invention of original sin, either in the Pentateuch, or in the prophets, or the gospels, whether apocryphal or canonical, or in any of the writers who are called the "first fathers of the Church."

It is not even related in the Book of Genesis that God condemned Adam to death for eating an apple. God says to him, indeed, "in the day that thou eatest thereof thou shalt surely die" [Gen. 2:17]. But the very same Book of Genesis makes Adam live nine hundred and thirty years after indulging in this criminal repast. The animals, the plants, which had not partaken of this fruit, died at the respective periods prescribed for them by nature. Man is evidently born to die, like all the rest.

Moreover, the punishment of Adam was never, in any way, introduced into the Jewish law. Adam was no more a Jew than he was a Persian or Chaldean.

The first chapters of Genesis—at whatever period they were composed—were regarded by all the learned Jews as an allegory, and even as a fable not a little dangerous, since that book was forbidden to be read by any before they had attained the age of twenty-one.

In a word, the Jews knew no more about original sin than they did about the Chinese ceremonies; and, although divines generally discover in Scripture everything they wish to find there, either *totidem verbis* [in so many words], or *totidem litteris* [in so many letters], we may safely assert that no reasonable divine will ever discover in it this surprising and overwhelming mystery.

We admit that St. Augustine was the first who brought this strange notion into credit; a notion worthy of the warm and romantic brain of an African debauchee and penitent, Manichean and Christian, tolerant and persecuting—who passed his life in perpetual self-contradiction.

What an abomination, exclaim the strict Unitarians, so atrociously to insult the Author of Nature as to impute to him perpetual miracles, in order that he may damn to all eternity the unhappy race of mankind, whom he introduces into the present life for so short a span! Either he created souls from all eternity, upon which system, as they must be infinitely more ancient than the sin of Adam, they can have no possible connection with it; or these souls are formed whenever man and woman sexually associate; in which case God must be supposed to be continually watching for all the various associations of this nature that take place, to create spirits that he will render eternally miserable; or, finally, God is himself the soul of all mankind, and upon this system damns himself. Which of these three suppositions is the most absurd and abominable? There is no fourth. For the opinion that God waits six weeks before he creates a damned soul in a fetus is, in fact, no other than that which creates it at the moment of sexual connection: the difference of six weeks cannot be of the slightest consequence in the argument. I have merely related the opinion of the Unitarians; but men have now attained such a degree of superstition that I can scarcely relate it without trembling.

It must be acknowledged that we are not acquainted with any father of the Church before St. Augustine and St. Jerome who taught the doctrine of original sin. St. Clement of Alexandria, notwithstanding his profound knowledge of antiquity, far from speaking in any one passage of his works of that corruption which has infected the whole human race, and rendered it guilty from its birth, says in express words, "What evil can a new-born infant commit? How could it possibly prevaricate? How could such a being, which has, in fact, as yet done no one thing, fall under the curse of Adam?"[8]

And it is worth observing that he does not employ this language in order to combat the rigid opinion of original sin, which was not at that time developed, but merely to show that the passions, which are capable of corrupting all mankind, have as yet taken no hold of this innocent infant. He does not say: This creature of a day would not be damned if it should now die, for no one had yet conjectured that it would be damned. St. Clement could not combat a system absolutely unknown.

The great Origen is still more decisive than St. Clement of Alexandria. He admits, indeed, in his exposition of the Epistle of Paul to the Romans, that sin entered into the world by Adam, but he maintains that it is the inclination to sin that thus entered; that it is very easy to commit evil, but that it is not on that account said that man will always commit evil and is guilty even as soon as he is born.

In short, original sin, in the time of Origen, consisted only in the misfortune of resembling the first man by being liable to sin like him. Baptism was necessary; it was the seal of Christianity; it washed away all sins, but no man had yet said that it washed away those which the subject of it had not committed. No one yet asserted that an infant would be damned, and burned in everlasting flames, as a result of its dying within two minutes of its birth. And an unanswerable proof on this point is that a long period passed away before the practice of baptizing infants became prevalent. Tertullian was averse to their being baptized; but, assuming that original sin—of which these poor innocents could not possibly be guilty— would affect their reprobation and expose them to suffer boundless and endless torture, for a deed of which it was impossible for them to have the slightest knowledge, to refuse them the consecrated bath of baptism would be willfully consigning them to eternal damnation. The souls of all the executioners in the world, condensed into the very essence of ingenious cruelty, could not have suggested a more execrable abomination. In a word, it is an incontestable fact that Christians did not for a certain period baptize their infants, and it is therefore equally incontestable that they were very far from damning them.

This, however, is not all; Jesus Christ never said: "The infant that is not baptized will be damned."[9] He came on the contrary to expiate all sins, to redeem mankind by His blood; therefore, infants could not be damned. Infants would, of course, *a fortiori*, and, preferably, enjoy this privilege. Our divine Savior never baptized any person. Paul circumcised his disciple Timothy, but is nowhere said to have baptized him.

In a word, during the two first centuries, the baptism of infants was not customary; it was not believed, therefore, that infants would become victims of the fault of Adam. At the end of four hundred years their salvation was considered in danger, and great uncertainty and apprehension existed on the subject.

In the fifth century appears Pelagius. He treated the opinion of original sin as monstrous. According to him, this dogma, like all others, was founded upon a mere ambiguity. God had said to Adam in the garden: "In the day in which thou shalt eat of the tree of knowledge, thou shalt die" [Gen. 2:17]. But he did not die; and God pardoned him. Why, then, should He not spare His race to the thousandth generation? Why should He consign to infinite and eternal torments the innocent infants whose father He received back into forgiveness and favor?

Pelagius considered God not merely as an absolute master, but as a parent, who left his children at perfect liberty, rewarded them beyond their merits, and punished them less than their faults deserved. The language used by him and his disciples was: "If all men are born objects of the eternal wrath of that Being who confers on them life; if they can possibly be guilty before they can even think, it is then a fearful and execrable offense to give them being, and marriage is the most atrocious of crimes. Marriage, on this system, is nothing more or less than an emanation from the Manichean principle of evil; and those who engage in it, instead of adoring God, adore the devil."

Pelagius and his partisans propagated this doctrine in Africa, where the reputation and influence of St. Augustine were unbounded. He had been a Manichean and seemed to think himself called upon to enter the lists against Pelagius. The latter was ill able to resist either Augustine or Jerome; various points, however, were contested, and the dispute proceeded so far that Augustine pronounced his sentence of damnation upon all children born, or to be born, throughout the world, in the following terms: "The Catholic faith teaches that all men are born so guilty that even infants are certainly damned when they die without having been regenerated in Jesus."[10]

It would be but a wretched compliment of condolence to offer to a queen of China, or Japan, or India, Scythia, or Gothia, who had just lost her infant son to say: "Be comforted, madam; his highness the prince royal is now in the clutches of five hundred devils, who turn him round and round in a great furnace to all eternity, while his body rests embalmed and in peace within the precincts of your palace."

The astonished and terrified queen inquires why these devils should eternally roast her dear son, the prince royal. She is answered that the reason of it is that his great-grandfather formerly ate of the fruit of knowledge, in a garden. Form an idea, if possible, of the looks and thoughts of the king, the queen, the whole council, and all the beautiful ladies of the court!

The sentence of the African bishop appeared to some divines—for there are some good souls to be found in every place and class—rather severe, and was therefore mitigated by one Peter Chrysologus, or Peter Golden-tongue, who invented a suburb to hell, called "limbo," where all the little boys and girls that died before baptism might be disposed of.[11] It is a place in which these innocents vegetate without sensation; the abode of apathy; the place that has been called "The paradise of fools." We find this very expression in Milton. He places this paradise somewhere near the moon![12]

From *The System of Nature* (1770)

PAUL-HENRI THIRY, BARON D'HOLBACH

[Paul-Henri Thiry, Baron d'Holbach (1723–1789) was born Paul Heinrich Dietrich in Edesheim, in the Rhenish Palatinate, but came to Paris as a youth and spent most of his life there. When he was thirty, his father and uncle both died, leaving him an immense fortune. He initiated a salon at his home in Paris, and many of the leading philosophes of the day attended. He wrote or translated many articles on religion and other subjects for the *Encyclopédie*, but he gained greater notoriety for his unrestrained polemics against religion, notably *Le Christianisme dévoilé* (1761; *Christianity Unveiled*) and *La Contagion sacrée* (1768; *The Sacred Contagion*). In *Système de la nature* (1770; translated as *The System of Nature*), d'Holbach openly espoused atheism. The treatise remains one of the most exhaustive discussions of atheism—from a scientific, philosophical, moral, and political perspective—ever written. In the following chapter from *The System of Nature*, d'Holbach argues that the immortality of the soul is a scientifically unwarranted assumption, and that the belief in an afterlife and in heaven and hell is morally and psychologically damaging.]

The reflections presented in this work show clearly what ought to be thought of the human soul, as well as of its operations and faculties: everything proves, in the most convincing manner, that it acts and moves according to laws similar to those prescribed to the other beings of nature; that it cannot be distinguished from the body; that it is born with it; that it is modified in the same progression; in short, everything ought to make man conclude that it perishes with it. This soul, as well as the body, passes through a state of weakness and infancy; it is in this stage of its existence that it is assailed by a multitude of modifications and of ideas it receives from exterior objects through the medium of the organs; that it amasses facts; that it collects experiences, whether true or false; that it forms to itself a system of conduct, according to which it thinks and acts, and from which results either its happiness or its misery, its reason or its delirium, its virtues or its vices. Arrived with the body at its full powers and maturity, it does not cease for an instant to share with it its sensations, either agreeable or disagreeable, its pleasures and its pains; as a result, it conjointly approves or disapproves its state; like it, it is either sound or diseased, active or languishing, awake or asleep. In old age, man is extinguished entirely, his fibers become rigid, his nerves lose their elasticity, his senses are blunted, his sight grows dim, his ears lose their sharpness, his ideas become unconnected, his memory fails, his imagination withers; what, then, becomes of his soul? Alas! it sinks down with the body; it gets benumbed as the body loses its feeling, becomes sluggish as the body decays in activity; like it, when enfeebled by years it fulfills its functions with pain; and this substance, which is deemed spiritual or immaterial, undergoes the same revolutions as the body itself.

In spite of this convincing proof of the materiality of the soul, and of its identity with the body, some thinkers have supposed that although the latter is perishable, the former does not perish; that this portion of man enjoys the especial privilege of *immortality*; that it is exempt from dissolution and free from those changes of form that all the beings in nature undergo. As a result of this, man has persuaded himself that this privileged soul does not die: its immortality above all appears indubitable to those who suppose it spiritual: after having made it a simple being, without extent, devoid of parts, totally different from anything of which he has knowledge, they claimed that it was not subject to the laws of decomposition common to all beings, whose continual operation experience has shown him.

Man, feeling within himself a concealed force that insensibly produced action, that imperceptibly gave direction to the motion of his machine, believed that all nature, of whose energies he is ignorant, with whose modes of action he is unacquainted, owed its motion to an agent analogous to his own soul, who acted upon the great macrocosm in the same manner that this soul acted upon his body. Man, having supposed himself double, made nature double also: he distinguished it from its own peculiar energy; he separated it from its mover, which by degrees he made spiritual. This being, distinguished from nature, was regarded as the soul of the world, and the soul of man was regarded as portions emanating from this universal soul. This opinion of the origin of the soul is of very remote antiquity. It was that of the Egyptians, of the Chaldeans, of the Hebrews, of the greater number of the wise men of the east. It was in these schools that Pherecydes, Pythagoras, and Plato drew up a doctrine so flattering to human vanity and imagination. Thus man believed himself a portion of the Divinity; immortal, like the Godhead, in one part of himself. Nevertheless, subsequently invented religions have renounced these advantages, which they judged incompatible with the other parts of their systems: they claimed that the sovereign of nature, or its contriver, was not its soul, but that in virtue of his omnipotence he created human souls in proportion as he produced the bodies they must animate; and they taught that these souls, once produced, by an effect of the same omnipotence enjoyed immortality.

However it may be with these variations upon the origin of souls, those who supposed them emanating from God himself believed that after the death of the body, which served them for an envelope or prison, they returned to their original source. Those who, without adopting the opinion of divine emanation, admired the spirituality and the immortality of the soul were obliged to suppose a region and abode for these souls, which their imagination painted to them each according to his fears, hopes, desires, and prejudices.

Nothing is more popular than the doctrine of the immortality of the soul; nothing is more universally diffused than the expectation of another life. Nature having inspired man with the most ardent love for his existence, the desire of preserving himself forever was a necessary consequence. This desire was presently converted into certainty; from the desire of existing eternally, which nature has implanted in him, he made an argument to prove that man would never cease to exist. Abbadie says: "Our soul has no useless desires, it desires naturally an eternal life";[1] and by a very strange logic he concludes that this desire could not fail to be fulfilled. However this may be, man, thus disposed, listened with avidity to those who announced to him systems so conformable with his wishes. Nevertheless, he ought not to regard as supernatural the desire of existing, which always was and always will be of the essence of man; it ought not to elicit surprise if he eagerly received a hypothesis that flattered his hopes by promising that his desire would one day be gratified; but let him beware how he concludes that this desire itself is an indubitable proof of the reality of this future life, with which, for his present happiness, he seems to be far too much occupied. The passion for existence is in man only a natural consequence of the tendency of a sensible being, whose essence it is to wish to conserve himself: in the human being, it follows the energy of his soul or keeps pace with the force of his imagination, always ready to realize what he strongly desires. He desires the life of the body, and yet this desire is frustrated; why should not the desire for the life of the soul be frustrated like the other?[2]

The simplest reflection upon the nature of his soul ought to convince us that the idea of its immortality is only an illusion. Indeed, what is his soul, save the principle of sensibility? What is it to think, to enjoy, to suffer; is it not to feel? What is life other than the assemblage of modifications, the congregation of motion, peculiar to an organized being? Thus, as soon as the body ceases to live, its sensibility can no longer exercise itself; therefore it can no longer have ideas, nor in consequence thoughts. Ideas, as we have proved, can only reach man through his senses; now how will they maintain that, once deprived of his senses, he is yet capable of receiving sensations, of having perceptions, of forming ideas? As they have made the soul of man an entity separated from the animated body, why have they not made life an entity distinguished from the living body? Life in a body is the totality of its motion; feeling and thought make a part of this motion: thus, in the dead man, these motions will cease like all the others.

Indeed, by what reasoning will it be claimed that this soul, which cannot feel, think, will, or act but by aid of man's organs, can experience pain or pleasure, or even have a consciousness of its own existence, when the organs that should warn it of their presence are decomposed or destroyed? Is it not evident that the soul depends on the arrangement of the various parts of the body, and on the order with which these parts conspire to perform their functions or motions? Thus, once the organic structure is destroyed, it cannot be doubted the soul will be destroyed also. Is it not seen that, during the whole course of human life, this soul is altered, disturbed, troubled by all the changes man's organs experience? And yet, it will be insisted that this soul acts, thinks, subsists when these same organs have entirely disappeared!

An organized being may be compared to a clock, which, once broken, is no longer suitable to the uses for which it was designed. To say that the soul shall feel, think, enjoy, suffer after the death of the body is to pretend that a clock, shivered into a thousand pieces, will continue to strike the hour or mark the progress of time. Those who say that the soul of man is able to subsist notwithstanding the destruction of the body evidently support the position that the modification of a body will be enabled to conserve itself after the subject is destroyed: but this is completely absurd.

It will be said that the conservation of the soul after the death of the body is an effect of the divine power: but this is supporting an absurdity by a gratuitous hypothesis. It surely is not meant by divine power, of whatever nature it may be supposed, that a thing shall exist and not exist at the same time: that a soul shall feel and think without the intermediates necessary to thought.

Let them, then, at least forbear asserting that reason is not wounded by the doctrine of the immortality of the soul, or by the expectation of a future life. These notions, formed solely to flatter or to disturb the imagination of the uninformed who do not reason, cannot appear either convincing or probable to enlightened minds. Reason, exempted from the illusions of prejudice, is without doubt wounded by the supposition of a soul that feels, that thinks, that is afflicted, that rejoices, that has ideas, without having organs; that is to say, destitute of the only known and natural means by which it is possible for it to feel sensations, have perceptions, or form ideas. If it is replied that other means are able to exist that are *supernatural* or *unknown*, it may be answered that these means of transmitting ideas to the soul separated from the body are not better known to, nor more within the reach of, those who suppose it than they are of other men. It is at least very certain that all those who reject the system of innate ideas cannot, without contradicting their own principles, admit the groundless doctrine of the immortality of the soul.

In spite of the consolation that so many persons claim to find in the notion of an eternal existence; in spite of that firm persuasion that so many men assure us they have that their souls will survive their bodies, they seem so alarmed at the dissolution of this body that they do not contemplate their end, which they ought to desire as the period of so many miseries, except with the greatest inquietude. So true it is that the real, the present, even accompanied with pain, has much more influence over mankind than the most beautiful chimeras of the future, which he never views except through the clouds of uncertainty. Indeed, the most religious men, notwithstanding the conviction they express of a blessed eternity, do not find these flattering hopes sufficiently consoling to repress their fears and trembling when they think on the necessary dissolution of their bodies. Death is always for mortals the most frightful point of view; they regard it as a strange phenomenon, contrary to the order of things, opposed to nature; in a word, as an effect of the celestial vengeance, as the *wages of sin*. Although everything proves to man that death is inevitable, he is never able to familiarize himself with this idea; he never thinks on it without shuddering, and the assurance of possessing an immortal soul only feebly indemnifies him for the grief he feels at the deprivation of his perishable body. Two causes contribute to strengthen and nourish his alarm: the one is that this death, commonly accompanied with pain, wrests from him an existence that pleases him, with which he is acquainted, and to which he is accustomed; the other is the uncertainty of the state that must succeed his actual existence.

The illustrious Bacon has said that "Men fear death for the same reason that children dread being alone in darkness."[3] Man naturally challenges everything with which he is unacquainted; he wishes to see clearly, so that he may guarantee himself against those objects that may menace his safety, or that he may be able to procure for himself those that may be useful to him. The man who exists cannot form to himself any idea of nonexistence; as this circumstance disturbs him, for lack of experience his imagination sets to work; this points out to him, either well or ill, this uncertain state. Accustomed to think, to feel, to be active, to enjoy society, he contemplates as the greatest misfortune a dissolution that will strip him of these objects and deprive him of those sensations which his present nature has rendered necessary to him; that will prevent his being warned of his own existence; that shall bereave him of his pleasures to plunge him into nonexistence. In supposing it even exempt from pain, he always looks upon this nonexistence as an afflicting solitude, as a heap of profound darkness; he sees himself in a state of general desolation, destitute of all assistance, and feeling the rigor of this frightful situation. But does not a profound sleep help to give him a true idea of this nonexistence? Does not that deprive him of everything? Does it not appear to annihilate the universe to him, and him to the universe? Is death anything more than a profound and permanent sleep? It is for lack of being able to form an idea of death that man dreads it; if he could grasp a true idea of it he would from that point onward cease to fear it; but he is unable to conceive a state in which there is no feeling; he therefore believes that when he shall no longer exist, he will have the same feelings and the same consciousness of things that during his existence appear to his mind in such gloomy colors. Imagination pictures to him his funeral pomp; the grave they are digging for him; the lamentations that will accompany him to his last abode; he persuades himself that these hideous objects will affect him as painfully, even after his decease, as they do in his present condition in which he is in full possession of his senses.

Mortal, led astray by fear! After your death your eyes will see no more; your ears will hear no longer; in the depth of your grave, you will no more be witness to this scene that your imagination at present represents to you under such black colors; you will no longer take part in what shall be done in the world; you will no more be occupied with what may befall your inanimate remains than you were able to be the day previous to that which ranked you among the beings of your species. To die is to cease to think, to feel, to enjoy, to suffer; your ideas will perish with you; your sorrows will not follow you to the tomb. Think of death, not to feed your fears and your melancholy, but to accustom yourself to look upon it with a placid eye, and to reassure yourself against those false terrors with which the enemies to your repose toil to inspire you!

The fears of death are vain illusions that must disappear as soon as we learn to contemplate this necessary event under its true point of view. A great man has defined philosophy to be a *meditation on death*.[4] He does not wish by that to have it understood that we ought to occupy ourselves sorrowfully with our end, with a view to nourish our fears; on the contrary, he wishes to invite us to familiarize ourselves with an object that nature has rendered necessary to us, and to accustom ourselves to expect it with a serene countenance. If life is a benefit, if it is necessary to love it, it is no less necessary to quit it, and reason ought to teach us a calm resignation to the decrees of fate. Our welfare requires that we should develop the habit of contemplating without alarm an event that our essence has rendered inevitable; our interest demands that we should not by continual dread embitter our life, the charms of which we must inevitably destroy, if we can never view its termination except with trepidation. Reason and his interest concur to assure us against those vague terrors with which our imagination inspires us in this respect. If we were to call them to our assistance, they would reconcile us to an object that only startles us because we have no knowledge of it, or because it is only shown to us with those hideous accompaniments with which superstition has clothed it. Let us, then, endeavor to rid death of these vain illusions, and we will perceive that it is only the sleep of life; that this sleep will not be disturbed with disagreeable dreams, and that an unpleasant awakening will never follow it. To die is to sleep; it is to re-enter into that state of insensibility in which we were previous to our birth; before we had senses, before we were conscious of our actual existence. Laws, as necessary as those which gave us birth, will make us return into the bosom of nature whence we were drawn, in order to reproduce us afterwards under some new form, which it would be useless for us to know. Without consulting us, nature places us for a season in the order of organized beings; without our consent, it will oblige us to quit it to occupy some other order.

Let us not complain, then, that nature is callous; she only makes us undergo a law from which she does not exempt any single being she contains. If all are born and perish; if everything is changed and destroyed; if the birth of a being is never more than the first step toward its end; how is it possible to expect that man, whose machine is so frail, whose parts are so mobile and complicated, should be exempt from the common law that decrees that even the solid earth he inhabits shall experience change, shall undergo alteration—perhaps be destroyed! Feeble mortal! you claim to exist forever; do you wish, then, that for you alone eternal nature shall change its undeviating course? Do you not behold in those eccentric comets with which your eyes are sometimes astonished that the planets themselves are subject to death? Live then in peace, for the season that nature permits you; and if your mind is enlightened by reason, you will die without terror.

Notwithstanding the simplicity of these reflections, nothing is rarer than the sight of men truly fortified against the fears of death. The wise man himself turns pale at its approach; he has occasion to collect the whole force of his mind to await it with serenity. It cannot then be surprising if the idea of death is so revolting to the generality of mortals; it terrifies the young; it redoubles the chagrin and sorrow of the old, who are worn down with infirmity: indeed, the aged, although enfeebled by time, dread it much more than the young who are in the full vigor of life. The man of many decades is more accustomed to live; the powers of his mind are weakened; he has less energy: at length disease consumes him; yet the unhappy wretch thus plunged into misfortune, and laboring under excruciating tortures, has scarcely ever dared to contemplate death, which he ought to regard as the end of all his anguish.

If we seek the source of this cowardice, we will find it in our nature, which attaches us to life, and in that deficiency of energy in our soul which hardly anything tends to corroborate, but which everything strives to enfeeble and bruise. All human institutions, all our opinions, conspire to augment our fears and to render our ideas of death more terrible and revolting. Indeed, superstition pleases itself with exhibiting death under the most frightful traits; as a dreadful moment, which not only puts an end to our pleasures, but gives us up without defense to the strange rigor of a pitiless despot, which nothing can soften. According to this superstition, the most virtuous man is never sure of pleasing him, but has reason to tremble for the severity of his judgments; to fear the dreadful torments and endless punishments that await the victims of his caprice, for involuntary weaknesses or the necessary faults of a short-lived existence. This implacable tyrant will avenge himself of man's infirmities, of his momentary offenses, of the propensities that have been planted in his heart, of the errors of his mind, the opinions, ideas, and passions he has imbibed in the society in which he was born without his own consent, and above all, his not being able to comprehend an inconceivable being and all the extravagant dogmas offered to his acceptance, his daring to think for himself and refusing to listen to enthusiastic or erroneous guides, and his having the boldness to consult reason, which would have given him the means to regulate his conduct in the path of life.

Such, then, are the afflicting objects with which religion occupies its unhappy and credulous disciples; such are the fears that the tyrant of human thoughts points out to them as *salutary*. In spite of the meagerness of the effect that these notions produce on the greater number of those who say they are, or who believe themselves persuaded, they are held forth as the most powerful rampart that can be opposed to the things that disturb us. Nevertheless, as will be seen presently, it will be found that these systems, or rather these chimeras so terrible to behold, have little or no efficacy on the larger portion of mankind, who think of them but seldom, and never in the moment that passion, interest, pleasure, or example hurries them along. If these fears act, it is commonly on those who have little need to abstain from evil. They make honest hearts tremble, but have no effect on the perverse; they torment sensible souls, but leave in repose those that are hardened; they disturb tractable and gentle minds, but cause no trouble to rebellious spirits: thus they alarm none but those who are already sufficiently alarmed; they coerce only those who are already restrained.

These notions, then, make no impression on the wicked; when by accident they do act on them, it is only to redouble the wickedness of their natural character, to justify them in their own eyes, to furnish them with pretexts to exercise it without fear and without scruple. Indeed, the experience of a great number of ages has shown to what excess the wickedness and passions of man have carried him, when they have been authorized and unchained by religion; or, at least, when he has been enabled to cover himself with its mantle. Man has never been more ambitious, never more covetous, never more crafty, never more cruel, never more seditious, than when he has persuaded himself that religion permitted or commanded him to be so: thus religion did nothing more than lend an invincible force to his natural passions, which, under its sacred auspices, he could exercise with impunity and without remorse. Still more, the greatest villains, in giving free rein to the detestable propensities of their natural wickedness, have believed that by displaying an overheated zeal they merited well of heaven; that they exempted themselves by crimes from that chastisement at the hand of a God whom they thought their prior conduct had richly merited.

These, then, are the effects that the salutary notions of theology produce on mortals! These reflections will furnish an answer to those who say that "if religion promised heaven equally to the wicked as to the righteous, there would be no disbelievers in another life." We reply that, in point of fact, religion does accord heaven to the wicked, since it frequently places in this happy abode the most useless and the most depraved of men. Thus religion, as we have seen, sharpens the passions of evil-disposed men, by legitimating those crimes that without this sanction they would shudder to commit; or for which, at least, they would feel shame and experience remorse. In short, the ministers of religion furnish to the most profligate men the means of diverting from their own heads the thunderbolt that should strike their crimes, with the promise of an eternal happiness.

With respect to unbelievers, without doubt there may be among them wicked men, as well as among the most faithful; but unbelief no more supposes wickedness than belief supposes righteousness. On the contrary, the man who thinks and meditates knows far better the true motives to goodness than he who suffers himself to be blindly guided by uncertain motives or by the interest of others. Sensible men have the greatest advantage in examining opinions that it is claimed must have an influence over their eternal happiness: if these are found false or injurious to their present life, they will not therefore conclude that they have not another life either to fear or to hope; that they are permitted to deliver themselves up with impunity to vices that would do an injury to themselves, or would draw upon them the contempt and anger of society. The man who does not expect another life is the more interested in prolonging his existence in this one, and in rendering himself dear to his fellows in the only life he knows: he has made a great stride toward happiness in disengaging himself from those terrors that afflict others.

Superstition, in fact, takes a pride in rendering man slothful, credulous, and cowardly. It is its principle to afflict him without intermission; to redouble in him the horrors of death. Ever ingenious in tormenting him, it has extended his inquietudes beyond even his known existence; and its ministers, the more securely to dispose of him in this world, have invented future regions, reserving to themselves the privilege of awarding recompenses to those who yielded most implicitly to their arbitrary laws, and of having their god decree punishments to those refractory beings who rebelled against their power. Thus, far from holding forth consolation to mortals, far from cultivating man's reason, far from teaching him to yield under the hand of necessity, religion strives to render death still more bitter to him, to make its yoke sit heavy, to fill up its retinue with a multitude of hideous phantoms, and to render its approach terrible. By this means it has crowded the world with enthusiasts, whom it seduces by vague promises; with contemptible slaves, whom it coerces with the fear of imaginary evils. It has at length persuaded man that his actual existence is only a journey by which he will arrive at a more important life. This irrational dogma of a future life prevents him from occupying himself with his true happiness; from thinking of ameliorating his institutions, his laws, his morals, his sciences. Empty chimeras have absorbed his attention: he consents to groan under religious and political tyranny, to live in error, to languish in misfortune, in the hope of someday being happier; in the firm confidence that his calamities, his stupid patience, will conduct him to a never-ending happiness. He has believed himself subject to a cruel god who is willing to make him purchase his future welfare at the expense of everything most dear to him here below: his god has been depicted as the sworn enemy of the human race, as irritated against him, as disposed to appease himself by punishing him eternally for any efforts he should make to withdraw himself from his power. It is thus that the dogma of a future life has been one of the most fatal errors with which the human species has been infected: it plunged whole nations into sloth, languor, and indifference to their present welfare; or else precipitated them into the most furious enthusiasm, which hurried them on to tear each other to pieces in order to merit heaven.

It will be asked, perhaps, by what road has man been led to form to himself these gratuitous and bizarre ideas of another world. I reply that it is a truth that we have no idea of a future life, which does not exist for us; it is our ideas of the past and the present that furnish our imagination with the materials of which it constructs the edifice of the regions of futurity. Hobbes says, "We believe that that which is will always be, and that the same causes will have the same effects."[5] Man in his actual state has two modes of feeling, one that he approves, another that he disapproves: thus, persuaded that these two modes of feeling must accompany him, even beyond his present existence, he placed in the regions of eternity two distinguished abodes; one destined to happiness, the other to misery. The one will contain the friends of his God; the other is a prison, destined to avenge him for the outrages that his unhappy subjects have inflicted on him.[6]

Such is the true origin of the ideas upon a future life, so diffused among mankind. Everywhere may be seen an *Elysium* and a *Tartarus*; a *Paradise* and a *Hell*; in a word, two distinct abodes, constructed according to the imagination of the knaves or enthusiasts who have invented them, and who have accommodated them to the peculiar prejudices, ideas, hopes, and fears of the people who believe in them. Indians figure the first of these abodes as one of inaction and of permanent repose, because, being the inhabitants of a hot climate, they have learned to contemplate rest as the ultimate happiness; Muslims promise themselves corporeal pleasures similar to those that actually constitute the object of their search in this life; Christians hope for ineffable and spiritual pleasures—in a word, for a happiness of which they have no idea.

Of whatever nature these pleasures may be, man perceived that a body was needed in order that his soul might be able to enjoy the pleasures or to experience the pains reserved for him by the divinity: from hence the doctrine of the *resurrection*, by which it was imagined that the body—which was seen to putrefy, decompose, and dissolve—would one day be reconstituted by an act of divine omnipotence, to form afresh an envelope for the soul, in order to receive conjointly with it the rewards and punishments that both would have merited during their original union. This incomprehensible opinion is said to have originated in Persia, among the Magi, and finds a great number of adherents who have never given it a serious examination. Others, incapable of elevating themselves to these sublime notions, believed that, under various forms, man successively occupied different animals, of various species, and that he never ceased to be an inhabitant of the earth; such was the opinion of those who believed in *metempsychosis*.

As for the miserable abode of souls, the imagination of fanatics, who wanted to govern the people, strove to assemble the most frightful images to render it still more terrible. Fire is of all entities that which produces in man the most pungent sensation; it was therefore supposed that divine omnipotence could not invent anything more cruel to punish his enemies: then fire was the point at which their imagination was obliged to stop; and it was agreed pretty generally that fire would one day avenge the offended divinity, as, by human cruelty and madness, this element so often avenged them on this earth. Thus they painted the victims of God's anger as confined in fiery dungeons; as perpetually rolling in a vortex of flames; as plunged in gulfs of sulfur and bitumen; and making the infernal caverns resound with their useless groanings, and with their gnashing of teeth.

But it will perhaps be inquired how could man reconcile himself to the belief in an existence accompanied with eternal torments; above all, as many according to their own religious systems had reason to fear it for themselves? Many causes have concurred to make him adopt so revolting an opinion. In the first place, very few thinking men have ever believed such an absurdity, when they have deigned to make use of their reason; or, when they have credited it, the atrocity of this notion was always counterbalanced by the idea of the mercy and the goodness that they attributed to their God.[7] In the second place, those who were blinded by their fears never rendered to themselves any account of these strange doctrines, which they either received with awe from their legislators or which were transmitted to them by their fathers. In the third place, each sees the object of his terrors only at a favorable distance; moreover, superstition promises him the means of escaping the tortures he believes he has merited. Finally, like those sick people whom we see cling fondly even to the most painful life, man preferred the idea of an unhappy though unknown existence to that of nonexistence, which he looked upon as the most frightful evil that could befall him, either because he could form no idea of it or because his imagination painted to him this nonexistence, this nothingness, as the confused assemblage of all evils. A known evil, of whatever magnitude, alarmed him less, above all when there remained the hope of being able to avoid it, than an evil of which he knew nothing, upon which consequently his imagination was painfully employed, but to which he knew not how to oppose a remedy.

It will be seen, then, that superstition, far from consoling man upon the necessity of death, only redoubles his terrors, by the evils it claims will follow his decease: these terrors are so strong that the miserable wretches who believe strictly in these formidable doctrines pass their days in bitterness and tears. What shall we say of an opinion so destructive to society, yet adopted by so many nations, which announces to them that a severe God may at each instant, *like a thief*, take them unprovided; that at each moment they are liable to pass under the most rigorous judgment? What idea can be better suited to terrify man, what more likely to discourage him, what more calculated to dampen the desire of ameliorating his condition, than the afflicting prospect of a world always on the brink of dissolution and of a divinity seated upon the ruins of nature, ready to pass judgment on the human species? Such are, nevertheless, the fatal opinions with which the mind of nations has been fed for thousands of years; they are so dangerous that if, by a happy absence of just inference, he did not derogate in his conduct from these afflicting ideas, he would fall into the most abject stupidity. How could man occupy himself with a perishable world, ready every moment to crumble into atoms? How think of rendering himself happy on earth, when it is only the porch to an eternal kingdom? Is it, then, surprising that the superstitions to which such dogmas serve for a basis have prescribed to their disciples a total detachment from things below, an entire renunciation of the most innocent pleasures; and have given birth to a sluggishness, a cowardice, an abjection of soul, an insociability, that renders him useless to himself and dangerous to others? If necessity did not oblige man to depart in his practice from these irrational systems; if his needs did not bring him back to reason, in spite of his religious dogmas, the whole world would presently become a vast desert, inhabited by a few isolated savages, who would not even have the courage to multiply themselves. What kind of notions are these that must necessarily be put aside in order that human association may subsist?

Nevertheless, the dogma of a future life, accompanied with rewards and punishments, has been regarded for a great number of ages as the most powerful, or even as the only, motive capable of containing the passions of man— as the sole means that can force him to be virtuous. By degrees, this dogma has become the basis of almost all religious and political systems, so much so that at this day it is said this prejudice cannot be attacked without absolutely rending asunder the bonds of society. The founders of religions have made use of it to bind their credulous disciples; legislators have looked at it as the curb best calculated to keep mankind under the yoke. Many philosophers themselves have believed with sincerity that this doctrine was requisite to terrify man and thus divert him from crime.

It must indeed be allowed that this dogma has been of the greatest utility to those who have given religions to nations and made themselves its ministers: it was the foundation of their power; the source of their wealth; the permanent cause of that blindness and those terrors that it was in their interest to nourish in the human race. It was by this dogma the priest became first the rival, then the master of kings; that nations are filled with enthusiasts drunk with religion, always more disposed to listen to its menaces than to the counsels of reason, the orders of the sovereign, the cries of nature, or the laws of society. Politics itself was enslaved to the caprice of the priest; the temporal monarch was obliged to bend under the yoke of the eternal monarch. The one only disposed of this perishable world; the other extended his power into the world to come, much more important for man than the earth, on which he is only a pilgrim, a mere passenger. Thus the doctrine of another life placed the government itself in a state of dependence upon the priest; the monarch was nothing more than his first subject, and he was never obeyed except when the two were in accord to oppress the human race. Nature in vain cried out to man to be careful of his present happiness; the priest ordered him to be unhappy, in the expectation of future felicity. Reason in vain exhorted him to be peaceable, the priest breathed forth fanaticism and fury and obliged him to disturb the public tranquility, every time there was a question of the interests of the invisible monarch of another life or the real interests of his ministers in this one.

Such is the fruit that politics has gathered from the dogma of a future life. The regions of the world to come have enabled the priesthood to conquer the present world. The expectation of celestial happiness, and the dread of future tortures, only served to prevent man from seeking after the means to render himself happy here below. Thus error, under whatever aspect it is considered, will never be more than a source of evil for mankind. The dogma of another life, in presenting to mortals an ideal happiness, will render them enthusiasts; in overwhelming them with fears, it will make useless beings, cowards, atrabilarious or furious men, who will lose sight of their present abode to occupy themselves with the fancied regions of a world to come, and with those dreadful evils that they must fear after their death.

If it is insisted that the dogma of future rewards and punishments is the most powerful curb to restrain the passions of man, we shall reply by calling in daily experience. If we only cast our eyes around, we shall see this assertion contradicted; and we shall find that these marvelous speculations, incapable of changing the temperament of man, of annihilating those passions that the vices of society engender in his heart, do not in any manner diminish the number of the wicked. In those nations that appear the most thoroughly convinced of this future punishment may be seen assassins, thieves, crafty knaves, oppressors, adulterers, voluptuaries. All these pretend they are firmly persuaded of the reality of a hereafter; yet in the whirlwind of dissipation and pleasure, in the fury of their passions, they no longer behold this formidable future existence, which in those moments has no kind of influence over their earthly conduct.

In short, in many of those countries where the dogma of another life is so firmly established that each individual is annoyed with whoever may have the temerity to combat the opinion, or even to doubt it, we see that it is utterly incapable of impressing anything on rulers who are unjust, negligent, or debauched; on eager and dissolute prostitutes; on covetous misers; on flinty extortioners who fatten on the substance of a nation; on women without modesty; on a vast multitude of drunken and vicious men; on great numbers even among those priests whose function it is to announce the vengeance of heaven. If it is inquired of them how they dare to give themselves up to such actions, which they ought to know are certain to draw upon them eternal punishment, they will reply that the madness of their passions, the force of their habits, the contagion of example, or even the power of circumstances have hurried them along and have made them forget the dreadful consequences in which their conduct is likely to involve them; besides, they will say that the treasures of the divine mercy are infinite, and that repentance suffices to efface the blackest and most enormous crimes.[8] In this multitude of wretched beings, who, each after his own manner, ravages society, you will find only a small number who are sufficiently intimidated by the fears of a miserable hereafter to resist their evil propensities. What did I say? These propensities are in themselves too weak to carry them forward, and without the aid of the dogma of another life, the law and the fear of censure would have been motives sufficient to prevent them from rendering themselves criminal.

It is, indeed, fearful, timorous souls upon whom the terrors of another life make a profound impression. Men of this sort come into the world with moderate passions, a sickly organization, and a cool imagination; it is not therefore surprising that in such men, who are already restrained by their nature, the fear of future punishment counterbalances the weak efforts of their feeble passions. But it is by no means the same with those hardened criminals, with those men who are habitually vicious, whose unseemly excesses nothing can arrest, and who, in their violence, shut their eyes to the fear of the laws of this world, despising still more those of the other.

Nevertheless, how many persons say they are, and even believe themselves, restrained by the fears of the life to come! But either they deceive us or they impose upon themselves, by attributing to these fears what is only the effect of motives much nearer at hand, such as the feebleness of their machine, the mildness of their temperament, the slender energy of their souls, their natural timidity, the ideas imbibed in their education, the fear of immediate and physical consequences resulting from their irregularities or their evil actions. These are the true motives that restrain them, and not the notions of a future life, which men who say they are most firmly persuaded of its existence forget whenever a powerful interest solicits them to sin. If for a time man would pay attention to what passes before his eyes, he would perceive that he ascribes to the fear of his God what is in reality only the effect of his own weakness, cowardice, and the small interest found to commit evil: these men would not act otherwise than they do if they had not this fear before them; if therefore he reflected, he would feel that it is always necessity that makes men act as they do.

Man cannot be restrained when he does not find within himself motives sufficiently powerful to conduct him back to reason. There is nothing, either in this world or in the other, that can render him virtuous when an unhappy organization, a mind badly cultivated, a violent imagination, inveterate habits, fatal examples, powerful interests, invite him from every quarter to the commission of crime. No speculations are capable of restraining the man who braves public opinion, who despises the law, who is careless of its censure, who turns a deaf ear to the cries of conscience, whose power in this world places him out of the reach of punishment.[9] In the violence of his transports he will fear still less a distant futurity, the idea of which always recedes before what he believes necessary to his immediate and present happiness. All lively passions blind man to everything that is not its immediate object; the terrors of a future life, the probability of which his passions always possess the secret to diminish, can effect nothing upon the wicked man who does not fear even the much nearer punishment of the law—who sets at naught the assured hatred of those by whom he is surrounded. Man, when he delivers himself up to crime, sees nothing certain except the supposed advantage that attends it; the rest always appear to him either false or problematical.

If man would only open his eyes, he would clearly perceive that to effect anything upon hearts hardened by crime, he must not reckon upon the chastisement of an avenging God, which the self-love natural to man always shows him as pacified in the long run. He who has arrived at persuading himself that he cannot be happy without crime will always readily deliver himself up to it notwithstanding the menaces of religion. Whoever is sufficiently blind not to read his infamy in his own heart, to see his own condemnation in the faces of his associates, the indignation and anger in the eyes of the judges established to punish the offenses he may commit; such a man, I say, will never feel the impression his crimes shall make on the features of a judge that is either hidden from his view, or that he only contemplates at a distance. The tyrant, who with dry eyes can hear the cries of the distressed, who with callous heart can behold the tears of a whole people of whose misery he is the cause, will not see the angry eyes of a more powerful master. When an arrogant monarch pretends to be accountable for his actions to God alone, it is because he fears his nation more than he does his God.

On the other hand, does not religion itself annihilate the effects of those fears that it announces as salutary? Does it not furnish its disciples with the means of extricating themselves from the punishments with which it has so frequently menaced them? Does it not tell them that a sterile repentance will, even at the moment of death, disarm the celestial wrath and purify the filthy souls of sinners? Do not even the priests, in some superstitions, arrogate to themselves the right of remitting to the dying the punishment due to the crimes committed during the course of a disorderly life? In short, do not the most perverse men, encouraged in iniquity, debauchery, and crime, reckon, even to the last moment, upon the aid of a religion that promises them the infallible means of reconciling themselves to the God whom they have irritated, and of avoiding his rigorous punishments?

As a result of these notions, so favorable to the wicked, so suitable to tranquilize them, we see that the hope of an easy expiation, far from correcting man, engages him to persist until death in the most flagrant disorders. Indeed, in spite of the numberless advantages that he is assured flow from the dogma of a life to come, in spite of its purported efficacy in repressing the passions of men, do not the priests themselves, although so interested in the maintenance of this system, every day complain of its insufficiency? They acknowledge that mortals whom from their infancy they have imbued with these ideas are not less hurried forward by their evil propensities, less sunk in the vortex of dissipation, less the slaves to their pleasures, less captivated by bad habits, less driven along by the torrent of the world, less seduced by their present interest, which make them forget equally the rewards and punishments of a future life. In a word, the ministers of heaven allow that their disciples, for the most part, conduct themselves in this world as if they had nothing either to hope or to fear in another.

But let it be supposed for a moment that the dogma of eternal punishments was of some utility, and that it really restrained a small number of individuals; what are these feeble advantages compared to the numberless evils that flow from it? Against one timid man whom this idea restrains, there are thousands upon whom it has no effect; there are millions whom it makes irrational, fanatical, useless, and wicked; there are millions whose mind it disturbs, and whom it diverts from their duties toward society; there are an infinity whom it afflicts and troubles, without producing any real good for their associates.

"Conversation between the Abbé Barthélemy and Diderot" (1772–73)

DENIS DIDEROT

[Denis Diderot (1713–1784) was a leading French intellectual of his day. He spent most of his life as a professional writer. His works were increasingly bold and controversial, from *Les Bijoux indiscrets* (1748; *The Indiscreet Jewels*), a collection of bawdy stories, to *Lettre sur les aveugles* (1749; *Letter on the Blind*), which rejected divine providence and propounded a rudimentary version of natural selection, to *La Religieuse* (1760; *The Nun*), a pungent satire on corruption in the Catholic Church. But his greatest achievement was the editing (in part with Jean le Rond d'Alembert) of the *Encyclopédie* (1751–72; *Encyclopedia*), a landmark that expressed religious skepticism throughout its thousands of entries. A materialist, Diderot all but openly espoused atheism. In the following text (written in 1772–73 but not published until 1921), purporting to be a dialogue with a French Catholic clergyman, Diderot covers a wide range of religious subjects but focuses on such topics as the efficacy of prayer, heaven and hell, and religious toleration.]

Diderot: However, Abbé, you would not like to converse with someone who never answered?

Barthélemy: Certainly not.

Diderot: Well then, when you pray, that is to say, when you address words to God or to the Virgin Mary, what answer do you get?

Barthélemy: But I don't expect an answer.

Diderot: What's the good of conversing, then?

Barthélemy: You are confused, my dear philosopher, you misapprehend. Prayer is not a conversation.

Diderot: It is a monologue?

Barthélemy: If you like. It is an elevation of our soul to God, it is an effusion, it is the evidence and the tribute of our adoration and our gratitude; very often also it is an entreaty, a supplication.

Diderot: But what is the object of this petition, what is its guarantee and its sanction, since it always remains obstinately and invariably without an answer? Your God, in fact, my dear Abbé, is ETERNAL SILENCE. The phrase is Flechier's, I believe.[1] You never hear his voice. You may well cry to him: "My Father, my Father! Have pity! . . . Mercy! I beseech you! . . ." Never, however ardent and vehement, however tearful, moving, and irresistible your prayers may be, you will never draw from him even a single acknowledgment, you will never hear this Father, so much besought and so merciful, answer you: "My child!" Do you recall that woman we saw one afternoon, at St. Roch, prostrate before a statue of the Virgin, praying, weeping, sobbing? . . . It was enough to break one's heart. It moved you so much that you approached her, and questioned her.

Barthélemy: I remember. She was praying for her daughter, a child of fifteen, who was dying.

Diderot: How she prayed and sobbed, the poor thing! She would have softened a heart of stone. But the stone Virgin did not wince, did not flinch . . . or at least we did not notice anything like that, I think. And was the child saved?

Barthélemy: No, she died; died precisely while the mother was kneeling there.

Diderot: No doubt God had hastened to call this young soul to him. He lacked angels.

Barthélemy: Perhaps. Without a doubt, she went to heaven. That is a favor that the Lord did to her.

Diderot: To the mother?

Barthélemy: To the mother and to the daughter, both of them. Do we know our needs? Does not the Almighty, in his infinite wisdom, know better than we what is good for us?

Diderot: Why doesn't he tell us then? Why leave this poor woman to lament and sigh and to be wrung with anguish? You remember? It was heart-rending, frightful. And one word would have been enough: "I take back to me those I value. Rejoice therefore, woman, instead of grieving."

Barthélemy: Yes, that is the truth. It is indeed.

Diderot: And that is what this mother did not admit, what she could not understand. And how many others share her blindness and like to keep their children near them in this vale of tears, rather than see them carried off to the heavenly abode! Moreover, when I say see, "see them carried off," that's just a way of speaking, for we see nothing at all. . . . The eyelids fall, the voice becomes weak and stilled, the mind darkens and becomes nothing, there is no movement, nothing. . . .

Barthélemy: In fact, for you, Diderot, death is the end of everything.

Diderot: Don't make me say that, Abbé. Don't let us go so far. Although I might very well quote against you a certain legend, a corollary of the resurrection of Lazarus by the Christ: "What did you see down there, when you were dead?"—"Nothing, Master; there is nothing," answered Lazarus. And Jesus whispered in his ear: "No, there is nothing; but do not tell."

Barthélemy: Legend, assuredly! Pure legend!

Diderot: Agreed! But for myself, I hold to what we have before our eyes. Our soul, its essence, its origin, its destiny, what it will become after us, and in the very first place, if we really have one . . . for, indeed, I don't know. I can affirm nothing about it, and I've an idea that those who speak so freely and so willingly about it *ex cathedra* do not know any more about it than I do.

Barthélemy: However, if you abolish the soul . . .

Diderot: I abolish nothing at all: I do not know.

Barthélemy: . . . you will have to abolish God.

Diderot: That would not be a reason. But, once again, I want to abolish nothing, Abbé, I am only an ignorant person who has the frankness and courage of this ignorance; I dare to say: "I do not know." And I note that we are discussing endlessly a number of things that we not only do not know, but cannot know, that are beyond our understanding—which ought, it may be said in parenthesis, to convince us that they are hardly necessary to us, for everything that is an everlasting subject of dispute is necessarily of everlasting uselessness for us, as Voltaire wrote recently. And, by a sort of calamity, it is precisely those things that are most spoken about that are least understood. How many of our most common phrases mean absolutely nothing! "God has recalled her to him." How do you know? Has God taken you into his confidence? "God has hastened to have him near him." Not so much haste, since this dead man had seen ninety-one springtimes. "She has ascended to heaven," you just said to me, about the little girl torn from her pious mother. But what is heaven? Where is it situated? Does one go up at first? You say "above." But "above" now will be "below" this evening, since the earth revolves. At least, you don't deny the movement of the earth, with Pope Urban and the Holy Inquisition?[2]

Barthélemy: I have not come to that, dear friend.

Diderot: The ancients knew at least where to put their paradise, or at least they tried. . . . For some, it was in the Canary Islands, which they called the Fortunate Isles, *Arva beata*; for others, higher up, in Ireland; for others . . .

Barthélemy: In fact, there was hardly any agreement among them, on this point as on so many others.

Diderot: Just like us, Abbé. I was reading this morning in a history of Sweden that the king, the king of that country, had triumphed over his enemies by providential good fortune; while, for the same victory, contested and denied by the Turks, the latter declared that Providence had not allowed . . . and that the Spaniards claimed in the same way that the aforesaid Providence had remained dumb. . . . See how each one judges Providence after his own fashion, gauges it by his own standards, makes it act and express itself after his own fancy! There should be a Lutheran Providence (or at least a Swedish one), a Muslim or Turkish Providence, a Spanish Providence, without counting all the others, Russian Providence, Polish Providence, English Providence, French Providence. Just think a little of the embarrassment of Providence, if there were only one, when each nation invoked it for the same purpose, with opposed interests and contrary intentions! And would it not first be necessary to be certain that this sovereign with so many and diverse faces, this Divine Providence, consents to be troubled with our little affairs, which appears to me to be excessively problematical; for how many crimes, shames, and abominations we should then have to place on the shoulders of this sacrosanct princess! The easiest thing, in my opinion, would be to concern ourselves with her no more than she concerns herself with us. Yes, Abbé, that's the great thing wrong with us, and it will be so for a long time, I fear; we discuss ceaselessly numerous subjects beyond our understanding, beyond our faculties, consequently without in any sense being able to attain a certain and practical conclusion, and getting no other result but discord and hatred—horrible hatreds accompanied by the cruelest persecutions. Aren't these hatreds between nations most often engendered by religious differences, and in direct proportion to the zeal for the cause of God which animates these people? If only we had the good wit and the good sense to stop ourselves in time on this odious slope, and not to tear each other, cut throats, or burn each other alive because we do not envisage the Absolute from the same point of view, or do not think the same about the mystery of the Incarnation or the sacrament of the Eucharist! Why lose ourselves in these clouds and not keep ourselves quite frankly to questions of current life, to what we can see, observe, and control. It is the pursuit and passion for the supernatural that causes misery to so many people.

Barthélemy: And their consolation also, and their joy.

Diderot: There are consoling errors, I don't deny. A doctor tells a sick man that he is better, a dying man that he will get back his health and that he will be on his feet within a week, and he dies the same evening; but during that day a ray of hope has warmed his heart and comforted him. The doctor's lie has sweetened the last moments of the patient. That is something. But don't let the good prevent us from recognizing that it comes from something wrong, a lie.

Barthélemy: Wait a moment! The consolations of religion and the promises that accompany them are not in the least lies.

Diderot: Evidently, Abbé, and I shall be far from contesting it. . . . But these promises are without guarantee and without proof; without evident and tangible proofs, I mean. You assure this mother we were talking of just now that her daughter has gone straight to heaven and rests in the bosom of the Eternal. These are simply words, this: *hæc sunt verba*, nothing more. In reality, the poor child has been nailed up in a pine or oaken box, then buried in the earth. That is all that is permissible to say. All the rest beyond that is an affair of the imagination, of supposition, of hope. . . . It is dreaming!

That you have consoled the mother by guaranteeing resurrection and the salvation of her daughter, "whom she will one day find again above, in the home of the blessed," is very fine, it is perfect; but, once more, you have asked to be believed on your word. Now, the wise man is not content with a simple assertion: *Sapiens nihil affirmat quod non probet. . . . Quod gratis asseritur gratis negatur.* [The wise man affirms nothing that he cannot prove. What is freely asserted is freely denied.] We may permit a little Latin between ourselves, may we not, Monsignore?

Barthélemy: You will never prevent the crowd from seeking these superior consolations, from having a liking for the supernatural and delighting therein.

Diderot: It's possible! But are these always consolations that you offer to your flock? Oh, no, not always! See our poor friend Desmahis:[3] he, with such a cheerful, gracious, and charming character, so naturally happy, there now, if he isn't in a blue funk at going to grill in hell, even imagining that he's grilling and roasting already, plunged in eternal flames for the expiation of his sins? Isn't it horrible?

Barthélemy: It is madness.

Diderot: Madness or not, do you believe that he will be consoled, he? And how many, how many others are like him, and experience this very explicable but abominable terror of the aforesaid eternal flames? Think of Massillon preaching at St. Eustache his sermon "On the small number of the elect."[4] Many are called but few are chosen [Matt. 22:14], Abbé! Then it is always, in spite of all the merits of our Redeemer, always Master Satan who carries him off? . . . Yes, the general fear, the terrible panic that seized the congregation at this sermon of Massillon! They did not think themselves consoled, those people. You offer to your clients two perspectives, two solutions, paradise and hell. It is hell that imposes itself and triumphs; you do not console, you terrify, you appall. Now, in order to abolish radically these very legitimate fears and to play a trick on Satan, as soon as a newborn has received this sacrament of baptism, which makes a Christian of him and opens wide the gates of heaven to him, wouldn't it be more prudent, wiser, to send him speedily above or below . . . ?

Barthélemy: Send him? How's that? Kill him?

Diderot: Quite simply. The English writer Jonathan Swift suggested, not long ago, in his *Modest Proposal* relative to the poor children of Ireland, that the little children of indigent Irish families, destined to die of hunger, should be carefully fattened, then they should be bled like calves or sheep, and butcheries for infants' flesh should be established for the use of gentlemen whose taste is particularly delicate. I am not so exacting, and I spare you the fattening. I only ask you to dispatch all these little angels to the good God as promptly as possible, in order to spare them the half-certainty they have, by living on earth, of going after their death to boil and roast for all eternity. The thing is worth the trouble, Abbé. Eternal flames! Where there shall be wailing and gnashing of teeth! And for ever! for ever! Now see, would it not be a thousand times better to dispatch them to the good God at once? . . . I go even further. Could we not act in the same way toward adults, charge a confessor to put them in a state of grace, and as soon as the absolution is received, hasten them off. . . . Ah! There must be no dallying, there!

Barthélemy: But this is madness!

Diderot: An error! On the contrary, it would be very wise. Torture for all eternity, think of it! And would it not be the best method—a supremely radical method I agree, but, once more, to flame for all eternity!—whereby to cheat, to get the better of and beat the angel of darkness, Satan, always on the watch for souls he can clutch and impale on his prongs? You have not forgotten the criminal at the theatre in Rouen who stabbed his neighbor, a young girl he did not know and had never seen before, who killed her without any motive, except to be condemned to death and to be able, before being broken on the wheel or hanged, to receive absolution, while if he had committed suicide, he would have departed this life in a state of mortal sin?

Barthélemy: Let us talk seriously, Diderot.

Diderot: But that is what we are doing.

Barthélemy: You wriggle and chop logic in vain. I tell you again you will never take from the crowd its taste for the supernatural. The human mind is made that way; it is carried of its own accord toward what is beyond it, beyond its understanding. . . .

Diderot: Yes, everything that dazzles and enchants it. The crowd loves the marvelous, and the more strange, inconceivable, and fabulous the miracle is, the better it is pleased and is delighted. But we philosophers, whose role it is to see clearly in our business—which is devilish difficult, I agree—we try to reduce the number of these dupes as much as possible. We think that the greatest service to be done to men is to teach them to use their reason, to accept as the truth only what they have verified and proved. You are compelled to agree, aren't you, that the more a nation educates itself and improves itself, the more the belief in the supernatural is moderated and reduced? Greater or lesser belief in the supernatural is always the index of lesser or greater civilization. Consider the savages encountered by Bougainville:[5] everything was witchcraft, magic, sorcery, and miracle with them. Miracles, a rare commodity with us, eh, Abbé? in spite of this craze for the marvelous, the incomprehensible? But there are miracles wherever they are believed in, and the more they are believed in, the more there are of them. Is that true? You see, Abbé, once one sets foot in this realm of the supernatural, there are no bounds, one doesn't know where one is going nor what one may meet. Someone affirms that five thousand persons have been fed with five small loaves; this is fine! But tomorrow another will assure you to have fed five thousand people with one small loaf, and the following day a third will have fed five thousand with the wind. Medallions hung from the neck and other amulets guard you from all accidents or cure you from all ills. If one wants to calm the attack of madness of one of those lunatics called "possessed," a clyster of holy water is administered—infallible remedy. In the countryside, in many places, it is sufficient to carry around the relics of a saint—in Burgundy, those of St. Potentien, for example—to obtain sun or rain, warmth or moisture, at will. And good St. Denis walks, carrying his cut-off head in his hands, a phenomenon that St. Savinien hastened to reproduce after his decapitation by the Emperor Aurelius. And St. Nicolas who began to fast from the day of his birth: Wednesdays and Fridays he only took the breast of his nurse once a day. And that pious noblewoman who, finding herself pregnant during the absence of her husband, obtained from her celestial patroness, with the aid of God, that her pregnancy not only disappeared, but passed into the body of the said patroness, St. Pelagia or someone, who would thus take the sin upon herself, or at least the consequences of sin. And what do you think about the two skulls of St. Pancras, which are honored and feasted in two of our rival parishes, his skull when he was twenty-two and his skull when he was thirty-six? There is nothing more diverting than the lives of the saints, my dear Abbé, and I've often wished to write all that. . . . But it's already done: we have the *Golden Legend*.[6]

Barthélemy: Which nothing obliges you to believe.

Diderot: I beg your pardon! It is your most eminent hagiographers who utter this nonsense to us.

Barthélemy: These are not articles of faith.

Diderot: There you are, already backing out; Abbé, you are shirking. If, among all your prodigies and miracles, one can choose . . .

Barthélemy: Certainly, one can choose; one ought, even.

Diderot: Go and persuade our country clergy of that! They all have their St. Potentiens. And even your dogmas, obligatory to faith, your God in three people, your wicked angels who revolt against their Creator and try to dethrone him, your Eve drawn out of Adam's side, your Virgin who receives the visit of a young man and a bird and who becomes pregnant, not by the young man, but by the bird; this Virgin who bears a child and remains a virgin; this God who dies on the cross to appease God, then comes to life again and ascends into heaven (where, to heaven?), all that is mythology, my dear Abbé, it is paganism, it is worthy of Uranus, Saturn, and the Titans, Minerva springing fully armed from the head of Jupiter, Juno pregnant with Mars from having breathed the perfume of a flower, Phoebus-Apollo driving the chariot of the sun. . . . These are the same delirious adventures. Our friend d'Holbach freely declares that the supernatural does not interest him. No, it tells him nothing; it is aberration, unreason. Isn't it really folly, now, to go imagining that with simple words, that is to say, moving the air with the tip of the tongue, one is going to change the laws of the universe and what one calls the decrees of Providence?

Barthélemy: No, philosopher, indeed no, for these words are addressed to a supreme Being, all-powerful, infinitely perfect, a Father infinitely good, who listens to them, notes them . . .

Diderot: And grants them; so be it! Example: the unfortunate woman we noticed at St. Roch. But where is the proof that he hears you, this Father, so good and so merciful, to whom you have recourse? No one has this proof, which, for my part, I should be truly delighted to possess. But nothing, always nothing, always the unfathomable and inviolable silence. I do not recall what governor of a province it was, or even some bishop or cardinal perhaps, who reproached another bishop for having exceeded his instructions. "Monseigneur, I have prayed, I have asked God's advice," the accused replied with noble assurance, "I have consulted my crucifix. . . ." "Well then, imbecile, you must do what God and your crucifix answered to you!" interrupted the other. That is to say, keep silent and do nothing at all. What is God but a word, a simple vocable to explain the existence of the world? And note well that, after all, this word explains nothing; for if you object that no clock has ever been made without a clockmaker, I shall ask you who made the clockmaker, so that we are back at the same mark—at the same question-mark.

Barthélemy: However, haven't you yourself, Diderot, sometimes proclaimed the existence of this clockmaker?

Diderot: Proclaimed! That is saying a great deal.

Barthélemy: A certain letter of yours has been circulated in which you clearly say: "I believe in God, although I get along very well with the atheists."

Diderot: A letter to Voltaire. . . . That was to please him. . . . Ah! so you saw that scribble. This is what happens, Abbé: when I am with atheists, since there are atheists, all the arguments in favor of the existence of God spring up in my mind; when I happen to be with believers, it's the opposite: I see rise up before me, and in spite of myself, everything that combats, saps, and demolishes the Divinity.

Barthélemy: After this avowal, you will no longer say, my dear Diderot, that you are not endowed with the spirit of contradiction?

Diderot: It is certain that contradiction, or at least opposition, is the stimulant, also the embellishment and spice of conversation. If we were always of the same opinion, what monotony, what feebleness, what platitude! The world would not be habitable. Diversity of opinion is as necessary, as inevitable, as diversity of features and characters. We have to recognize and admit that what pleases some cannot please all the others. But no, my dear friend, no; it is not only for the vain pleasure of contradicting that I thus see rise up in my mind all the arguments contrary to the thesis of my opponent; it is because of a peculiarity of my nature, a strangeness that I record and suffer, without being able to explain it at all. That's how it is!

Barthélemy: See all the advantages of faith! If you possessed it . . .

Diderot: All difficulties would disappear, evidently. That is the way Pascal reasoned: whether it is true or false, you never risk anything in believing our holy religion to be true, and you risk everything in believing it false. But a Jew can say as much, a Muslim even, and similarly a Huguenot. It's a saddle that fits all horses, a barber's chair that suits all bottoms. Unfortunately, dear Abbé, I do not possess this sovereign remedy, this panacea you call faith, that is to say, the ability to believe things we know are manifestly false, inadmissible, unbelievable. A table for me is only a table, a chair only a chair, bread is only bread, and wine, equally, is only wine. I cannot tell you that this lack of faith bothers me very much, that it obsesses, distracts, poisons, and torments my days and nights, and that I lose the desire to eat and drink because of it! No, alas! I cannot tell you that, for, on the contrary, this incredulity or ignorance leaves me absolutely calm and indifferent. But to affirm and maintain certain facts that are beyond our reason, that escape us entirely; to certify and to proclaim them stubbornly—that is what seems as arrogant as it is ridiculous. And if one furiously sets about imposing these supernatural things on people, as always happens with those who are convinced that they alone hold the inborn science, the absolute truth, the truth on which depends our eternal happiness, then . . . "Think as I do, or the good God will damn you. . . . Think as I do or I kill you!" That is the necessary conclusion and final point. Does not the Bible, in Deuteronomy, command the massacre of those of our fellow-citizens who do not share our religious beliefs?[7] "Brother, son, daughter, mother, wife; do not discuss with them: kill them at once!" It is clear and plain. A charming plan, and drawn up in the name of the Lord! And note well, Abbé, that in thus asking that someone should change his religious beliefs, you ask him, in brief, to do something which you yourself refuse to do. What logic, eh?

Barthélemy: But . . .

Diderot: Yes, I know, I guess what you are going to say. It's that your own cult is the good one, the true one, the only true and the only good one, while mine is not worth a fig. Do you recall the letters once exchanged between the Pope and the Duke of Sully? The Holy Father complimented the Huguenot minister on his politics and his excellent government, and he finished, like a good shepherd who wants to bring back a strayed ewe into the fold, by beseeching him to open his eyes to the divine light, to see the truth where it is, and to re-enter the bosom of the Church. "Exactly, this is also what I pray to Heaven for, about you," Sully replied to him. "I never cease to pray for the conversion of Your Holiness."[8]

Barthélemy: What cynicism!

Diderot: It is the answer of the shepherdess to the shepherd. But let's return . . . return to our other sheep. Now, every consideration and reflection being taken into account, does God manifest himself to us otherwise than through the worship we offer him? Do you see him manifest himself otherwise, Abbé?

Barthélemy: But, my dear philosopher, one need only open one's eyes and look around. The whole of nature . . .

Diderot: Then the blind who, never having seen anything, cannot render an account to themselves. . . .

Barthélemy: Let's leave the blind out of it.

Diderot: Very well then, for us, for all who can see, isn't it our prayers, our offerings, our religious practices solely, you understand, Abbé, solely, which attest to us the existence of God? Now, I will not hide from you that for myself and some others, this is not enough. We wish that these evidences should not always come from ourselves, but sometimes a little from this Divinity, so much celebrated and glorified, hymned and entreated.

Barthélemy: These evidences have already been collected. They exist in the holy books.

Diderot: Yes, but your holy books are not those of other nations, and they differ even among themselves. And then, I should very much like to have been there, to verify for myself. . . . For, after all, it is always men who speak in the name of God, who claim to be the representatives here on earth of the Most High; but these representatives never show us their credentials, never!

Barthélemy: Indeed they do! Only you obstinately refuse to see them.

Diderot: I would only ask this, however, that they should be only the least bit clear, precise, and convincing—which they never are, alas! And again, note this, which is hardly to the credit of the Divinity, at least as it shows itself to us: that wherever there is a God, there is a religious cult, and wherever there is a cult, the natural order of moral duties is overturned.

Barthélemy: Overturned? But how is that?

Diderot: Without any doubt. To go without Mass on Sunday or to eat a slice of veal on Friday becomes a more horrible crime than to steal a neighbor's purse or to debauch his daughter. And that is to be understood! In the first case it is God personally whom you offend; in the second case it is only your neighbor. You have read the story of that herdsman on the outskirts of Naples who carried on brigandage on every possible occasion, and at confession only accused himself of having broken a fast by inadvertently drinking a little soup. At the tribunal of penitence it was never a question of his ravages, shootings, and killings. That didn't count. And that other man, all stained with blood his dagger had just shed, scrupling on a Friday to put any bacon on his bread. With us it is enough to receive absolution before dying in order to go straight to heaven, whatever life one may have led, whatever scandals and horrors one may have perpetrated. With the Indians, provided one dies on the banks of the Ganges so that one's ashes are thrown into that river, then you are saved, admitted at once into paradise. See just a little, my dear Abbé, how much this idea of God and of religion falsifies and vitiates all our reasoning. Isn't it precisely this, according to the *Spirit of Laws*, which by making us regard as necessary what is or ought to be indifferent, makes us consider as indifferent what is absolutely necessary?[9] Again, isn't it this that drives us to massacre thousands of men because they haven't the same beliefs as ourselves? The Vaudois, the Albigenses, St. Bartholomew's Night, the Inquisition, the Dragonnades,[10] how many others, are the proof of it. And what about human sacrifices designed to appease the Supreme Being, the

God of clemency and mercy? I remember in one of your memoirs that you yourself, Abbé, said: "For long no better way for averting celestial anger was known than shedding on the altars the blood of men. . . . "

Barthélemy: Those were pagans.

Diderot: We have not changed, and we have burnt enough Jews, tortured enough infidels. . . . Even one of your colleagues and rivals, the Abbé of Longuerue, who is concerned with Chaldeans and ancient France, as you are with the Greeks, estimates that religions, by all the blood which they have caused to be shed, have caused more evil than good in the world.[11]

Barthélemy: Longuerue, a learned man, yes, but a hothead. In any case, my dear philosopher, you cannot do without these religions, whatever they are.

Diderot: We cannot?

Barthélemy: No, and you never will be able to. People will always want some ceremonial for their marriages and their births, funeral hymns and the trappings of mourning at the burial of their dead, and holy water on their tombs. Otherwise they would fear to resemble too closely the animals who couple and die without any ceremony and are flung on the dung-heap.

Diderot: Now let us see, Abbé, don't we procreate exactly like animals? Don't we breathe, eat, and function in everything exactly as they do? Did not Solomon teach us that the condition of man in no way differs from that of animals, and that what remains of the one is no more than remains of the other? Then why this demarcation and this contempt? Animals are, and ought to be, only younger brothers for us, having a little less reason, but the same needs, the same appetites, the same passions. . . . According to you, then, in order not to resemble animals, we ought not to eat?

Barthélemy: We ought to make ourselves not resemble their bad sides, but to uplift our intellect as high as possible towards heaven.

Diderot: And our gaze also: *Os sublime dedit.* [He (God) gave to man a face that looks to the skies.][12]

Barthélemy: Yes, certainly.

Diderot: There is yet another point that troubles me: among all these millions and billions of stars that race through space, and which, like our little terrestrial globe, are inhabited worlds—one supposes so at least—have their inhabitants also committed original or queer—yes, queer!—sin? do they also need a Messiah, a virgin birth? . . .

Barthélemy: You ask too much of me, my dear philosopher, and it is for inquisitive people of your kind that hell was created.

Diderot: Joker! You're confusing me with Desmahis.

Barthélemy: Not at all. But I ask you, since you yourself recognize that these questions have been discussed without any result as long as the universe has existed, what is the good of discussing them again?

Diderot: Ah! now you are speaking wisely, Abbé. We are wasting our time. Pascal has clearly forewarned us of it: all philosophical discussion, the whole of philosophy even, is not worth an hour's trouble.

Barthélemy: Our human and earthly philosophy; but . . .

Diderot: Oh! theology; that's a thousand times worse!

Barthélemy: But instinctively, inevitably, once again, man looks, and will ever look, higher than himself; his hope for the Beyond will never leave him, and will never be quenched. And note, moreover, that we Christians have a base of operations, we have a body of doctrines, a code, a catechism to give it its proper name; while you do not and cannot have one.

Diderot: Hey! Hey!

Barthélemy: No, impossible; for one does not make laws and one converts nobody with negation and doubt. In order to teach and to make laws there must be a collection of incontestable facts, above all concerning those things that affect us most closely, our most constant and essential preoccupations, our origin, our creation, the creation of the universe. . . .

Diderot: In six days, and rest on the seventh day.

Barthélemy: We possess a catechism, and it is what gives us our strength.

Diderot: And you also have those ceremonies of which you were speaking just now, your processions, your feasts, your hymns, your organs, all your music, all these shows, so well contrived to attract the crowd, to ensnare and to keep it. That is another of the elements of your success, of your power. I am not hiding from myself, my dear Abbé, any of your advantages. But neither let us deny our own, those of the philosophers, and let us testify that we are making progress, the greatest and most incontestable progress. Recently at Grandval, Father Hoop told me that he had seen in a Swiss village when the curé was away or ill, a Protestant pastor replace the curé in his offices, teaching the catechism to the Catholic children in the evening, after having given his lesson of religious instruction to the little Protestants in the morning; and thus in the same locality serving at the same time, or rather, successively, the church and the temple.

Barthélemy: This pastor did not go so far as to celebrate Mass, I imagine?

Diderot: Not yet, but we are coming to it. Tolerance is permeating and penetrating little by little everywhere. Catholics and Huguenots are beginning not to burn one another; that's something. And since tolerance necessarily leads to indifference, I calculate that Christianity has still two or three centuries. . . .

Barthélemy: For a little longer, if you please. *Tu es Petrus et super hanc petram.* [You are Peter and upon this rock I will build my church.][13]

Diderot: Alas! there is nothing everlasting here below, Abbé. Montesquieu gives you still five hundred years of existence as a maximum; the Scotsman, John Craig,[14] dead, it is true, over a century and a half ago, allowed you three hundred and fifty years; for myself, I am less generous, I grant you two or three hundred. Perhaps I am wrong, and you deserve more. What is certain is that everything changes, everything varies, on our globe, everything fades, weakens, is extinguished, falls, and disappears. That is the general law, and you will not escape it, in spite of your predictions, your *Tu es Petrus.* What a fall you had there! Where are the days when through your popes and their influence and preponderance, you were as masters of the earth! And before you, wasn't Jupiter also enthroned in his Olympus with all his fellow-gods? He reigned so well and was so powerful that during the Council of Trent, that is to say barely two centuries ago, two learned men testified to it and besought him, and actually at Trent: "They may well perorate and do all that in there. We shall be obliged to return to thy worship sooner or later. Yea, Jupiter, we have faith in thee. When thou shalt have regained thy rank and grasped thy sovereignty again, in thy turn forget us not! Deign, oh Jupiter! deign to remember that we have remained faithful unto thee!".

Barthélemy: Dreamers! Visionaries!

Diderot: Yes, certainly! But so far as dreamers and visionaries go, to you the palm, to you and yours, monsieur l'Abbé! And if you have to be reminded of all the metamorphoses that your Church has undergone since St. Peter, how much it differs today from what it was at its beginning . . . St. Peter himself would not recognize it; you know it as well as I do. And you who know very well that this code or catechism which makes your strength is a tissue of impossibilities, of humbug, of . . .

Barthélemy: Of whatever you please, my dear philosopher. But this tissue holds together from one end to the other. It forms a solid whole. . . .

Diderot: Solid!

Barthélemy: For the masses it answers and suffices for everything; while as for you others, you gentlemen of the *Encyclopedia*, you answer and can answer none of the great questions that haunt the human mind: "How was the world created? By whom? What is God? How did man appear on earth? And so on." You philosophers, or at least part of you . . . oh! I don't accuse you of being swollen with pride and boasting! No, on the contrary! You have forever on your lips your "I do not know . . . I am ignorant!"

Diderot: That is true, and I am the most often like that, among them. But with you, Abbé, it's just the opposite; you always know everything, you others, and you never question anything.

Barthélemy: Precisely!

Diderot: You continually affirm things that are contradicted more and more by science.

Barthélemy: Human science!

Diderot: Don't speak ill of it. . . . You have recourse to it when you discourse and debate. And you, least of all, Abbé, should disparage science, you who pass your life surrounded with your books and manuscripts, your medallions and all the remains of Roman and Greek antiquity. You know in what high esteem you are held by those whom you call the Encyclopedists?

Barthélemy: I know how forbearing you are, Diderot, how sensitive and tender your soul is.

Diderot: Well, would you believe, my dear friend, sometimes I suspect you of having, besides your profound learning, too much good sense not to be enlightened about the value of these Catholic dogmas, and to be decided, in this respect, just as I am? Naturally you will not agree to this, and in your conscience you think me terribly indiscreet. . . . But finally, yes—why are you a Catholic?

Barthélemy: What! Why?

Diderot: Yes!

Barthélemy: But . . .

Diderot: Well then, I'll tell it you. It is solely—solely!—because you were born in France and were brought up, "nourished," by Catholics. Exactly! Suppose yourself for a moment a native of the Antipodes, of Zanzibar, of Cathay, of Patagonia, and see what would have become of you. You would be perhaps not even an Israelite, Lutheran, Calvinist, or Muslim, but very likely a Buddhist, Brahmin, idolater, or animal-worshipper for all I know! We have the choice. You see, my dear Abbé, all that is an affair of latitude, a pure chance, luck.

Barthélemy: You said the word, Diderot: luck! So be it. And I profit by this luck.

Diderot: Much good may it do you! But state with me that the most important thing for man, his eternal salvation, his religion in other words, depends solely on chance, on a caprice of fate. What fine desserts, eh?

Barthélemy: So I bless Providence. . . .

Diderot: And you are right Abbé. I, an unbeliever, don't profit from this windfall. . . . But pardon me, forgive my questions. . . . I hardly ever restrain myself, and speak freely what is in my mind.

Barthélemy: I live apart from all discussions. I work and associate more with the sages of Athens and of Rome, and indeed with those of Palestine, than with my contemporaries.

Diderot: Work, eh? Yes, that's our lot and our role here below. To try to leave after us a little more light and comfort than there was before, to improve and increase the heritage we have received; it is to that we should apply ourselves. I add: to do as much good as possible, and to spare as much suffering as possible around us, to all our companions on the way. Benevolence is better than anything. Work and benevolence, there are my sole two articles of faith, Abbé. For the rest . . . For myself, no more than for d'Holbach, the infinite does not preoccupy me, not in the least.

When and by whom was the world created? Where shall we go after our death? What shall we become? All these problems, which you think of such capital importance, don't in the least disturb my sleep. For hundreds and thousands of centuries, nobody has been able to solve them, but only to clarify them. So . . . . God, the soul, the future life. I neither believe nor disbelieve them; I eliminate these questions, I stick to life in the present, and I consider, with Spinoza, that all meditation about the Beyond and about death is useless, vain, and depressing.

Barthélemy: Ah, my poor Diderot! how far we are out in our reckoning! Is not true wisdom, on the contrary, a continual meditation on death, as our Bourdaloue has demonstrated in such masterly fashion?[15]

Diderot: The Lord bless him! As for myself, I haven't got such penetrating and far-seeing vision, and limit myself to the present, to what I am and what I see, and I do not feel any more in despair at not knowing what to think about the existence of the Supreme Being and of the immortality of the soul, than at not having two heads, three arms, or four legs. I take existence as it is, trying to pass through it as honestly and as comfortably and agreeably as I can, and if later on I encounter what I hardly expect, I confess it, namely a judge beyond the Styx, I have confidence in his wisdom and mercy; he will not punish me for my ignorance and my humility, any more than for my frankness. Otherwise I should have the right to answer him: "You had only to speak more clearly, Lord. Is it my fault that I know not how to unravel these enigmas? How could I suspect that in order to guide myself through the darkness into which you plunged me, I ought to have begun by blowing out my lantern, my sole torch, this feeble candle-end, this poor little reason with which you have favored me?"

From *Critique of Pure Reason* (1781)

IMMANUEL KANT

[Immanuel Kant (1724–1804) was the leading German thinker of the Enlightenment. An early work, dating to 1755, laid out an early version of the nebular hypothesis later devised by Laplace, in which the solar system was shown to have developed naturally without the intervention of a god. Another early work, *The Only Possible Argument in Support of a Demonstration of the Existence of God* (1763), anticipates the arguments in the *Kritik der reinen Vernunft* (1781; *Critique of Pure Reason*). In that work, Kant proved to his satisfaction that many of the standard proofs of the existence of God—the ontological (the notion that a perfect being must exist), the cosmological (the notion of a prime mover, or an absolutely necessary being), and the physico-theological (the argument from design)—are either false or unprovable. This stance conformed to the agnosticism that Kant developed from an early age. In the later *Kritik der praktischen Vernunft* (1788; *Critique of Practical Reason*), Kant maintained that the idea of God, even if unprovable, is necessary for morality as an embodiment of the "ideal of the supreme good." The following extract from the *Critique of Pure Reason* exhibits the density of Kant's language and thought in his proofs against the existence of God.]

OF THE ARGUMENTS EMPLOYED BY SPECULATIVE REASON TO PROVE A SUPREME BEING'S EXISTENCE

Notwithstanding the pressing necessity that reason feels to form some presupposition that shall serve the understanding as a proper basis for the complete determination of its conceptions, the idealistic and factitious nature of such a presupposition is too evident to allow reason for a moment to persuade itself into a belief of the objective existence of a mere creation of its own thought. But there are other considerations that compel reason to seek out some resting-place in the regress from the conditioned to the unconditioned, which is not given as an actual existence from the mere conception of it, although it alone can give completeness to the series of conditions. And this is the natural course of every human reason, even of the most uneducated, although it does not always continue to follow the path entered at the start. It does not begin from conceptions, but from common experience, and requires a basis in actual existence. But this basis is insecure, unless it rests upon the immovable rock of absolute necessity. And this foundation is itself unworthy of trust, if it leaves under and above it empty space, if it does not fill all and leave no room for a *why* or a *wherefore*, if it is not, in a word, infinite in its reality.

If we admit the existence of some one thing, whatever it may be, we must also admit that there is something that exists *necessarily*. For what is contingent exists only under the condition of some other thing, which is its cause; and from this we must go on to conclude the existence of a cause that is not contingent, and which consequently exists necessarily and unconditionally. Such is the argument by which reason justifies its advances toward a primal being.

Now reason looks around for the conception of a being that may be admitted, without inconsistency, to be worthy of the attribute of absolute necessity—not for the purpose of inferring *a priori*, from the conception of such a being, its objective existence (for if reason allowed itself to take this course, it would not require a basis in given and actual existence, but merely the support of pure conceptions), but for the purpose of discovering, among all our conceptions of possible things, that conception which possesses no element inconsistent with the idea of absolute necessity. For that there must be some absolutely necessary existence is a truth that it regards as already established. Now, if it can remove every existence incapable of supporting the attribute of absolute necessity, excepting one—this must be the absolutely necessary being, whether its necessity is comprehensible by us, that is, deducible from the conception of it alone, or not.

Now that being, the conception of which contains a *therefore* to every *wherefore*, which is not defective in any respect whatever, which is all-sufficient as a condition, seems to be the being of which we can justly predicate absolute necessity—for this reason, that, possessing the conditions of all that is possible, it does not and cannot itself require any condition. And thus it satisfies, in one respect at least, the requirements of the conception of absolute necessity. In this view, it is superior to all other conceptions, which, being deficient and incomplete, do not possess the characteristic of independence of all higher conditions. It is true that we cannot infer from this that what does not contain in itself the supreme and complete condition—the condition of all other things—must possess only a conditioned existence; but we can as little assert the contrary, for this supposed being does not possess the only characteristic that can enable reason to understand by means of an *a priori* conception the unconditioned and necessary nature of its existence.

The conception of a being of the highest reality is that which best agrees with the conception of an unconditioned and necessary being. The former conception does not satisfy all the requirements of the latter; but we have no choice, we are obliged to adhere to it, for we find that we cannot do without the existence of a necessary being; and even although we admit it, we find it beyond our power to discover in the whole sphere of possibility any being that can advance well-grounded claims to such a distinction.

The following is, therefore, the natural course of human reason. It begins by persuading itself of the existence of some necessary being. In this being it recognizes the characteristics of unconditioned existence. It then seeks the conception of that which is independent of all conditions, and finds it in that which is itself the sufficient condition of all other things—in other words, in that which contains all reality. But the unlimited all is an absolute unity, and is conceived by the mind as a being one and supreme; and thus reason concludes that the supreme being, as the primal basis of all things, possesses an existence that is absolutely necessary.

This conception must be regarded as in some degree satisfactory, if we admit the existence of a necessary being and consider that there exists a necessity for a definite and final answer to these questions. In such a case, we cannot make a better choice, or rather we have no choice at all, but feel ourselves obliged to declare in favor of the absolute unity of complete reality, as the highest source of the possibility of things. But if there exists no motive for coming to a definite conclusion, and we may leave the question unanswered till we have fully weighed both sides—in other words, when we are merely called upon to decide how much we happen to know about the question, and how much we merely flatter ourselves that we know—the above conclusion does not appear to such great advantage, but, on the contrary, seems defective in the grounds upon which it is supported.

For admitting the truth of all that has been said, namely, that the inference from a given existence (my own, for example) to the existence of an unconditioned and necessary being is valid and unassailable; that, in the second place, we must consider a being that contains all reality, and consequently all the conditions of other things, to be absolutely unconditioned; and admitting too, that we have thus discovered the conception of a thing to which may be attributed, without inconsistency, absolute necessity—it does not follow from all this that the conception of a limited being, in which the supreme reality does not reside, is therefore incompatible with the idea of absolute necessity. For, although I do not discover the element of the unconditioned in the conception of such a being—an element that is manifestly existent in the sum total of all conditions—I am not entitled to conclude that its existence is therefore conditioned; just as I am not entitled to affirm, in a hypothetical syllogism, that where a certain condition does not exist (in the present case, completeness, as far as pure conceptions are concerned), the conditioned does not exist either. On the contrary, we are free to regard all limited beings as likewise unconditionally necessary, although we are unable to infer this from the general conception we have of them. Thus conducted, this argument is incapable of giving us the least notion of the properties of a necessary being and must be in every respect without result.

This argument continues, however, to possess a weight and an authority that, in spite of its objective insufficiency, it has never been divested of. For, granting that certain responsibilities lie upon us, which, as based on the ideas of reason, deserve to be respected and submitted to, although they are incapable of a real or practical application to our nature, or, in other words, would be responsibilities without motives, except upon the supposition of a Supreme

Being to give effect and influence to the practical laws: in such a case we should be bound to obey our conceptions, which, although objectively insufficient, do, according to the standard of reason, preponderate over and are superior to any claims that may be advanced from any other quarter. The equilibrium of doubt would in this case be destroyed by a practical addition; indeed, reason would be compelled to condemn itself, if it refused to comply with the demands of the judgment, no superior to which we know—however defective its understanding of the grounds of these demands might be.

This argument, although in fact transcendental, inasmuch as it rests upon the intrinsic insufficiency of the contingent, is so simple and natural that the commonest understanding can appreciate its value. We see things around us change, arise, and pass away; they, or their condition, must therefore have a cause. The same demand must again be made of the cause itself—as a datum of experience. Now it is natural that we should place the *highest* causality just where we place *supreme* causality, in that being which contains the conditions of all possible effects, and the conception of which is so simple as that of an all-embracing reality. This highest cause, then, we regard as absolutely necessary, because we find it absolutely necessary to rise to it, and do not discover any reason for proceeding beyond it. Thus, among all nations, through the darkest polytheism glimmer some faint sparks of monotheism, to which these idolaters have been led, not from reflection and profound thought, but by the study and natural progress of the common understanding.

There are only three modes of proving the existence of a Deity, on the grounds of speculative reason.

All the paths conducting to this end begin either from determinate experience and the peculiar constitution of the world of sense, and rise, according to the laws of causality, from it to the highest cause existing apart from the world—or from a purely indeterminate experience, that is, some empirical existence—or abstraction is made of all experience, and the existence of a supreme cause is concluded from *a priori* conceptions alone. The first is the *physico-theological* argument, the second the *cosmological*, the third the *ontological*. More there are not, and more there cannot be.

I shall show it is as unsuccessful on the one path (the empirical) as on the other (the transcendental), and that it stretches its wings in vain, to soar beyond the world of sense by the mere might of speculative thought. As regards the order in which we must discuss those arguments, it will be exactly the reverse of that in which reason, in the progress of its development, attains to them—the order in which they are placed above. For it will be made manifest to the reader that, although experience presents the occasion and the starting-point, it is the *transcendental idea* of reason that guides it in its pilgrimage and is the goal of all its struggles. I shall therefore begin with an examination of the transcendental argument and afterwards inquire what additional strength has accrued to this mode of proof from the addition of the empirical element.

OF THE IMPOSSIBILITY OF AN ONTOLOGICAL PROOF OF THE EXISTENCE OF GOD

It is evident from what has been said that the conception of an absolutely necessary being is a mere idea, the objective reality of which is far from being established by the mere fact that it is a need of reason. On the contrary, this idea serves merely to indicate a certain unattainable perfection and rather limits the operations than, by the presentation of new objects, extends the sphere of the understanding. But a strange anomaly meets us at the very threshold; for the inference from a given existence in general to an absolutely necessary existence seems to be correct and unavoidable, while the conditions of the *understanding* refuse to aid us in forming any conception of such a being.

Philosophers have always talked of an *absolutely necessary* being and have nevertheless declined to take the trouble of conceiving whether—and how—a being of this nature is even conceivable, not to mention that its existence is actually demonstrable. A verbal definition of the conception is certainly easy enough; it is something, the nonexistence of which is impossible. But does this definition throw any light upon the conditions that render it impossible to contemplate the nonexistence of a thing—conditions that we wish to ascertain, so that we may discover whether we think anything in the conception of such a being or not? For the mere fact that I throw away, by means of the word *unconditioned*, all the conditions that the understanding habitually requires in order to regard anything as necessary is very far from making clear whether, by means of the conception of the unconditionally necessary, I think of something or really of nothing at all.

Nay, more, this chance conception, now become so current, is one that many have tried to explain by examples that seemed to render any inquiries regarding its intelligibility quite needless. It was said that every geometrical proposition—a triangle has three angles—is absolutely necessary; and thus people talked of an object that lay out of the sphere of our understanding as if it were perfectly plain what the conception of such a being meant.

All the examples adduced have been drawn, without exception, from *judgments*, and not from *things*. But the unconditioned necessity of a judgment does not form the absolute necessity of a thing. On the contrary, the absolute necessity of a judgment is only a conditioned necessity of a thing, or of the predicate in a judgment. The above-mentioned proposition does not declare that three angles necessarily exist, but, upon condition that a triangle exists, three angles must necessarily exist—in it. And thus this logical necessity has been the source of the greatest delusions. Having formed an *a priori* conception of a thing, the content of which was made to embrace existence, we believed ourselves safe in concluding that, because existence belongs necessarily to the object of the conception (that is, under the condition of my positing this thing as given), the existence of the thing is also posited necessarily, and that it is therefore absolutely necessary—merely because its existence has been contemplated in the conception.

If, in an identical judgment, I annihilate the predicate in thought and retain the subject, a contradiction is the result; and hence I say, the former belongs necessarily to the latter. But if I suppress both subject and predicate in thought, no contradiction arises; for there is nothing at all, and therefore no means of forming a contradiction. To suppose the existence of a triangle and not that of its three angles is self-contradictory; but to suppose the non-existence of both triangle and angles is perfectly admissible. And so is it with the conception of an absolutely necessary being. Annihilate its existence in thought, and you annihilate the thing itself with all its predicates; how then can there be any room for contradiction? Externally, there is nothing to give rise to a contradiction, for a thing cannot be necessary externally;

nor internally, for, by the annihilation or suppression of the thing itself, its internal properties are also annihilated. God is omnipotent—that is a necessary judgment. His omnipotence cannot be denied, if the existence of a Deity is posited—the existence, that is, of an infinite being, the two conceptions being identical. But when you say, "God does not exist," neither omnipotence nor any other predicate is affirmed; they must all disappear with the subject, and in this judgment there cannot exist the least self-contradiction.

You have thus seen that when the predicate of a judgment is annihilated in thought along with the subject, no internal contradiction can arise, whatever the predicate may be. There is no possibility of evading the conclusion; you would find yourself compelled to declare, "There are certain subjects that cannot be annihilated in thought." But this is nothing more than saying: "There exist subjects that are absolutely necessary"—the very hypothesis you are called upon to establish. For I find myself unable to form the slightest conception of a thing that, when annihilated in thought with all its predicates, leaves behind a contradiction; and contradiction is the only criterion of impossibility, in the sphere of pure *a priori* conceptions.

Against these general considerations, the justice of which no one can dispute, one argument is adduced that is regarded as furnishing a satisfactory demonstration from the fact. It is affirmed that there is one and only one conception in which the non-being or annihilation of the object is self-contradictory, and this is the conception of a most real being (*ens realissimum*). It possesses, you say, all reality, and you feel yourself justified in admitting the possibility of such a being. (This I am willing to grant for the present, although the existence of a conception that is not self-contradictory is far from being sufficient to prove the possibility of an object.) Now the notion of all reality embraces in it that of existence; the notion of existence lies, therefore, in the conception of this possible thing. If this thing is annihilated in thought, the internal possibility of the thing is also annihilated, which is self-contradictory.

I answer: It is absurd to introduce—disguised under whatever term— into the conception of a thing, which is to be contemplated solely in reference to its possibility, the conception of its existence. If this is admitted, you will have apparently gained the day, but in reality have expressed nothing but a mere tautology. I ask, is the proposition, "*this or that thing* (which I am admitting to be possible) exists," an analytic or a synthetic proposition? If the former, there is no addition made to the subject of your thought by the affirmation of its existence; but then the conception in your mind is identical with the thing itself, or you have supposed the existence of a thing to be possible and then inferred its existence from its internal possibility—which is simply a miserable tautology. The word *reality* in the conception of the thing, and the word *existence* in the conception of the predicate, will not help you out of the difficulty. For, supposing you were to term all positing of a thing as *reality*, you have thereby posited the thing with all its predicates in the conception of the subject and assumed its actual existence, and this you merely repeat in the predicate. But if you confess, as every reasonable person must, that every existential proposition is synthetic, how can it be maintained that the predicate of existence cannot be denied without contradiction—a property that is the characteristic of analytical propositions alone?

I should have a reasonable hope of putting an end forever to this sophistical mode of argumentation by a strict definition of the conception of existence, if my own experience did not teach me that the illusion arising from our confounding a logical with a real predicate (a predicate that aids in the determination of a thing) resists almost all the endeavors of explanation and illustration. A *logical predicate* may be whatever you please, even the subject may be predicated of itself; for logic pays no regard to the content of a judgment. But the determination of a conception is a predicate that adds to and enlarges the conception. It must not, therefore, be contained in the conception.

Being is evidently not a real predicate, that is, a conception of something that is added to the conception of some other thing. It is merely the positing of a thing, or of certain determinations in it. Logically, it is merely the copula of a judgment. The proposition, "God is omnipotent," contains two conceptions that have a certain object or content; the word *is* is no additional predicate—it merely indicates the relation of the predicate to the subject. Now, if I take the subject (God) with all its predicates (omnipotence being one), and say, "God is," or, "There is a God," I add no new predicate to the conception of God, I merely posit or affirm the existence of the subject with all its predicates—I posit the *object* in relation to my *conception*. The content of both is the same; and there is no addition made to the conception, which expresses merely the possibility of the object, by my contemplating the object—in the expression, it *is*—as absolutely given or existing. Thus the real contains no more than the possible. A hundred real dollars contain no more than a hundred possible dollars. For, as the latter indicate the conception, and the former the object, on the supposition that the content of the former was greater than that of the latter, my conception would not be an expression of the whole object, and would consequently be an inadequate conception of it. But in reckoning my wealth there may be said to be more in a hundred real dollars than in a hundred possible dollars—that is, in the mere conception of them. For the real object—the dollars—is not analytically contained in my conception, but forms a synthetic addition to my conception (which is merely a determination of my mental state), although this objective reality—this existence—apart from my conception does not in the least increase the aforesaid hundred dollars.

By whatever and by whatever number of predicates—even to the complete determination of it—I may contemplate a thing, I do not in the least augment the object of my conception by the addition of the statement, "This thing exists." Otherwise, not exactly the same, but something more than what was contemplated in my conception would exist, and I could not affirm that the exact object of my conception had real existence. If I contemplate a thing as containing all modes of reality except one, the mode of reality that is absent is not added to the conception of the thing by the affirmation that the thing exists; on the contrary, the thing exists—if it exists at all—with the same defect as that contemplated in its conception; otherwise not what was contemplated, but something different, exists. Now, if I contemplate a being as the highest reality, without defect or imperfection, the question still remains—whether this being exists or not? For although no element is lacking in the possible real content of my conception, there is a defect in its relation to my mental state; that is, I am ignorant whether the cognition of the object indicated by the conception is possible *a posteriori*. And here the cause of the present difficulty becomes apparent. If the question regarded only an object of sense, it would be impossible for me to confound the conception with the existence of a thing. For the conception merely enables me to contemplate an object as according with the general conditions of experience; while the existence of the object permits me to contemplate it as contained in the sphere of actual experience. At the same time, this connection with the world of experience does not in the least augment the conception, although a possible perception has been added to the experience of the mind. But if we contemplate existence by the pure category alone, it is not to be wondered at that we should find ourselves unable to present any criterion sufficient to distinguish it from mere possibility.

Whatever be the content of our conception of an object, it is necessary to go beyond it if we wish to predicate existence of the object. In the case of objects of the senses, this is attained by their connection according to empirical laws with some one of my perceptions; but there is no means of cognizing the existence of objects of pure thought, because it must be cognized completely *a priori*. But all our knowledge of existence (be it immediately by perception or by inferences connecting some object with a perception) belongs entirely to the sphere of experience—which is in perfect unity with itself—and although an existence out of this sphere cannot be absolutely declared to be impossible, it is a hypothesis the truth of which we have no means of ascertaining.

The notion of a supreme being is in many respects a highly useful idea; but for the very reason that it is an idea, it is incapable of enlarging our cognition with regard to the existence of things. It is not even sufficient to instruct us as to possibility. The analytic criterion of possibility, which consists in the absence of contradiction in propositions, cannot be denied it. But the connection of real properties in a thing is a synthesis of the possibility of which an *a priori* judgment cannot be formed, because these realities are not presented to us specifically; and even if this were to happen, a judgment would still be impossible, because the criterion of the possibility of synthetic cognitions must be sought for in the world of experience, to which the object of an idea cannot belong. And thus the celebrated Leibniz has utterly failed in his attempt to establish upon *a priori* grounds the possibility of this sublime ideal being.[1]

The celebrated ontological or Cartesian argument for the existence of a Supreme Being is therefore insufficient; and we may as well hope to increase our stock of knowledge by the aid of mere ideas as the merchant to augment his wealth by the addition of zeros to his cash-account.

OF THE IMPOSSIBILITY OF A COSMOLOGICAL PROOF OF THE EXISTENCE OF GOD

It was by no means a natural course of proceeding, but, on the contrary, an invention entirely due to the subtlety of the schools, to attempt to draw from a mere idea a proof of the existence of an object corresponding to it. Such a course would never have been pursued were it not for that need of reason which requires it to suppose the existence of a necessary being as a basis for the empirical regress, and that, as this necessity must be unconditioned and *a priori*, reason is bound to discover a conception that shall satisfy, if possible, this requirement and enable us to attain to the *a priori* cognition of such a being. This conception was thought to be found in the idea of an *ens realissimum*, and thus this idea was employed for the attainment of a better defined knowledge of a necessary being, of the existence of which we were convinced, or persuaded, on other grounds. Thus reason was seduced from her natural course; and, instead of concluding with the conception of an *ens realissimum*, an attempt was made to begin with it, for the purpose of inferring from it that idea of a necessary existence which it was in fact called in to complete. Thus arose that unfortunate ontological argument which neither satisfies the healthy common sense of humanity nor sustains the scientific examination of the philosopher.

The *cosmological proof*, which we are about to examine, retains the connection between absolute necessity and the highest reality; but, instead of reasoning from this highest reality to a necessary existence, like the preceding argument, it concludes from the given unconditioned necessity of some being its unlimited reality. The track it pursues, whether rational or sophistical, is at least natural and not only goes far to persuade the common understanding, but shows itself deserving of respect from the speculative intellect; while it contains, at the same time, the outlines of all the arguments employed in natural theology—arguments that always have been, and still will be, in use and authority. These, however adorned and hidden under whatever embellishments of rhetoric and sentiment, are at bottom identical with the arguments we will now discuss. This proof, termed by Leibniz the *argumentum a contingentia mundi* [argument from the contingency of the world], I shall now lay before the reader and subject to a strict examination.

It is framed in the following manner: If something exists, an absolutely necessary being must likewise exist. Now I, at least, exist. Consequently, there exists an absolutely necessary being. The minor premise contains an experience, the major premise reasons from a general experience to the existence of a necessary being. Thus this argument really begins at experience and is not completely *a priori*, or ontological. The object of all possible experience being the world, it is called the *cosmological* proof. It contains no reference to any peculiar property of objects of experience, by which this world of sense might be distinguished from other possible worlds; and in this respect it differs from the physico-theological proof, which is based upon the consideration of the peculiar constitution of our world of sense.

The proof proceeds thus: A necessary being can be determined only in one way, that is, it can be determined by only one of all possible opposed predicates; consequently, it must be *completely* determined in and by its conception. But only a single conception of a thing is possible that completely determines the thing *a priori*: that is, the conception of the *ens realissimum*. It follows that the conception of the *ens realissimum* is the only conception by and in which we can contemplate a necessary being. Consequently, a supreme being necessarily exists.

In this cosmological argument are assembled so many sophistical propositions that speculative reason seems to have exerted in it all its dialectical skill to produce a transcendental illusion of the most extreme character. We shall postpone an investigation of this argument for the present, confining ourselves to exposing the stratagem by which it imposes upon us an old argument in a new dress and appeals to the agreement of two witnesses, the one with the credentials of pure reason, and the other with those of empiricism; while, in fact, it is only the former that has changed its dress and voice, for the purpose of passing itself off as an additional witness. That it may possess a secure foundation, it bases its conclusions upon experience and thus appears to be completely distinct from the ontological argument, which places its confidence entirely in pure *a priori* conceptions. But this experience merely aids reason in making one step—to the existence of a necessary being. What the properties of this being are cannot be learned from experience; and therefore reason abandons it altogether and pursues its inquiries in the sphere of pure conceptions, for the purpose of discovering what the properties of an absolutely necessary being ought to be, that is, what among all possible things contain the conditions (*requisita*) of absolute necessity. Reason believes that it has discovered these requisites in the conception of an *ens realissimum* and in it alone, and hence concludes: The *ens realissimum* is an absolutely necessary being. But it is evident that reason has here presupposed that the conception of an *ens realissimum* is perfectly adequate to the conception of a being of absolute necessity, that is, that we may infer the existence of the latter from that of the former—a proposition that formed the basis of the ontological argument, and which is now employed in the support of the cosmological argument, contrary to the wish and professions of its inventors. For the existence of an absolutely necessary being is given in conceptions alone. But if I say that the conception of the *ens realissimum* is a conception of this kind, and in fact the only conception that is adequate to our idea of a necessary being, I am obliged to admit that the latter may be inferred from the former. Thus it is properly the ontological argument that figures in the cosmological and constitutes the whole strength of the latter; while the spurious basis of experience has been of no further use than to conduct us to the conception of absolute necessity, being utterly insufficient to demonstrate the presence of this attribute in any determinate existence or thing. For when we propose to ourselves an aim of this character, we must abandon the sphere of experience and rise to that of pure conceptions, which we examine with the purpose of discovering whether any one contains the conditions of the possibility of an absolutely necessary being. But if the possibility of such a being is thus demonstrated, its existence is also proved; for we may then assert that, of all possible beings, there is one that possesses the attribute of necessity—in other words, this being possesses an absolutely necessary existence.

All illusions in an argument are more easily detected when they are presented in the formal manner employed by the schools, which we now proceed to do.

If the proposition, "Every absolutely necessary being is likewise an *ens realissimum*," is correct (and it is this which constitutes the *nervus probandi* [the nerve (i.e., essence) of the proof] of the cosmological argument), it must, like all affirmative judgments, be capable of conversion—the *conversio per accidens* [the conversion by accident (i.e., by limitation)], at least. It follows, then, that some *entia realissima* are absolutely necessary beings. But no *ens realissimum* is in any respect different from another, and what is valid for some is valid for all. In this present case, therefore, I may employ simple conversion and say, "Every *ens realissimum* is a necessary being." But as this proposition is determined *a priori* by the conceptions contained in it, the mere conception of an *ens realissimum* must possess the additional attribute of absolute necessity. But this is exactly what was maintained in the ontological argument and not recognized by the cosmological, although it formed the real ground of its disguised and illusory reasoning.

Thus the second mode employed by speculative reason of demonstrating the existence of a Supreme Being is not only, like the first, illusory and inadequate, but possesses the additional blemish of an *ignoratio elenchi* [ignorance of the course (i.e., of an argument)]—professing to conduct us by a new road to the desired goal, but bringing us back, after a short circuit, to the old path that we had deserted at its call.

I mentioned above that this cosmological argument contains a perfect nest of dialectical assumptions that transcendental criticism does not find it difficult to expose and dissipate. I shall merely enumerate these, leaving it to the reader, who must by this time be well practiced in such matters, to investigate the fallacies residing therein.

The following fallacies, for example, are discoverable in this mode of proof: 1. The transcendental principle, "Everything that is contingent must have a cause"—a principle without significance, except in the world of sense. For the purely intellectual conception of the contingent cannot produce any synthetic proposition, like that of causality, which is itself without significance or distinguishing characteristic except in the phenomenal world. But in the present case it is employed to help us beyond the limits of its sphere. 2. From the impossibility of an infinite ascending series of causes in the world of sense a first cause is inferred; a conclusion that the principles of the employment of reason do not justify even in the sphere of experience, and still less when an attempt is made to pass the limits of this sphere. 3. Reason allows itself to be satisfied on insufficient grounds with regard to the completion of this series. It removes all conditions (without which, however, no conception of necessity can take place); and, as after this it is beyond our power to form any other conception, it accepts this as a completion of the conception it wishes to form of the series. 4. The logical possibility of a conception of the totality of reality (the criterion of this possibility being the absence of contradiction) is confounded with the transcendental, which requires a principle of the practicability of such a synthesis—a principle that again refers us to the world of experience. And so on.

The aim of the cosmological argument is to avoid the necessity of proving the existence of a necessary being *a priori* from mere conceptions—a proof that must be ontological, and of which we feel ourselves quite incapable. With this purpose, we reason from an actual existence—an experience in general—to an absolutely necessary condition of that existence. It is in this case unnecessary to demonstrate its possibility. For after having proved that it exists, the question regarding its possibility is superfluous. Now, when we wish to define more strictly the nature of this necessary being, we do not look out for some being the conception of which would enable us to comprehend the necessity of its being—for if we could do this, an empirical presupposition would be unnecessary; no, we try to discover merely the negative condition (*conditio sine qua non*), without which a being would not be absolutely necessary. Now this would be perfectly admissible in every sort of reasoning from a consequence to its principle; but in the present case it unfortunately happens that the condition of absolute necessity can be discovered in only a single being, the conception of which must consequently contain all that is requisite for demonstrating the presence of absolute necessity, and thus entitle me to infer this absolute necessity *a priori*. That is, it must be possible to reason conversely and say, "The thing, to which the conception of the highest reality belongs, is absolutely necessary." But if I cannot reason thus—and I cannot, unless I believe in the sufficiency of the ontological argument—I find insurmountable obstacles in my new path and am really no further than the point from which I set out. The conception of a Supreme Being satisfies all questions *a priori* regarding the internal determinations of a thing, and is for this reason an ideal without equal or parallel, the general conception of it indicating it as at the same time an individual being among all possible things. But the conception does not satisfy the question regarding its existence—which was the purpose of all our inquiries; and, although the existence of a necessary being was admitted, we should find it impossible to answer the question: What of all things in the world must be regarded as such?

It is certainly allowable to *admit* the existence of an all-sufficient being—a cause of all possible effects—for the purpose of enabling reason to introduce unity into its mode and grounds of explanation with regard to phenomena. But to assert that such a being *necessarily exists* is no longer the modest enunciation of an admissible hypothesis, but the boldest declaration of an apodictic certainty; for the cognition of that which is absolutely necessary must itself possess that character.

The aim of the transcendental ideal formed by the mind is either to discover a conception that shall harmonize with the idea of absolute necessity or a conception that shall contain that idea. If the one is possible, so is the other; for reason recognizes that alone as absolutely necessary which is necessary from its conception. But both attempts are equally beyond our power—we find it impossible to *satisfy* the understanding upon this point, and as impossible to induce it to remain at rest in relation to this incapacity.

Unconditioned necessity—which, as the ultimate support and stay of all existing things, is an indispensable requirement of the mind—is an abyss on the verge of which human reason trembles in dismay. Even the idea of eternity, terrible and sublime as it is, as depicted by Haller,[2] does not produce upon the mental vision such a feeling of awe and terror; for, although it measures the duration of things, it does not *support* them. We cannot bear, nor can we rid ourselves of the thought, that a being whom we regard as the greatest of all possible existences should *say to himself*: "I am from eternity to eternity; beside me there is nothing, except that which exists by my will; *but whence then am I?*" Here all sinks away from under us; and the greatest, as the smallest, perfection hovers without stay or footing in the presence of the speculative reason, which finds it as easy to part with the one as with the other.

Many physical powers, which manifest their existence by their effects, are perfectly inscrutable in their nature; they elude all our powers of observation. The transcendental object that forms the basis of phenomena, and, in connection with it, the reason why our sensibility possesses this rather than that particular kind of conditions, are and must ever remain hidden from our mental vision; the fact is there, the reason for the fact we cannot see. But an ideal of pure reason cannot be termed mysterious or *inscrutable*, because the only credential of its reality is the need of it felt by reason, for the purpose of giving completeness to the world of synthetic unity. An ideal is not even given as a contemplatable *object*, and therefore cannot be inscrutable; on the contrary, it must, as a mere idea, be based on the constitution of reason itself, and on this account must be capable of explanation and solution. For the very essence of reason consists in its ability to give an account of all our conceptions, opinions, and assertions—upon objective or, when they happen to be illusory and fallacious, upon subjective grounds.

Detection and Explanation of the Dialectical Illusion in All Transcendental Arguments for the Existence of a Necessary Being

Both of the above arguments are transcendental; in other words, they do not proceed upon empirical principles. For, although the cosmological argument professed to lay a basis of experience for its edifice of reasoning, it did not ground its procedure upon the peculiar constitution of experience, but upon pure principles of reason—in relation to an existence given by empirical consciousness; utterly abandoning its guidance, however, for the purpose of supporting its assertions entirely upon pure conceptions. Now what is the cause, in these transcendental arguments, of the dialectical but natural illusion that connects the conceptions of necessity and supreme reality and hypostatizes what cannot be anything but an idea? What is the cause of this unavoidable step on the part of reason of admitting that some one among all existing things must be necessary, while it falls back from the assertion of the existence of such a being as from an abyss? And how does reason proceed to explain this anomaly to itself, and from the wavering condition of a timid and reluctant approbation—always again withdrawn—arrive at a calm and settled insight into its cause?

It is very remarkable that, on the supposition that something exists, I cannot avoid the inference that something exists necessarily. Upon this perfectly natural—but not on that account reliable—inference does the cosmological argument rest. But if I form any conception whatever of a thing, I find that I cannot contemplate the existence of the thing as absolutely necessary, and that nothing prevents me—be the thing or being what it may—from contemplating its nonexistence. I may thus be obliged to admit that all existing things have a necessary basis, while I cannot contemplate any single or individual thing as necessary. In other words, I can never *complete* the regress through the conditions of existence without admitting the existence of a necessary being; but, on the other hand, I cannot make a *commencement* from this beginning.

If I must contemplate something as existing necessarily as the basis of existing things, and yet am not permitted to contemplate any individual thing as in itself necessary, the inevitable inference is that necessity and contingency are not properties of things themselves—otherwise an internal contradiction would result; that consequently neither of these principles are objective, but merely subjective principles of reason—the one requiring us to seek for a necessary ground for everything that exists, that is, to be satisfied with no other explanation than what is complete *a priori*, the other forbidding us ever to hope for the attainment of this completeness, that is, to regard no member of the empirical world as unconditioned. In this mode of viewing them, both principles, in their purely heuristic and regulative character, and as concerning merely the formal interest of reason, are quite consistent with each other. The one says, "You must philosophize upon nature as if there existed a necessary primal basis of all existing things, solely for the purpose of introducing systematic unity into your knowledge, by pursuing an idea of this character"—a foundation that is arbitrarily admitted to be ultimate; while the other warns you to consider no individual determination concerning the existence of things as such an ultimate foundation, that is, as absolutely necessary, but to keep the way always open for further progress in the deduction and to treat every determination as determined by some other. But if all that we perceive must be regarded as conditionally necessary, it is impossible that anything that is empirically given should be absolutely necessary.

It follows from this that you must accept the absolutely necessary as *out of* and beyond the world, inasmuch as it is useful only as a principle of the highest possible unity in experience, and you cannot discover any such necessary existence in the *world*, the second rule requiring you to regard all empirical causes of unity as themselves deduced.

The philosophers of antiquity regarded all the forms of nature as contingent; while matter was considered by them, in accordance with the judgment of the common reason of mankind, as primal and necessary. But if they had regarded matter, not relatively—as the substratum of phenomena, but absolutely and *in itself*—as an independent existence, this idea of absolute necessity would have immediately disappeared. For there is nothing absolutely connecting reason with such an existence; on the contrary, it can annihilate it in thought, always and without self-contradiction. But in thought alone lay the idea of absolute necessity. A regulative principle must, therefore, have been at the foundation of this opinion. In fact, extension and impenetrability—which together constitute our conception of matter—form the supreme empirical principle of the unity of phenomena, and this principle, insofar as it is empirically unconditioned, possesses the property of a regulative principle. But as every determination of matter that constitutes what is real in it—and consequently impenetrability—is an effect that must have a cause, and is for this reason always derived, the notion of matter cannot harmonize with the idea of a necessary being, in its character of the principle of all derived unity. For every one of its real properties, being derived, must be only conditionally necessary, and can therefore be annihilated in thought; and thus the whole existence of matter can be so annihilated or suppressed. If this were not the case, we should have found in the world of phenomena the highest ground or condition of unity—which is impossible, according to the second regulative principle. It follows that matter and, in general, all that forms part of the world of sense cannot be a necessary primal being, nor even a principle of empirical unity, but that this being or principle must have its place assigned without the world. And, in this way, we can proceed in perfect confidence to deduce the phenomena of the world and their existence from other phenomena, just as if there existed no necessary being; and we can at the same time strive ceaselessly toward the attainment of completeness for our deduction, just as if such a being—the supreme condition of all existences—were presupposed by the mind.

These remarks will have made it evident to the reader that the ideal of the Supreme Being, far from being a declaration of the existence of a being in itself necessary, is nothing more than a *regulative principle* of reason, requiring us to regard every connection existing between phenomena as if it had its origin from an all-sufficient necessary cause, and basing upon this the rule of a systematic and necessary unity in the explanation of phenomena. We cannot at the same time avoid regarding, by a transcendental misrepresentation, this formal principle as constitutive and hypostatizing this unity. Precisely similar is the case with our notion of space. Space is the primal condition of all forms, which are properly just so many different limitations of it; and thus, although it is merely a principle of sensibility, we cannot help regarding it as an absolutely necessary and self-subsistent thing—as an object given *a priori* in itself. In the same way, it is quite natural that, as the systematic unity of nature cannot be established as a principle for the empirical employment of reason unless it is based upon the idea of an *ens realissimum* as the supreme cause, we should regard this idea as a real object, and this object, in its character of supreme condition, as absolutely necessary, and that in this way a *regulative* principle should be transformed into a *constitutive* principle. This interchange becomes evident when I regard this supreme being, which, relatively to the world, was absolutely (unconditionally) necessary, as a thing *per se*. In this case, I find it impossible to represent this necessity in or by any conception, and it exists merely in my own mind, as the formal condition of thought, but not as a material and hypostatic condition of existence.

OF THE IMPOSSIBILITY OF A PHYSICO-THEOLOGICAL PROOF

If, then, neither a pure conception nor the general experience of an existing being can provide a sufficient basis for the proof of the existence of the Deity, we can make the attempt by the only other mode—that of grounding our argument upon a *determinate experience* of the phenomena of the present world, their constitution and disposition, and discover whether we can thus attain to a sound conviction of the existence of a Supreme Being. This argument we shall term the *physico-theological* argument. If it is shown to be insufficient, speculative reason cannot present us with any satisfactory proof of the existence of a being corresponding to our transcendental idea.

It is evident from the remarks that have been made in the preceding sections that an answer to this question will be far from being difficult or unconvincing. For how can any experience be adequate with an idea? The very essence of an idea consists in the fact that no experience can ever be discovered congruent or adequate with it. The transcendental idea of a necessary and all-sufficient being is so immeasurably great, so high above all that is empirical, which is always conditioned, that we hope in vain to find materials in the sphere of experience sufficiently ample for our conception, and in vain seek the unconditioned among things that are conditioned, while examples, nay, even guidance, is denied us by the laws of empirical synthesis.

If the Supreme Being forms a link in the chain of empirical conditions, it must be a member of the empirical series, and, like the lower members that it precedes, have its origin in some higher member of the series. If, on the other hand, we disengage it from the chain and contemplate it as an intelligible being, apart from the series of natural causes, how shall reason bridge the abyss that separates the latter from the former? All laws respecting the regress from effects to causes, all synthetic additions to our knowledge relate solely to possible experience and the objects of the world of sense, and apart from them are without significance.

The world around us opens before our view so magnificent a spectacle of order, variety, beauty, and conformity to ends that, whether we pursue our observations into the infinity of space in the one direction, or into its illimitable divisions in the other, whether we regard the world in its greatest or its least manifestations—even after we have attained to the highest summit of knowledge that our weak minds can reach, we find that language in the presence of wonders so inconceivable has lost its force, and number its power to reckon; nay, even thought fails to conceive adequately, and our conception of the whole dissolves into an astonishment without the power of expression—all the more eloquent in that it is mute. Everywhere around us we observe a chain of causes and effects, of means and ends, of death and birth; and, as nothing has entered of itself into the condition in which we find it, we are constantly referred to some other thing that itself suggests the same inquiry regarding its cause, and thus the universe must sink into the abyss of nothingness unless we admit that, besides this infinite chain of contingencies, there exists something that is primal and self-subsistent—something that, as the cause of this phenomenal world, secures its continuance and preservation.

This highest cause—what magnitude shall we attribute to it? Of the content of the world we are ignorant; still less can we estimate its magnitude by comparison with the sphere of the possible. But this supreme cause being a necessity of the human mind, what is there to prevent us from attributing to it such a degree of perfection as to place it above the sphere of all that is possible? This we can easily do, although only by the aid of the faint outline of an abstract conception, by representing this being to ourselves as containing in itself, as an individual substance, all possible perfection—a conception that satisfies that requirement of reason which demands parsimony in principles, which is free from self-contradiction, which even contributes to the extension of the employment of reason in experience, by means of the guidance afforded by this idea to order and system, and which in no respect conflicts with any law of experience.

This argument always deserves to be mentioned with respect. It is the oldest, the clearest, and the one most in conformity with the common reason of humanity. It animates the study of nature, as it itself derives its existence and draws ever new strength from that source. It introduces aims and ends into a sphere in which our observation could not of itself have discovered them, and extends our knowledge of nature by directing our attention to a unity, the principle of which lies beyond nature. This knowledge of nature again reacts upon this idea—its cause; and thus our belief in a divine author of the universe rises to the power of an irresistible conviction.

For these reasons it would be utterly hopeless to attempt to rob this argument of the authority it has always enjoyed. The mind, unceasingly elevated by these considerations, which, although empirical, are so remarkably powerful, and continually adding to their force, will not suffer itself to be depressed by the doubts suggested by subtle speculation; it tears itself out of this state of uncertainty at the very moment it casts a look upon the wondrous forms of nature and the majesty of the universe, and rises from height to height, from condition to condition, till it has elevated itself to the supreme and unconditioned author of all.

But although we have nothing to object to the reasonableness and utility of this procedure, but have rather to commend and encourage it, we cannot approve of the claims this argument advances to demonstrative certainty and to a reception upon its own merits, apart from favor or support by other arguments. Nor can it injure the cause of morality to try to lower the tone of the arrogant sophist and to teach him that modesty and moderation which are the properties of a belief that brings calm and content into the mind without prescribing to it an unworthy subjection. I maintain, then, that the physico-theological argument is insufficient of itself to prove the existence of a Supreme Being, that it must entrust this to the ontological argument—to which it serves merely as an introduction, and that, consequently, this argument contains the *only possible ground of proof* (possessed by speculative reason) for the existence of this being.

The chief elements in the physico-theological argument are as follows: 1. We observe in the world manifest signs of an arrangement full of purpose, executed with great wisdom, and existing in a whole of a content indescribably various, and of an extent without limits. 2. This arrangement of means and ends is entirely foreign to the things existing in the world—it belongs to them merely as a contingent attribute; in other words, the nature of different things could not of itself, whatever means were employed, harmoniously tend toward certain purposes, were they not chosen and directed for these purposes by a rational and disposing principle, in accordance with certain fundamental ideas. 3. There exists, therefore, a sublime and wise cause (or several), which is not merely a blind, all-powerful nature, producing the beings and events that fill the world in unconscious *fecundity*, but a *free* and intelligent cause of the world. 4. The unity of this cause may be inferred from the unity of the reciprocal relation existing between the parts of the world as portions of an artistic edifice—an inference that all our observation favors, and all principles of analogy support.

In the above argument, it is inferred from the analogy of certain products of nature with those of human art, when it compels nature to bend herself to its purposes, as in the case of a house, a ship, or a watch, that the same kind of causality—namely, understanding and will—resides in nature. It is also declared that the internal possibility of this freely acting nature (which is the source of all art, and perhaps also of human reason) is derivable from another and superhuman art—a conclusion that would perhaps be found incapable of standing the test of subtle transcendental criticism. But to neither of these opinions shall we at present object. We shall only remark that it must be confessed that, if we are to discuss the subject of cause at all, we cannot proceed more securely than with the guidance of the analogy subsisting between nature and such products of design—these being the only products whose causes and modes of origination are completely known to us. Reason would be unable to satisfy its own requirements if it passed from a causality that it does know to obscure and indemonstrable principles of explanation that it does not know.

According to the physico-theological argument, the connection and harmony existing in the world demonstrate the contingency of the form merely, but not of the matter, that is, of the substance of the world. To establish the truth of the latter opinion, it would be necessary to prove that all things would be in themselves incapable of this harmony and order unless they were, even as regards their *substance*, the product of a supreme wisdom. But this would require very different grounds of proof from those presented by the analogy with human art. This proof can at most, therefore, demonstrate the existence of an *architect of the world*, whose efforts are limited by the capabilities of the material with which he works, but not of a *creator of the world*, to whom all things are subject. Thus this argument is utterly insufficient for the task before us—a demonstration of the existence of an all-sufficient being. If we wish to prove the contingency of matter, we must have recourse to a transcendental argument, which the physico-theological was constructed expressly to avoid.

We infer, from the order and design visible in the universe, as a disposition of a thoroughly contingent character, the existence of a cause *proportionate thereto*. The conception of this cause must contain certain *determinate* qualities, and it must therefore be regarded as the conception of a being that possesses all power, wisdom, and so on, in one word, all perfection—the conception, that is, of an all-sufficient being. For the predicates of *very great*, astonishing, or immeasurable power and excellence give us no determinate conception of the thing, nor do they inform us what the thing may be in itself. They merely indicate the relation existing between the magnitude of the object and the observer, who compares it with himself and with his own power of comprehension, and are mere expressions of praise and reverence, by which the object is either magnified, or the observing subject depreciated in relation to the object. Where we have to do with the magnitude (of the perfection) of a thing, we can discover no determinate conception, except what comprehends all possible perfection or completeness, and it is only the totality (*omnitudo*) of reality that is completely determined in and through its conception alone.

Now it cannot be expected that anyone will be bold enough to declare that he has a perfect insight into the relation that the magnitude of the world he contemplates bears (in its extent as well as in its content) to omnipotence, into that of the order and design in the world to the highest wisdom, and that of the unity of the world to the absolute unity of a Supreme Being. Physico-theology is therefore incapable of presenting a determinate conception of a supreme cause of the world, and is therefore insufficient as a principle of theology—a theology that is itself to be the basis of religion.

The attainment of absolute totality is completely impossible on the path of empiricism. And yet, this is the path pursued in the physico-theological argument. What means shall we employ to bridge the abyss?

After elevating ourselves to admiration of the magnitude of the power, wisdom, and other attributes of the author of the world, and finding we can advance no further, we leave the argument on empirical grounds and proceed to infer the contingency of the world from the order and conformity to aims that are observable in it. From this contingency we infer, by the help of transcendental conceptions alone, the existence of something absolutely necessary; and, still advancing, proceed from the conception of the absolute necessity of the first cause to the completely determined or determining conception thereof—the conception of an all-embracing reality. Thus the physico-theological, failing in its undertaking, recurs in its embarrassment to the cosmological argument; and, as this is merely the ontological argument in disguise, it executes its design solely by the aid of pure reason, although it at first professed to have no connection with this faculty and to base its entire procedure upon experience alone.

The physico-theologians have therefore no reason to regard with such contempt the transcendental mode of argument, and to look down upon it, with the conceit of clear-sighted observers of nature, as the brain-cobweb of obscure speculatists. For if they reflect upon and examine their own arguments, they will find that, after following for some time the path of nature and experience and discovering themselves no nearer their object, they suddenly leave this path and pass into the region of pure possibility, where they hope to reach upon the wings of ideas what had eluded all their empirical investigations. Gaining, as they think, a firm footing after this immense leap, they extend their determinate conception—into the possession of which they have come, they know not how—over the whole sphere of creation and explain their ideal, which is entirely a product of pure reason, by illustrations drawn from experience—though in a degree miserably unworthy of the grandeur of the object—while they refuse to acknowledge that they have arrived at this cognition or hypothesis by a very different road from that of experience.

Thus the physico-theological is based upon the cosmological, and this upon the ontological proof of the existence of a Supreme Being; and as besides these three there is no other path open to speculative reason, the ontological proof, on the ground of pure conceptions of reason, is the only possible one, if any proof of a proposition so far transcending the empirical exercise of the understanding is possible at all.

PART 2

THE BRITISH ENLIGHTENMENT

"Of Faith and Reason, and Their Distinct Provinces" (1690)

JOHN LOCKE

[John Locke (1632–1704) was a pioneering British philosopher who, although by no means an atheist or even an agnostic, laid the groundwork for much freethought during the Enlightenment. His chief philosophical work is *An Essay concerning Human Understanding* (1690), which advocated a strictly empiricist theory of mind by asserting that the mind was a *tabula rasa* (blank slate) and that all knowledge is the ultimate result of sense impressions. In the realm of religion, Locke's *Letters concerning Toleration* (1689–92) was a landmark in arguing against legal penalties for dissenting religious views, although this tolerance was not to be extended to atheists. In *The Reasonableness of Christianity* (1695), he contended that all aspects of Christian doctrine were acceptable to human reason. In the following chapter from *An Essay concerning Human Understanding,* Locke lays down a clear distinction between faith and reason, adding that reason can only accept those elements of revelation that conform to its dictates.]

1. It has been above shown, 1. That we are of necessity ignorant, and want knowledge of all sorts, where we want ideas. 2. That we are ignorant, and want rational knowledge, where we want proofs. 3. That we want certain knowledge and certainty, as far as we want clear and determined specific ideas. 4. That we want probability to direct our assent in matters where we have neither knowledge of our own nor testimony of other men to bottom our reason upon.

From these things thus premised, I think we may come to lay down *the measures and boundaries between faith and reason*: the want whereof may possibly have been the cause, if not of great disorders, yet at least of great disputes, and perhaps mistakes in the world. For till it be resolved how far we are to be guided by reason, and how far by faith, we shall in vain dispute, and endeavour to convince one another in matters of religion.

2. I find every sect, as far as reason will help them, make use of it gladly: and where it fails them, they cry out, It is matter of faith, and above reason. And I do not see how they can argue with any one, or ever convince a gain-sayer who makes use of the same plea, without setting down strict boundaries between faith and reason; which ought to be the first point established in all questions where faith has anything to do.

Reason, therefore, here, as contradistinguished to *faith*, I take to be the discovery of the certainty or probability of such propositions or truths, which the mind arrives at by deduction made from such ideas, which it has got by the use of its natural faculties; viz. by sensation or reflection.

Faith, on the other side, is the assent to any proposition, not thus made out by the deductions of reason, but upon the credit of the proposer, as coming from God, in some extraordinary way of communication. This way of discovering truths to men, we call *revelation*.

3. *First*, Then I say, that *no man inspired by God can by any revelation communicate to others any new simple ideas which they had not before from sensation or reflection*. For, whatsoever impressions he himself may have from the immediate hand of God, this revelation, if it be of new simple ideas, cannot be conveyed to another, either by words or any other signs. Because words, by their immediate operation on us, cause no other ideas but of their natural sounds: and it is by the custom of using them for signs, that they excite and revive in our minds latent ideas; but yet only such ideas as were there before. For words, seen or heard, recal to our thoughts those ideas only which to us they have been wont to be signs of, but cannot introduce any perfectly new, and formerly unknown simple ideas. The same holds in all other signs; which cannot signify to us things of which we have before never had any idea at all.

Thus whatever things were discovered to St. Paul, when he was rapt up into the third heaven;[1] whatever new ideas his mind there received, all the description he can make to others of that place, is only this, That there are such things, "as eye hath not seen, nor ear heard, nor hath it entered into the heart of man to conceive."[2] And supposing God should discover to any one, supernaturally, a species of creatures inhabiting, for example, Jupiter or Saturn, (for that it is possible there may be such, nobody can deny,) which had six senses; and imprint on his mind the ideas conveyed to theirs by that sixth sense: he could no more, by words, produce in the minds of other men those ideas imprinted by that sixth sense, than one of us could convey the idea of any colour, by the sound of words, into a man who, having the other four senses perfect, had always totally wanted the fifth, of seeing. For our simple ideas, then, which are the foundation, and sole matter of all our notions and knowledge, we must depend wholly on our reason, I mean our natural faculties; and can by no means receive them, or any of them, from traditional revelation. I say, *traditional revelation*, in distinction to *original revelation*. By the one, I mean that first impression which is made immediately by God on the mind of any man, to which we cannot set any bounds; and by the other, those impressions delivered over to others in words, and the ordinary ways of conveying our conceptions one to another.

4. *Secondly*, I say that *the same truths may be discovered, and conveyed down from revelation, which are discoverable to us by reason, and by those ideas we naturally may have.* So God might, by revelation, discover the truth of any proposition in Euclid; as well as men, by the natural use of their faculties, come to make the discovery themselves. In all things of this kind there is little need or use of revelation, God having furnished us with natural and surer means to arrive at the knowledge of them. For whatsoever truth we come to the clear discovery of, from the knowledge and contemplation of our own ideas, will always be certainer to us than those which are conveyed to us by *traditional revelation*. For the knowledge we have that this revelation came at first from God, can never be so sure as the knowledge we have from the clear and distinct perception of the agreement or disagreement of our own ideas: v.g. if it were revealed some ages since, that the three angles of a triangle were equal to two right ones, I might assent to the truth of that proposition, upon the credit of the tradition, that it was revealed: but that would never amount to so great a certainty as the knowledge of it, upon the comparing and measuring my own ideas of two right angles, and the three angles of a triangle. The like holds in matter of fact knowable by our senses; v.g. the history of the deluge is conveyed to us

by writings which had their original from revelation: and yet nobody, I think, will say he has as certain and clear a knowledge of the flood as Noah, that saw it; or that he himself would have had, had he then been alive and seen it. For he has no greater an assurance than that of his senses, that it is writ in the book supposed writ by Moses inspired: but he has not so great an assurance that Moses wrote that book as if he had seen Moses write it. So that the assurance of its being a revelation is less still than the assurance of his senses.

5. In propositions, then, whose certainty is built upon the clear perception of the agreement or disagreement of our ideas, attained either by immediate intuition, as in self-evident propositions, or by evident deductions of reason in demonstrations we need not the assistance of revelation, as necessary to gain our assent, and introduce them into our minds. Because the natural ways of knowledge could settle them there, or had done it already; which is the greatest assurance we can possibly have of anything, unless where God immediately reveals it to us: and there too our assurance can be no greater than our knowledge is, that it *is* a revelation from God. But yet nothing, I think, can, under that title, shake or overrule plain knowledge; or rationally prevail with any man to admit it for true, in a direct contradiction to the clear evidence of his own understanding. For, since no evidence of our faculties, by which we receive such revelations, can exceed, if equal, the certainty of our intuitive knowledge, we can never receive for a truth anything that is directly contrary to our clear and distinct knowledge; v.g. the ideas of one body and one place do so clearly agree, and the mind has so evident a perception of their agreement, that we can never assent to a proposition that affirms the same body to be in two distant places at once, however it should pretend to the authority of a divine revelation: since the evidence, first, that we deceive not ourselves, in ascribing it to God; secondly, that we understand it right; can never be so great as the evidence of our own intuitive knowledge, whereby we discern it impossible for the same body to be in two places at once. And therefore *no proposition can be received for divine revelation, or obtain the assent due to all such, if it be contradictory to our clear intuitive knowledge.* Because this would be to subvert the principles and foundations of all knowledge, evidence, and assent whatsoever: and there would be left no difference between truth and falsehood, no measures of credible and incredible in the world, if doubtful

propositions shall take place before self-evident; and what we certainly know give way to what we may possibly be mistaken in. In propositions therefore contrary to the clear perception of the agreement or disagreement of any of our ideas, it will be in vain to urge them as matters of faith. They cannot move our assent under that or any other title whatsoever. For faith can never convince us of anything that contradicts our knowledge. Because, though faith be founded on the testimony of God (who cannot lie) revealing any proposition to us: yet we cannot have an assurance of the truth of its being a divine revelation greater than our own knowledge. Since the whole strength of the certainty depends upon our knowledge that God revealed it; which, in this case, where the proposition supposed revealed contradicts our knowledge or reason, will always have this objection hanging to it, viz. that we cannot tell how to conceive that to come from God, the bountiful Author of our being, which, if received for true, must overturn all the principles and foundations of knowledge he has given us; render all our faculties useless; wholly destroy the most excellent part of his workmanship, our understandings; and put a man in a condition wherein he will have less light, less conduct than the beast that perisheth. For if the mind of man can never have a clearer (and perhaps not so clear) evidence of anything to be a divine revelation, as it has of the principles of its own reason, it can never have a ground to quit the clear evidence of its reason, to give a place to a proposition, whose revelation has not a greater evidence than those principles have.

6. Thus far a man has use of reason, and ought to hearken to it, even in immediate and original revelation, where it is supposed to be made to himself. But to all those who pretend not to immediate revelation, but are required to pay obedience, and to receive the truths revealed to others, which, by the tradition of writings, or word of mouth, are conveyed down to them, reason has a great deal more to do, and is that only which can induce us to receive them. For matter of faith being only divine revelation, and nothing else, faith, as we use the word, (called commonly *divine faith*), has to do with no propositions, but those which are supposed to be divinely revealed. So that I do not see how those who make revelation alone the sole object of faith can say, That it is a matter of faith, and not of reason, to believe that such or such a proposition, to be found in such or such a book, is of divine inspiration; unless it be revealed

that that proposition, or all in that book, was communicated by divine inspiration. Without such a revelation, the believing, or not believing, that proposition, or book, to be of divine authority, can never be matter of faith, but matter of reason; and such as I must come to an assent to only by the use of my reason, which can never require or enable me to believe that which is contrary to itself: it being impossible for reason ever to procure any assent to that which to itself appears unreasonable.

In all things, therefore, where we have clear evidence from our ideas, and those principles of knowledge I have above mentioned, reason is the proper judge; and revelation, though it may, in consenting with it, confirm its dictates, yet cannot in such cases invalidate its decrees: nor can we be obliged, where we have the clear and evident sentence of reason, to quit it for the contrary opinion, under a pretence that it is matter of faith: which can have no authority against the plain and clear dictates of reason.

7. But, *Thirdly*, There being many things wherein we have very imperfect notions, or none at all; and other things, of whose past, present, or future existence, by the natural use of our faculties, we can have no knowledge at all; these, being beyond the discovery of our natural faculties, and *above reason*, are, when revealed, *the proper matter of faith*. Thus, that part of the angels rebelled against God, and thereby lost their first happy state: and that the dead shall rise, and live again: these and the like, being beyond the discovery of reason, are purely matters of faith, with which reason has directly nothing to do.

8. But since God, in giving us the light of reason, has not thereby tied up his own hands from affording us, when he thinks fit, the light of revelation in any of those matters wherein our natural faculties are able to give a probable determination; *revelation*, where God has been pleased to give it, *must carry it against the probable conjectures of reason*. Because the mind not being certain of the truth of that it does not evidently know, but only yielding to the probability that appears in it, is bound to give up its assent to such a testimony which, it is satisfied, comes from one who cannot err, and will not deceive. But yet, it still belongs to reason to judge of the truth of its being a revelation, and of the signification of the words wherein it is delivered. Indeed, if anything shall be thought revelation which is contrary to the plain principles of reason, and the evident knowledge the mind has of its own clear and distinct ideas;

there reason must be hearkened to, as to a matter within its province. Since a man can never have so certain a knowledge, that a proposition which contradicts the clear principles and evidence of his own knowledge was divinely revealed, or that he understands the words rightly wherein it is delivered, as he has that the contrary is true, and so is bound to consider and judge of it as a matter of reason, and not swallow it, without examination, as a matter of faith.

9. First, Whatever proposition is revealed, of whose truth our mind, by its natural faculties and notions, cannot judge, that is purely matter of faith, and above reason.

Secondly, All propositions whereof the mind, by the use of its natural faculties, can come to determine and judge, from naturally acquired ideas, are matter of reason; with this difference still, that, in those concerning which it has but an uncertain evidence, and so is persuaded of their truth only upon probable grounds, which still admit a possibility of the contrary to be true, without doing violence to the certain evidence of its own knowledge, and overturning the principles of all reason; in such probable propositions, I say, an evident revelation ought to determine our assent, even against probability. For where the principles of reason have not evidenced a proposition to be certainly true or false, there clear revelation, as another principle of truth and ground of assent, may determine; and so it may be matter of faith, and be also above reason. Because reason, in that particular matter, being able to reach no higher than probability, faith gave the determination where reason came short; and revelation discovered on which side the truth lay.

10. Thus far the dominion of faith reaches, and that without any violence or hindrance to reason; which is not injured or disturbed, but assisted and improved by new discoveries of truth, coming from the eternal fountain of all knowledge. Whatever God hath revealed is certainly true: no doubt can be made of it. This is the proper object of faith: but whether it be a *divine* revelation or no, reason must judge; which can never permit the mind to reject a greater evidence to embrace what is less evident, nor allow it to entertain probability in opposition to knowledge and certainty. There can be no evidence that any traditional revelation is of divine original, in the words we receive it, and in the sense we understand it, so clear and so certain as that of the principles of reason: and therefore *Nothing that is contrary to, and inconsistent*

with, the clear and self-evident dictates of reason, has a right to be urged or assented to as a matter of faith, wherein reason hath nothing to do. Whatsoever is divine revelation, ought to overrule all our opinions, prejudices, and interest, and hath a right to be received with full assent. Such a submission as this, of our reason to faith, takes not away the landmarks of knowledge: this shakes not the foundations of reason, but leaves us that use of our faculties for which they were given us.

11. If the provinces of faith and reason are not kept distinct by these boundaries, there will, in matters of religion, be no room for reason at all; and those extravagant opinions and ceremonies that are to be found in the several religions of the world will not deserve to be blamed. For, to this crying up of faith in *opposition* to reason, we may, I think, in good measure ascribe those absurdities that fill almost all the religions which possess and divide mankind. For men having been principled with an opinion, that they must not consult reason in the things of religion, however apparently contradictory to common sense and the very principles of all their knowledge, have let loose their fancies and natural superstition; and have been by them led into so strange opinions, and extravagant practices in religion, that a considerate man cannot but stand amazed at their follies, and judge them so far from being acceptable to the great and wise God, that he cannot avoid thinking them ridiculous and offensive to a sober good man. So that, in effect, religion, which should most distinguish us from beasts, and ought most peculiarly to elevate us, as rational creatures, above brutes, is that wherein men often appear most irrational, and more senseless than beasts themselves. *Credo, quia impossibile est* [I believe because it is impossible]:[3] I believe, because it is impossible, might, in a good man, pass for a sally of zeal; but would prove a very ill rule for men to choose their opinions or religion by.

From *A Discourse of Free-Thinking* (1713)

ANTHONY COLLINS

[Anthony Collins (1676–1729) was a British philosopher who advocated deism. He studied law and was a justice of the peace for much of his adult life. Building on the work of John Locke, a personal friend, Collins wrote his *Essay concerning the Use of Reason* (1707), in which he maintained that any doctrine derived from revelation should be conformable to reason. His major work was *A Discourse of Free-Thinking* (1713), in which he urged freedom of thought in the realm of religion. The treatise in no way advocated atheism or agnosticism, or even "freethought" in the contemporary sense of the term; rather, Collins believed that, extending the principles of Protestantism, an individual must be allowed the freedom to examine religious claims and that religion can be strengthened only by such scrutiny. Nevertheless, the treatise was attacked by numerous religious figures, including Jonathan Swift.

In *A Discourse on the Grounds and Reasons for the Christian Religion* (1724), Collins rejected the claim that the prophecies in the Old Testament were fulfilled by Jesus in the New Testament. Collins also advocated a strict determinism in *Inquiry concerning Human Liberty* (1715). In the following extract from *A Discourse of Free-Thinking*, Collins argues that the wide disagreement among authorities as to the veracity of key elements of Christian doctrine necessitates unhindered freedom of thought.]

The Subjects of which Men are deny'd the Right to think by the Enemys of Free-Thinking, are of all others those of which Men have not only a Right to think, but of which they are oblig'd in duty to think; viz. such as of the Nature and Attributes of the Eternal Being or God, of the Truth and Authority of

Books esteem'd Sacred, and of the Sense and Meaning of those Books; or, in one word, of Religious Questions.

A right Opinion in there matters is suppos'd by the Enemys of Free-Thinking to be absolutely necessary to Mens Salvation, and some Errors or Mistakes about them are suppos'd to be damnable. Now where a right Opinion is so necessary, there Men have the greatest Concern imaginable to think for themselves, as the best means to take up with the right side of the Question. For if they will not think for themselves, it remains only for them to take the Opinions they have imbib'd from their Grandmothers, Mothers or Priests, or owe to such like Accident, for granted. But taking that method, they can only be in the right by chance; whereas by Thinking and Examination, they have not only the mere accident of being in the right, but have the Evidence of things to determine them to the side of Truth: unless it be suppos'd that Men are such absurd Animals, that the most unreasonable Opinion is as likely to be admitted for true as the most reasonable, when it is judg'd of by the Reason and Understanding of Men. In that case indeed it will follow, That Men can be under no Obligation to think of these matters. But then it will likewise follow, That they can be under no Obligation to concern themselves about Truth and Falshood in any Opinions. For if Men are so absurd, as not to be able to distinguish between Truth and Falshood, Evidence and no Evidence, what pretence is there for Mens having any Opinions at all? Which yet none judg so necessary as the Enemys of Free-Thinking.

If the surest and best means of arriving at Truth lies in Free-Thinking, then the whole Duty of Man with respect to Opinions lies only in Free-Thinking. Because he who thinks freely does his best towards being in the right, and consequently does all that God, who can require nothing more of any Man than that he should do his best, can require of him. And should he prove mistaken in any Opinions, he must be as acceptable to God as if he receiv'd none but right Opinions. This is admirably express'd by that true Christian and Protestant (and by consequence great Free-Thinker) Mr. Chillingworth, who says, "That if Men do their best endeavours to free themselves from all Errors, and yet fail of it thro human Weakness; so well is he persuaded of the Goodness of God, that if in him alone should meet a Confluence of all such Errors of all the Protestants in the World that were thus qualify'd, he should not be so much afraid of them all, as he should be to ask pardon for them. For to ask pardon for such Errors, is tacitly to imply that God is angry with us for them; and that were to impute to him the strange Tyranny of requiring Brick where he gives no Straw; of expecting to gather where he strewed not; to reap where he sowed not; being offended with us for not doing what he knows we cannot do."[1]

On the other side, the whole Crime of Man, with respect to Opinions, must lie in his not thinking freely. He who is in the right by accident only, and does but suppose himself to be so without any Thinking, is really in a dangerous state, as, having taken no pains and used no endeavours towards being in the right, and consequently as having no Merit; nay, as being on the same foot with the most stupid Papist and Heathen. For when once Men refuse or neglect to think, and take up their Opinions upon trust, they do in effect declare they would have been Papists or Heathens, had they had Popish or Heathen Priests for their Guides, or Popish or Heathen Grandmothers, to have taught them their Catechisms.

Superstition is an Evil, which either by the means of Education, or the natural Weakness of Men, oppresses almost all Mankind. And how terrible an Evil it is, is well describ'd by the antient Philosophers and Poets. Tully says, "If you give way to Superstition it will ever haunt and plague you. If you go to a Prophet, or regard Omens; if you sacrifice or observe the Flight of Birds; if you consult an Astrologer or Haruspex; if it thunders or lightens, or any place is consum'd with Lightning, or such-like Prodigy happens (as it is necessary some such often should) all the Tranquillity of the Mind is destroy'd. And Sleep it self, which seems to be an Asylum and Refuge from all Trouble and Uneasiness, does by the aid of Superstition increase your Troubles and Fears."[2]

Horace ranks Superstition with Vice; and as he makes the Happiness of Man in this Life to consist in the practice of Virtue and Freedom from Superstition, so he makes the greatest Misery of this Life to consist in being vicious and superstitious. "You are not covetous," says he; "that's well: But are you as free from all other Vices? Are you free from Ambition, excessive Anger, and the Fear of Death? Are you so much above Superstition, as to laugh at all Dreams, panick Fears, Miracles, Witches, Ghosts, and Prodigys?"[3]

This was the state of Superstition among the Antients; but since

Uncharitableness and damning to all eternity for Trifles, has (in opposition both to Reason and Revelation) come into the World, the Evil of Superstition is much increas'd, and Men are now under greater Terrors and Uneasiness of Mind than they possibly could be when they thought they hazarded less.

Now there is no just Remedy to this universal Evil but Free-Thinking. By that alone can we understand the true Causes of things, and by consequence the Unreasonableness of all superstitious Fears. "Happy is the Man," says the Divine Virgil, "who has discover'd the Causes of Things, and is thereby cured of all kind of Fears, even of Death it self, and all the Noise and Din of Hell."[4] For by Free-Thinking alone Men are capable of knowing, that a perfectly Good, Just, Wise and Powerful Being made and governs the World; and from this Principle they know, that he can require nothing of Men in any Country or Condition of Life, but that whereof he has given them an opportunity of being convinc'd by Evidence and Reason in the Place where they are, and in that Condition of Life to which Birth or any other Chance has directed them; that an honest and rational Man can have no just reason to fear any thing from him: nay, on the contrary, must have so great a Delight and Satisfaction in believing such a Being exists, that he can much better be suppos'd to fear lest no such Being should exist, than to fear any harm from him. And lastly, That God being incapable of having any addition made either to his Power or Happiness, and wanting nothing, can require nothing of Men for his own sake, but only for Man's sake; and consequently, that all Actions and Speculations which are of no use to Mankind, [as for instance, Singing or Dancing, or wearing of Habits, or Observation of Days, or eating or drinking, or slaughtering of Beasts (in which things the greatest part of the Heathen Worship consisted) or the Belief of Transubstantiation or Consubstantiation or of any Doctrines not taught by the Church of England] either signify nothing at all with God, or else displease him, but can never render a Man more acceptable to him.

By means of all this, a Man may possess his Soul in peace, as having an expectation of enjoying all the good things which God can bestow, and no fear of any future Misery or Evil from his hands; and the very worst of his State can only be, that he is pleasantly deceiv'd.

Whereas superstitious Men are incapable of believing in a perfectly just and good God. They make him talk to all Mankind from corners, and consequently require things of Men under the Sanction of Misery in the next World, of which they are incapable of having any convincing Evidence that they come from him. They make him (who equally beholds all the Dwellers upon earth) to have favourite Nations and People, without any Consideration of Merit. They make him put other Nations under Disadvantages without any Demerit. And so they are more properly to be stil'd Demonists than Theists. No wonder therefore if such Wretches should be so full of Fears of the Wrath of God, that they are sometimes tempted (with the Vicious) to wish there was no God at all; a Thought so unnatural and absurd, that even Speculative Atheists would abhor it. These Men have no quiet in their own Minds; they rove about in search of saving Truth thro the dark Corners of the Earth, and are so foolish as to hope to find it (if I may so say) hid under the Sands of Africa, where Cato scorn'd to look for it: and neglecting what God speaks plainly to the whole World, take up with what they suppose he has communicated to a few; and thereby believe and practise such things, in which they can never have Satisfaction. For suppose Men take up with a Religion which consists in Dancing or Musick, or such-like Ceremonys, or in useless and unintelligible Speculations; how can they be assur'd they believe and perform as they ought? What Rule can such Men have to know whether other Ceremonys, and useless and unintelligible Speculations, may not be requir'd of them instead of those they perform and believe? And how can they be sure that they believe rightly any unintelligible Speculations? Here is a foundation laid for nothing but endless Scruples, Doubts, and Fears. Wherefore I conclude, that every one, out of regard to his own Tranquillity of Mind, which must be disturb'd as long as he has any Seeds of Superstition, is oblig'd to think freely on Matters of Religion.

The infinite number of Pretenders in all Ages to Revelations from Heaven, supported by Miracles, containing new Notions of the Deity, new Doctrines, new Commands, new Ceremonys, and new Modes of Worship, make thinking on the foregoing Heads absolutely necessary, if a Man be under an obligation to listen to any Revelation at all. For how shall any Man distinguish between the true Messenger from Heaven and the Impostor, but by considering the Evidence produc'd by the one, as freely as of the other? Nay, a Reverend

Divine of our Church not only contends for Free-Thinking in this case, but goes further, and says, "Men are ever to be suspected, when they make extraordinary Pretences. For," adds he, "when Men pretend to work Miracles, and talk of immediate Revelations, of knowing the Truth by Inspiration, and of more than ordinary Illumination; we ought not to be frighted with those big words from looking what is under them, nor to be afraid of calling those things into question, which are set off with such high-flown Pretences. From hence it has come to pass, that Superstition and Idolatry, Enthusiasms and Impostures, have so much prevail'd in the World. It is somewhat strange, that we should believe Men the more, for that very reason upon which we should believe them the less."[5]

We have here in England a Society supported by the Encouragement of her Most Excellent Majesty, and the Contributions of many Divines and Ladys of our Establish'd Church, in effect for the Propagation of Free-Thinking in matters of Religion throughout the World; and whose Design supposes that it is all Mens Duty to think freely about matters of Religion. For how can the Society for propagating the Gospel in foreign Parts[6] hope to have any effect on Infidel Nations, without first acquainting them that it is their duty to think freely both on the Notions of God and Religion, which they have receiv'd from their Ancestors, or which are establish'd by Law among them, and on those new Notions of God and Religion brought to them by the Missionarys of the Church of England? Can it be suppos'd, that our Missionarys would begin with telling 'em, that they ought not to think freely of their own, or our Religion; or that after they have by the means of Free-Thinking embrac'd our Religion, they ought then to cease from Free-Thinking? This were to proceed very inconsistently in the Work of Conversion, while no other Arms but Reason and Evidence were made use of to convert. On the contrary, every Missionary must as a first Principle insist on the Duty of Free-Thinking; in order to be hearken'd to by them. Nay, should the King of Siam (or any other infidel Prince) in return for the Favour of our Endeavours to convert him and his Kingdom to our Religion, desire to send us a parcel of his Talapoins (so the Priests of Siam are call'd) to convert us to the Religion by Law establish'd in Siam; I cannot see but that our Society for propagating the Gospel, and all the Contributors and Well-wishers to it, must acknowledge the King's Request to be highly reasonable, and perfectly of a-piece with their own Project; and particularly must allow to the King of Siam, that it is as much the Duty of the Members of the Church of England to think freely on what the Missionary Talapoins shall propose to them, as it is the Duty of the Members of the Church of Siam to think freely on what shall be propos'd by the Missionary Priests of England: And therefore no doubt all they who sincerely desir'd the Conviction of the Siamese, would give their Missionarys the same Encouragement here, which we expect for ours in Siam. The Institution therefore of this Society supposes Free-Thinking in matters of Religion to be the Duty of all Men on the face of the Earth. And upon that account I cannot sufficiently commend the Project.

And Oh! that the proper Persons were but employ'd for the Execution of so glorious a Design! That such zealous Divines as our S——ls, our At——ys, our Sm——ges, our St—bs's, our Higgins's, our M——rns, and our Sw—fts,[7] were drawn out annually, as our military Missionarys are, to be sent into foreign Parts to propagate the Gospel! (a Service in which such conscientious Men must rejoice, since preaching the Gospel to infidel Nations is no doubt contain'd in Christ's Commission, whatever haranguing upon a Text among Christians, falsly call'd preaching the Gospel, may be) we might then hope to see blessed Days, the Doctrine and Discipline of the Church of England triumph throughout the World, and Faction cease at home; as by the means of the others our Arms triumph abroad, and we securely take our rest at night, and travel by day unmolested.

And no doubt likewise, but it would be as beneficial to the Kingdom of Siam, to have a select number annually taken out of their vast Body of Talapoins.

As there can be no reasonable Change of Opinions among Men, no quitting of any old Religion, no Reception of any new Religion, or believing any Religion at all, but by means of Free-Thinking; so the Holy Scriptures agreeably to Reason, and to the Design of our Blessed Saviour of establishing his Religion throughout the whole Universe, imply every where and press in many places the Duty of Free-Thinking.

The Design of the Gospel was, by preaching, to set all Men upon Free-Thinking, that they might think themselves out of those Notions of God and Religion which were every where establish'd by Law, and receive an unknown God and an unknown Religion on the Evidence the Apostles, or first Messengers, produc'd to convince them. And accordingly the Apostles requir'd nothing to be receiv'd on their Authority, without an antecedent Proof given of their Authority. St. Paul even in his Epistles, which are all written to Men who were already Christians, offers many Arguments for their Confirmation in the true Faith, with respect to all the parts of the Christian Religion. Whereby he made them, and all his Readers for ever Judges of their Force: for whoever reasons, lays aide all Authority, and endeavours to force your Assent by Argument alone. St. Paul likewise went frequently into the Synagogues of the Jews, and reason'd with them [Acts 17:2–3]; which was not only putting the Jews upon Free-Thinking on matters of Religion, but taking (according to the present Notions of Christians) a very extraordinary step to put them upon Free-Thinking. For should William Penn the Quaker, or other religious Person differing from the Establish'd Church, come to St. Paul's during the time of Divine Service to reason with the Court of Aldermen, Preacher, and Singing-Men; or Mr. Whiston[8] into the Lower House of Convocation, to reason with them; it is certain, that pursuant to the false Notions which now universally prevail, the one would be treated as a Madman and Fanatick, and the other as a Disturber of the Proceedings of the Holy Synod, which assumes a right to determine without Reasoning with the Person whose Opinions they condemn.

Our Saviour particularly commands us to search the Scriptures [John 5:39], that is, to endeavour to find out their true meaning. And for fear we should surrender our Judgments to our Fathers, and Mothers, or Church-Rulers, or Preachers, he bids us take heed what we hear, and whom we hear, and to beware of their Doctrine [Mark 4:24; Luke 8:18; Matt. 16:12]. And why, says he, "even of your selves judge ye not what is right? If a Man come to me, and hate not his Father and Mother, he cannot be my Disciple" [Luke 12:56–57, 14:26; Matt. 19:29]. And he commanded his own Disciples not to be call'd Rabbi nor Masters [Matt. 21:1, 8:10]; by which last words our learned Commentator, the Reverend Dr. Whitby, understands, "That we should call no Man Guide, or Master upon earth, no Fathers, no Church, no Council."[9] And indeed whoever considers, that all the Priests upon earth were

Enemys to our Blessed Saviour and his Gospel, and that he giving the privilege of Infallibility to no body besides his holy Apostles, could not be secure that any Priests would ever be otherwise; I say, he who considers this, can never think it possible for Christ to give so partial a Command, as to contain a Reserve in behalf of any Set of Priests, in prejudice of the general Rules of Free-Thinking, on which the Gospel was to be built, and which he so particularly laid down and inculcated.

The Conduct of the Priests, who are the chief Pretenders to be Guides to others in matters of Religion, makes Free-Thinking on the Nature and Attributes of the Eternal Being or God, on the Authority of Scriptures, and on the Sense of Scriptures, unavoidable. And to prove this, I will give you an Induction of several Particulars of their Conduct.

It is well known that the Priests throughout the Universe are endlessly divided in Opinion about all these matters; and their Variety of Opinion is so great, as not possibly to be collected together: nay, even those kinds of Priests, with which we are more nearly concern'd, differ so much one among another on some of these heads, that it would be an impossible task to give you all their Differences. I will therefore out of this vast and spacious Field select such under each of these heads, as is most proper to affect us Englishmen.

As to the Nature of the Eternal Being or God, the antient and modern Pagan Priests had and have as many different Ideas of the Deity, as Wit, or Interest, or Folly can invent; and even the Christian Priests have been always, and still are, divided in their Notions of a Deity. Almost all the antient Priests and Fathers (who were most of them Priests) of the Christian Church conceiv'd God to be material; and several antient Christian Priests of Egypt were so gross, as to conceive him to be in the shape of Man, and from thence were Anthropomorphites. Most of the modern Priests contend that God is immaterial, but they differ in their Notion of Immateriality; some by Immaterial Being understanding "extended Substance without Solidity"; and others by Immaterial Being understanding "unextended Being."

If any regard is to be had to the malicious Books and Sayings of Priests one against another, several of them make the material Universe to be the Eternal Being or God, wherein consists the Essence of Atheism.

The Reverend Mr. William Carrol [*sic*] has wrote several Books to prove the Reverend Dr. Clark and the Reverend Mr. Samuel Bold Atheists in that sense.[10]

The Reverend Mr. Turner charges the Reverend Dr. Cudworth with Atheism for his *Intellectual System of the Universe:*[11] And a Great Prelate must suppose Atheism very far spread among the Priests, when he said, "It was a great Providence of God that so many of the Clergy swore to the Government" (under King William and Queen Mary) "lest the Church should be destroy'd: And it was the same Providence of God that so many of the Clergy refus'd the Oath, lest People should think that there was no such thing as Religion, and incline to Atheism."[12]

As the Christian Priests differ about the Nature or Essence of God, so they are infinitely more divided in their Notions about his Attributes.

The whole difference between the Arminians and Calvinists[13] is founded on different Notions of the Attributes of God; and this Dispute is kept up in most Christian Churches on the face of the earth. It is carry'd on in the Romish Church under the names of Jansenists and Jesuits, Thomists and Molinists; etc.[14] It has been for near a Century last past debated among the Divines of our Church, and is at this day between the Reverend Dr. Whitby and his Adversarys. Indeed the Differences among the Priests in every Church about the Attributes of God, are as numerous as the Priests who treat of the Divine Attributes; not one agreeing with another in his Notions of them all. I will therefore close this matter with one Instance of a most remarkable Difference.

It is the Opinion of many Divines, That when the Scriptures attribute Hands, and Eyes, and Feet, and Face to God, we are not to understand that God really has those parts, but only that he has a power to execute all those Actions, to the effecting of which those parts are necessary in us. And when the Scriptures attribute such Passions to God as Anger, Pleasure, Love, Hatred, Repentance, Revenge, and the like; the meaning is, that he will as certainly punish the Wicked, as if he was inflam'd with the Passion of Anger; that he will as infallibly reward the Good, as if he had a love for them; and that when Men turn from their Wickedness, he will suit Dispensations to them, as if he really repented or chang'd his Mind: So that these Scripture-Attributes belong not to God in a proper and just Sense, but only improperly, or as the Schools speak, *analogically.* But when the Scripture attributes to God an

Understanding, Wisdom, Will, Goodness, Holiness, Justice and Truth, these words are to be understood strictly and properly, or in their common sense. Dr. Tillotson, the late Archbishop of Canterbury, throughout his Works maintains this System of the Deity. I need only cite his words with respect to those Attributes last mention'd; his Notions, with respect to Parts or Passions in God, being sufficiently known without any proof. He says, "It is foolish for any Man to pretend he cannot know what Justice, and Goodness, and Truth in God are; for if we do not know this, it is all one to us whether God be good or not, nor could we imitate his Goodness; for he that imitates, endeavours to make himself like something that he knows, and must of necessity have some Idea of that to which he aims to be like. So that if we had no certain and settled Notion of the Goodness, and Justice, and Truth of God, he would be altogether an unintelligible Being; and Religion, which consists in the Imitation of him, would be utterly lost."[15] Thus that Religious and Free-Thinking Prelate. But on the other side, Dr. King the present Archbishop of Dublin tells us, "That the best Representations we can make of God, are infinitely short of Truth"; That "Wisdom, Understanding, and Mercy, Foreknowledge, Predestination, and Will, when ascrib'd to God, are not to be taken properly." Again, That "Justice and Virtue" (and by consequence all the moral Attributes of God) "are not to be understood to signify the same thing when apply'd to God and Man"; and "that they are of so different a nature from what they are in us, and so superiour to all that we can conceive, that there is no more likeness between them, than between our Hand and God's Power." But all these Attributes, according to his Grace, are to be understood in the same manner, as "when Men ascribe Hands, and Eyes, and Feet to God"; or as when "Men ascribe Anger, Love, Hatred, Revenge, Repentance, changing Resolutions, and in the same improper Analogical Sense."[16] So that as his Grace of Canterbury would define God to be a "Being without Parts and Passions, Holy, Wise, Just, True, and Good"; his Grace of Dublin must on the contrary define God to be a Being not only "without Parts and Passions," but "without Understanding, Wisdom, Will, Mercy, Holiness, Goodness, or Truth." [. . .]

I must observe, That the Priests of all Christian Churches differ among themselves in each Church about the Copys of the same Books of Scripture; some reading them according to one Manuscript, and others according to another. But the great Dispute of all, is concerning the Hebrew and Septuagint, between which two there is a great difference (the latter making the World 1500 Years older than the former:) to name no other Differences of greater or less importance.

Lastly, as the most antient Christian Churches and Priests receiv'd several Gospels and Books of Scripture which are now lost, such as the Gospel according to the Hebrews, the Gospel according to the Egyptians, the Traditions of Matthias, &c. and as not one of their Successors in the two first Centurys (whose Works now remain) but receiv'd Books of Scripture, which are either lost to us, or that we reject as Apocryphal: so the several Sects of Christians in the East and in Africa receive at this day some Books of Scripture, which are so far lost to us, that we know only their Names, and others which we have and reject. [. . .]

The same Books of Scripture have, among those Priests who receive them, a very different degree of Authority; some attributing more, and others less Authority to them.

The Popish Priests contend that the Text of Scripture is so corrupted, precarious, and unintelligible, that we are to depend on the Authority of their Church for the true Particulars of the Christian Religion. Others who contend for a greater Perfection in the Text of Scripture, differ about the Inspiration of those Books; some contending that every Thought and Word are inspir'd; some that the Thoughts are inspir'd, and not the Words; some that those Thoughts only are inspir'd, which relate to Fundamentals; and others that the Books were written by honest Men with great Care and Faithfulness, without any Inspiration either with respect to the Thoughts or Words. [. . .]

I might go on to assign other Instances of the Priests Conduct; such as their Declamations against Reason; their Arts and Methods of discouraging Examination into the Truths of Religion; and their encouraging Examination when Authority is against them, or when they think that Truth is clearly on their side; their instilling Principles into Youth, &c. But that I may not run this Letter into too great a length, I forbear insisting on these and many other Instances of their Conduct, which I could assign. And therefore shall now conclude from those foregoing, that since the Priests, not only of different Religions and Sects, but of the same Sect, are infinitely divided in Opinion

about the Nature of God, and the Authority and Meaning of Scriptures; since
we have Priests who acknowledge the Doctrines of our Church, which they
have solemnly sworn to preach up, to be contradictory to one another and to
Reason, and that several Abuses, Defects, and false Doctrines are crept into the
Church; since they profess they will not tell the Truth themselves, and make it
matter of Reproach in the Clergy to tell the Truth; since they prejudice Men
against their own Doctrines, by Insinuations of Infidelity and Heresy, against
all good Christians who are Men of Sense; since they render both the Canon
and Text of Scripture precarious and uncertain; since they fill Mens heads with
irreligious Notions, by publishing the Arguments of Infidels, and reviving the
old Systems of Atheism; and lastly, since they are guilty, on so many occasions,
of Frauds in the publishing of Books: we have no way of settling ourselves in a
right Notion of God; in the Reception of the present Canon of Scripture, and
that Sacred Greek Text of the New Testament which is commonly printed;
and in the Belief of the Doctrine and Practice of the Discipline and Worship
of the Church of England, as founded on that pure Text; nor can we be easy
in our own Minds, under the Prejudices and Difficultys which the Priests put
into us against these Truths, but by ceasing to rely on them, and thinking
freely for ourselves.

"Of Miracles" (1748)

DAVID HUME

[David Hume (1711–1776) was the leading British philosopher of the eighteenth century. His first major work, *A Treatise of Human Nature* (1739), was the culmination of a century of British empiricist thought but also injected a healthy dose of skepticism regarding the certainty of empirical knowledge. *An Enquiry concerning Human Understanding* (1748) is a reworking of his earlier treatise. Its tenth chapter, "Of Miracles," was immensely influential in casting doubt on the veracity of biblical miracles on grounds of probability, the unreliability of eyewitness accounts, and the conflict miracles present to the known course of natural phenomena. Hume went on to write several other important treatises on religion, including *The Natural History of Religion* (1757), which pioneered the anthropological approach to the origin and development of religious belief, and *Dialogues concerning Natural Religion* (1779), which attacks the argument from design. Hume also denied the immortality of the soul.]

PART I.

There is, in Dr. Tillotson's writings, an argument against the *real presence*,[1] which is as concise, and elegant, and strong as any argument can possibly be supposed against a doctrine, so little worthy of a serious refutation. It is acknowledged on all hands, says that learned prelate, that the authority, either of the scripture or of tradition, is founded merely in the testimony of the apostles, who were eye-witnesses to those miracles of our Saviour, by which he proved his divine mission. Our evidence, then, for the truth of the *Christian* religion is less than the evidence for the truth of our senses; because, even in the first authors of our religion, it was no greater; and it is evident it must diminish in passing from them to their disciples; nor can any one rest such confidence in their testimony, as in the immediate object of his senses. But a weaker evidence can never destroy a stronger; and therefore, were the doctrine of the real presence ever so clearly revealed in scripture, it were directly contrary to the rules of just reasoning to give our assent to it. It contradicts sense, though both the scripture and tradition, on which it is supposed to be built, carry not such evidence with them as sense; when they are considered merely as external evidences, and are not brought home to every one's breast, by the immediate operation of the Holy Spirit.

Nothing is so convenient as a decisive argument of this kind, which must at least *silence* the most arrogant bigotry and superstition, and free us from their impertinent solicitations. I flatter myself, that I have discovered an argument of a like nature, which, if just, will, with the wise and learned, be an everlasting check to all kinds of superstitious delusion, and consequently, will be useful as long as the world endures. For so long, I presume, will the accounts of miracles and prodigies be found in all history, sacred and profane.

Though experience be our only guide in reasoning concerning matters of fact; it must be acknowledged, that this guide is not altogether infallible, but in some cases is apt to lead us into errors. One, who in our climate, should expect better weather in any week of June than in one of December, would reason justly, and conformably to experience; but it is certain, that he may happen, in the event, to find himself mistaken. However, we may observe, that, in such a case, he would have no cause to complain of experience; because it commonly informs us beforehand of the uncertainty, by that contrariety of events, which we may learn from a diligent observation. All effects follow not with like certainty from their supposed causes. Some events are found, in all countries and all ages, to have been constantly conjoined together: Others are found to have been more variable, and sometimes to disappoint our expectations; so that, in our reasonings concerning matter of fact, there are all imaginable degrees of assurance, from the highest certainty to the lowest species of moral evidence.

A wise man, therefore, proportions his belief to the evidence. In such conclusions as are founded on an infallible experience, he expects the event with the last degree of assurance, and regards his past experience as a full *proof* of the future existence of that event. In other cases, he proceeds with more caution: He weighs the opposite experiments: He considers which side is supported by the greater number of experiments: to that side he inclines, with doubt and hesitation; and when at last he fixes his judgement, the evidence exceeds not what we properly call *probability*. All probability, then, supposes an opposition of experiments and observations, where the one side is found to overbalance the other, and to produce a degree of evidence, proportioned to the superiority. A hundred instances or experiments on one side, and fifty on another, afford a doubtful expectation of any event; though a hundred uniform experiments, with only one that is contradictory, reasonably beget a pretty strong degree of assurance. In all cases, we must balance the opposite experiments, where they are opposite, and deduct the smaller number from the greater, in order to know the exact force of the superior evidence.

To apply these principles to a particular instance; we may observe, that there is no species of reasoning more common, more useful, and even necessary to human life, than that which is derived from the testimony of men, and the reports of eye-witnesses and spectators. This species of reasoning, perhaps, one may deny to be founded on the relation of cause and effect. I shall not dispute about a word. It will be sufficient to observe that our assurance in any argument of this kind is derived from no other principle than our observation of the veracity of human testimony, and of the usual conformity of facts to the reports of witnesses. It being a general maxim, that no objects have any discoverable connexion together, and that all the inferences, which we can draw from one to another, are founded merely on our experience of their constant and regular conjunction; it is evident, that we ought not to make an exception to this maxim in favour of human testimony, whose connexion with any event seems, in itself, as little necessary as any other. Were not the memory tenacious to a certain degree; had not men commonly an inclination to truth and a principle of probity; were they not sensible to shame, when detected in a falsehood: Were not these, I say, discovered by *experience* to be qualities, inherent in human nature, we should never repose the least confidence in human testimony. A man delirious, or noted for falsehood and villany, has no manner of authority with us.

And as the evidence, derived from witnesses and human testimony, is founded on past experience, so it varies with the experience, and is regarded either as a *proof* or a *probability*, according as the conjunction between any particular kind of report and any kind of object has been found to be constant or variable. There are a number of circumstances to be taken into consideration in all judgements of this kind; and the ultimate standard, by which we determine all disputes, that may arise concerning them, is always derived from experience and observation. Where this experience is not entirely uniform on any side, it is attended with an unavoidable contrariety in our judgements, and with the same opposition and mutual destruction of argument as in every other kind of evidence. We frequently hesitate concerning the reports of others. We balance the opposite circumstances, which cause any doubt or uncertainty; and when we discover a superiority on any side, we incline to it; but still with a diminution of assurance, in proportion to the force of its antagonist.

This contrariety of evidence, in the present case, may be derived from several different causes; from the opposition of contrary testimony; from the character or number of the witnesses; from the manner of their delivering their testimony; or from the union of all these circumstances. We entertain a suspicion concerning any matter of fact, when the witnesses contradict each other; when they are but few, or of a doubtful character; when they have an interest in what they affirm; when they deliver their testimony with hesitation, or on the contrary, with too violent asseverations. There are many other particulars of the same kind, which may diminish or destroy the force of any argument, derived from human testimony.

Suppose, for instance, that the fact, which the testimony endeavours to establish, partakes of the extraordinary and the marvellous; in that case, the evidence, resulting from the testimony, admits of a diminution, greater or less, in proportion as the fact is more or less unusual. The reason why we place any credit in witnesses and historians, is not derived from any *connexion*, which we perceive *a priori*, between testimony and reality, but because we are accustomed to find a conformity between them. But when the fact attested is such a one as has seldom fallen under our observation, here is a contest of two opposite experiences; of which the one destroys the other, as far as its force goes, and the superior can only operate on the mind by the force, which remains. The very same principle of experience, which gives us a certain degree of assurance in the testimony of witnesses, gives us also, in this case, another degree of assurance against the fact, which they endeavour to establish; from which contradiction there necessarily arises a counterpoise, and mutual destruction of belief and authority.

I should not believe such a story were it told me by Cato, was a proverbial saying in Rome, even during the lifetime of that philosophical patriot.[2] The incredibility of a fact, it was allowed, might invalidate so great an authority.

The Indian prince, who refused to believe the first relations concerning the effects of frost, reasoned justly; and it naturally required very strong testimony to engage his assent to facts, that arose from a state of nature, with which he was unacquainted, and which bore so little analogy to those events, of which he had had constant and uniform experience. Though they were not contrary to his experience, they were not conformable to it.[3]

But in order to encrease the probability against the testimony of witnesses, let us suppose, that the fact, which they affirm, instead of being only marvellous, is really miraculous; and suppose also, that the testimony considered apart and in itself, amounts to an entire proof; in that case, there is proof against proof, of which the strongest must prevail, but still with a diminution of its force, in proportion to that of its antagonist.

A miracle is a violation of the laws of nature; and as a firm and unalterable experience has established these laws, the proof against a miracle, from the very nature of the fact, is as entire as any argument from experience can possibly be imagined. Why is it more than probable, that all men must die; that lead cannot, of itself, remain suspended in the air; that fire consumes wood, and is extinguished by water; unless it be, that these events are found agreeable to the laws of nature, and there is required a violation of these laws, or in other words, a miracle to prevent them? Nothing is esteemed a miracle, if it ever happen in the common course of nature. It is no miracle that a man, seemingly in good health, should die on a sudden: because such a kind of death, though more unusual than any other, has yet been frequently observed to happen. But it is a miracle, that a dead man should come to life; because that has never been observed in any age or country. There must, therefore, be a uniform experience against every miraculous event, otherwise the event would not merit that appellation. And as a uniform experience amounts to a proof, there is here a direct and full *proof*, from the nature of the fact, against the existence of any miracle; nor can such a proof be destroyed, or the miracle rendered credible, but by an opposite proof, which is superior.[4]

The plain consequence is (and it is a general maxim worthy of our attention), "That no testimony is sufficient to establish a miracle, unless the testimony be of such a kind, that its falsehood would be more miraculous, than the fact, which it endeavours to establish; and even in that case there is a mutual destruction of arguments, and the superior only gives us an assurance suitable to that degree of force, which remains, after deducting the inferior." When anyone tells me, that he saw a dead man restored to life, I immediately consider with myself, whether it be more probable, that this person should either deceive or be deceived, or that the fact, which he relates, should really have happened. I weigh the one miracle against the other; and according to the superiority, which I discover, I pronounce my decision, and always reject the greater miracle. If the falsehood of his testimony would be more miraculous, than the event which he relates; then, and not till then, can he pretend to command my belief or opinion.

PART II.

In the foregoing reasoning we have supposed, that the testimony, upon which a miracle is founded, may possibly amount to an entire proof, and that the falsehood of that testimony would be a real prodigy: But it is easy to shew, that we have been a great deal too liberal in our concession, and that there never was a miraculous event established on so full an evidence.

For *first*, there is not to be found, in all history, any miracle attested by a sufficient number of men, of such unquestioned good-sense, education, and learning, as to secure us against all delusion in themselves; of such undoubted integrity, as to place them beyond all suspicion of any design to deceive others; of such credit and reputation in the eyes of mankind, as to have a great deal to lose in case of their being detected in any falsehood; and at the same time, attesting facts performed in such a public manner and in so celebrated a part of the world, as to render the detection unavoidable: All which circumstances are requisite to give us a full assurance in the testimony of men.

Secondly. We may observe in human nature a principle which, if strictly examined, will be found to diminish extremely the assurance, which we might, from human testimony, have, in any kind of prodigy. The maxim, by which we commonly conduct ourselves in our reasonings, is, that the objects, of which we have no experience, resemble those, of which we have; that what we have found to be most usual is always most probable; and that where there is an opposition of arguments, we ought to give the preference to such as are founded on the greatest number of past observations. But though, in proceeding by this rule, we readily reject any fact which is unusual and incredible in an ordinary degree; yet in advancing farther, the mind observes not always the same rule; but when anything is affirmed utterly absurd and miraculous, it rather the more readily admits of such a fact, upon account of that very circumstance, which ought to destroy all its authority. The passion of *surprise* and *wonder*, arising from miracles, being an agreeable emotion, gives a sensible tendency towards the belief of those events, from which it is derived. And this goes so far, that even those who cannot enjoy this pleasure immediately, nor can believe those miraculous events, of which they are informed, yet love to partake of the satisfaction at second-hand or by rebound, and place a pride and delight in exciting the admiration of others.

With what greediness are the miraculous accounts of travellers received, their descriptions of sea and land monsters, their relations of wonderful adventures, strange men, and uncouth manners? But if the spirit of religion join itself to the love of wonder, there is an end of common sense; and human testimony, in these circumstances, loses all pretensions to authority. A religionist may be an enthusiast, and imagine he sees what has no reality: he may know his narrative to be false, and yet persevere in it, with the best intentions in the world, for the sake of promoting so holy a cause: or even where this delusion has not place, vanity, excited by so strong a temptation, operates on him more powerfully than on the rest of mankind in any other circumstances; and self-interest with equal force. His auditors may not have, and commonly have not, sufficient judgement to canvass his evidence: what judgement they have, they renounce by principle, in these sublime and mysterious subjects: or if they were ever so willing to employ it, passion and a heated imagination disturb the regularity of its operations. Their credulity increases his impudence: and his impudence overpowers their credulity.

Eloquence, when at its highest pitch, leaves little room for reason or reflection; but addressing itself entirely to the fancy or the affections, captivates the willing hearers, and subdues their understanding. Happily, this pitch it seldom attains. But what a Tully or a Demosthenes[5] could scarcely effect over a Roman or Athenian audience, every *Capuchin*,[6] every itinerant or stationary teacher can perform over the generality of mankind, and in a higher degree, by touching such gross and vulgar passions.

The many instances of forged miracles, and prophecies, and supernatural events, which, in all ages, have either been detected by contrary evidence, or which detect themselves by their absurdity, prove sufficiently the strong propensity of mankind to the extraordinary and the marvellous, and ought reasonably to beget a suspicion against all relations of this kind. This is our natural way of thinking, even with regard to the most common and most credible events. For instance: There is no kind of report which rises so easily, and spreads so quickly, especially in country places and provincial towns, as those concerning marriages; insomuch that two young persons of equal condition never see each other twice, but the whole neighbourhood immediately join them together. The pleasure of telling a piece of news so interesting, of propagating it, and of being the first reporters of it, spreads the intelligence. And this is so well known, that no man of sense gives attention to these reports, till he find them confirmed by some greater evidence. Do not the same passions, and others still stronger, incline the generality of mankind to believe and report, with the greatest vehemence and assurance, all religious miracles?

Thirdly. It forms a strong presumption against all supernatural and miraculous relations, that they are observed chiefly to abound among ignorant and barbarous nations; or if a civilized people has ever given admission to any of them, that people will be found to have received them from ignorant and barbarous ancestors, who transmitted them with that inviolable sanction and authority, which always attend received opinions. When we peruse the first histories of all nations, we are apt to imagine ourselves transported into some new world; where the whole frame of nature is disjointed, and every element performs its operations in a different manner, from what it does at present. Battles, revolutions, pestilence, famine and death, are never the effect of those natural causes, which we experience. Prodigies, omens, oracles, judgements, quite obscure the few natural events, that are intermingled with them. But as the former grow thinner every page, in proportion as we advance nearer the enlightened ages, we soon learn, that there is nothing mysterious or supernatural in the case, but that all proceeds from the usual propensity of mankind towards the marvellous, and that, though this inclination may at intervals receive a check from sense and learning, it can never be thoroughly extirpated from human nature.

It is strange, a judicious reader is apt to say, upon the perusal of these wonderful historians, *that such prodigious events never happen in our days*. But it is nothing strange, I hope, that men should lie in all ages. You must surely have seen instances enough of that frailty. You have yourself heard many such marvellous relations started, which, being treated with scorn by all the wise and judicious, have at last been abandoned even by the vulgar. Be assured, that those renowned lies, which have spread and flourished to such a monstrous height, arose from like beginnings; but being sown in a more proper soil, shot up at last into prodigies almost equal to those which they relate.

It was a wise policy in that false prophet, Alexander, who though now forgotten, was once so famous, to lay the first scene of his impostures in Paphlagonia, where, as Lucian tells us, the people were extremely ignorant and stupid, and ready to swallow even the grossest delusion.[7] People at a distance, who are weak enough to think the matter at all worth enquiry, have no opportunity of receiving better information. The stories come magnified to them by a hundred circumstances. Fools are industrious in propagating the imposture; while the wise and learned are contented, in general, to deride its absurdity, without informing themselves of the particular facts, by which it may be distinctly refuted. And thus the impostor above mentioned was enabled to proceed, from his ignorant Paphlagonians, to the enlisting of votaries, even among the Grecian philosophers, and men of the most eminent rank and distinction in Rome: nay, could engage the attention of that sage emperor

Marcus Aurelius; so far as to make him trust the success of a military expedition to his delusive prophecies.

The advantages are so great, of starting an imposture among an ignorant people, that, even though the delusion should be too gross to impose on the generality of them (*which, though seldom, is sometimes the case*) it has a much better chance for succeeding in remote countries, than if the first scene had been laid in a city renowned for arts and knowledge. The most ignorant and barbarous of these barbarians carry the report abroad. None of their countrymen have a large correspondence, or sufficient credit and authority to contradict and beat down the delusion. Men's inclination to the marvellous has full opportunity to display itself. And thus a story, which is universally exploded in the place where it was first started, shall pass for certain at a thousand miles distance. But had Alexander fixed his residence at Athens, the philosophers of that renowned mart of learning had immediately spread, throughout the whole Roman empire, their sense of the matter; which, being supported by so great authority, and displayed by all the force of reason and eloquence, had entirely opened the eyes of mankind. It is true; Lucian, passing by chance through Paphlagonia, had an opportunity of performing this good office. But, though much to be wished, it does not always happen, that every Alexander meets with a Lucian, ready to expose and detect his impostures.

I may add as a *fourth* reason, which diminishes the authority of prodigies, that there is no testimony for any, even those which have not been expressly detected, that is not opposed by an infinite number of witnesses; so that not only the miracle destroys the credit of testimony, but the testimony destroys itself. To make this the better understood, let us consider, that, in matters of religion, whatever is different is contrary; and that it is impossible the religions of ancient Rome, of Turkey, of Siam, and of China should, all of them, be established on any solid foundation. Every miracle, therefore, pretended to have been wrought in any of these religions (and all of them abound in miracles), as its direct scope is to establish the particular system to which it is attributed; so has it the same force, though more indirectly, to overthrow every other system. In destroying a rival system, it likewise destroys the credit of those miracles, on which that system was established; so that all the prodigies of different religions are to be regarded as contrary facts, and the evidences of these prodigies, whether weak or strong, as opposite to each other. According to this method of reasoning, when we believe any miracle of Mahomet[8] or his successors, we have for our warrant the testimony of a few barbarous Arabians: And on the other hand, we are to regard the authority of Titus Livius, Plutarch, Tacitus, and, in short, of all the authors and witnesses, Grecian, Chinese, and Roman Catholic, who have related any miracle in their particular religion; I say, we are to regard their testimony in the same light as if they had mentioned that Mahometan miracle, and had in express terms contradicted it, with the same certainty as they have for the miracle they relate. This argument may appear over subtile and refined; but is not in reality different from the reasoning of a judge, who supposes, that the credit of two witnesses, maintaining a crime against any one, is destroyed by the testimony of two others, who affirm him to have been two hundred leagues distant, at the same instant when the crime is said to have been committed.

One of the best attested miracles in all profane history, is that which Tacitus reports of Vespasian, who cured a blind man in Alexandria, by means of his spittle, and a lame man by the mere touch of his foot; in obedience to a vision of the god Serapis, who had enjoined them to have recourse to the Emperor, for these miraculous cures. The story may be seen in that fine historian;[9] where every circumstance seems to add weight to the testimony, and might be displayed at large with all the force of argument and eloquence, if any one were now concerned to enforce the evidence of that exploded and idolatrous superstition. The gravity, solidity, age, and probity of so great an emperor, who, through the whole course of his life, conversed in a familiar manner with his friends and courtiers, and never affected those extraordinary airs of divinity assumed by Alexander and Demetrius. The historian, a cotemporary writer, noted for candour and veracity, and withal, the greatest and most penetrating genius, perhaps, of all antiquity; and so free from any tendency to credulity, that he even lies under the contrary imputation, of atheism and profaneness: The persons, from whose authority he related the miracle, of established character for judgement and veracity, as we may well presume; eye-witnesses of the fact, and confirming their testimony, after the Flavian family was despoiled of the empire, and could no longer give any reward, as the price of a lie. *Utrumque, qui interfuere, aunt quoque memorant, postquam nullum mendacio pretium.* [Those who were present still remember (the miracles) today, when there is nothing to gain by lying.][10] To which if we add the public nature of the facts, as related, it will appear, that no evidence can well be supposed stronger for so gross and so palpable a falsehood.

There is also a memorable story related by Cardinal de Retz, which may well deserve our consideration.[11] When that intriguing politician fled into Spain, to avoid the persecution of his enemies, he passed through Saragossa, the capital of Arragon, where he was shewn, in the cathedral, a man, who had served seven years as a doorkeeper, and was well known to every body in town, that had ever paid his devotions at that church. He had been seen, for so long a time, wanting a leg; but recovered that limb by the rubbing of holy oil upon the stump; and the cardinal assures us that he saw him with two legs. This miracle was vouched by all the canons of the church; and the whole company in town were appealed to for a confirmation of the fact; whom the cardinal found, by their zealous devotion, to be thorough believers of the miracle. Here the relater was also cotemporary to the supposed prodigy, of an incredulous and libertine character, as well as of great genius; the miracle of so *singular* a nature as could scarcely admit of a counterfeit, and the witnesses very numerous, and all of them, in a manner, spectators of the fact, to which they gave their testimony. And what adds mightily to the force of the evidence, and may double our surprise on this occasion, is, that the cardinal himself, who relates the story, seems not to give any credit to it, and consequently cannot be suspected of any concurrence in the holy fraud. He considered justly, that it was not requisite, in order to reject a fact of this nature, to be able accurately to disprove the testimony, and to trace its falsehood, through all the circumstances of knavery and credulity which produced it. He knew, that, as this was commonly altogether impossible at any small distance of time and place; so was it extremely difficult, even where one was immediately present, by reason of the bigotry, ignorance, cunning, and roguery of a great part of mankind. He therefore concluded, like a just reasoner, that such an evidence carried falsehood upon the very face of it, and that a miracle, supported by any human testimony, was more properly a subject of derision than of argument.

There surely never was a greater number of miracles ascribed to one person, than those, which were lately said to have been wrought in France upon the tomb of Abbé Paris,[12] the famous Jansenist, with whose sanctity the people were so long deluded. The curing of the sick, giving hearing to the deaf, and sight to the blind, were every where talked of as the usual effects of that holy sepulchre. But what is more extraordinary; many of the miracles were immediately proved upon the spot, before judges of unquestioned integrity, attested by witnesses of credit and distinction, in a learned age, and on the most eminent theatre that is now in the world. Nor is this all; a relation of them was published and dispersed every where; nor were the *Jesuits*, though a learned body, supported by the civil magistrate, and determined enemies to those opinions, in whose favour the miracles were said to have been wrought, ever able distinctly to refute or detect them. Where shall we find such a number of circumstances, agreeing to the corroboration of one fact? And what have we to oppose to such a cloud of witnesses, but the absolute impossibility or miraculous nature of the events, which they relate? And this surely, in the eyes of all reasonable people, will alone be regarded as a sufficient refutation.

Is the consequence just, because some human testimony has the utmost force and authority in some cases, when it relates the battle of Philippi or Pharsalia for instance;[13] that therefore all kinds of testimony must, in all cases, have equal force and authority? Suppose that the Caesarean and Pompeian factions had, each of them, claimed the victory in these battles, and that the historians of each party had uniformly ascribed the advantage to their own side; how could mankind, at this distance, have been able to determine between them? The contrariety is equally strong between the miracles related by Herodotus or Plutarch, and those delivered by Mariana,[14] Bede, or any monkish historian.

The wise lend a very academic faith to every report which favours the passion of the reporter; whether it magnifies his country, his family, or himself, or in any other way strikes in with his natural inclinations and propensities. But what greater temptation than to appear a missionary, a prophet, an ambassador from heaven? Who would not encounter many dangers and difficulties, in order to attain so sublime a character? Or if, by the help of vanity and a heated imagination, a man has first made a convert of himself, and entered seriously into the delusion; who ever scruples to make use of pious frauds, in support of so holy and meritorious a cause?

The smallest spark may here kindle into the greatest flame; because the materials are always prepared for it. The *avidum genus auricularum*,[15] the gazing populace, receive greedily, without examination, whatever sooths superstition, and promotes wonder.

How many stories of this nature have, in all ages, been detected and exploded in their infancy? How many more have been celebrated for a time, and have afterwards sunk into neglect and oblivion? Where such reports, therefore, fly about, the solution of the phenomenon is obvious; and we judge in conformity to regular experience and observation, when we account for it by the known and natural principles of credulity and delusion. And shall we, rather than have a recourse to so natural a solution, allow of a miraculous violation of the most established laws of nature?

I need not mention the difficulty of detecting a falsehood in any private or even public history, at the place, where it is said to happen; much more when the scene is removed to ever so small a distance. Even a court of judicature, with all the authority, accuracy, and judgement, which they can employ, find themselves often at a loss to distinguish between truth and falsehood in the most recent actions. But the matter never comes to any issue, if trusted to the common method of altercation and debate and flying rumours; especially when men's passions have taken part on either side.

In the infancy of new religions, the wise and learned commonly esteem the matter too inconsiderable to deserve their attention or regard. And when afterwards they would willingly detect the cheat, in order to undeceive the deluded multitude, the season is now past, and the records and witnesses, which might clear up the matter, have perished beyond recovery.

No means of detection remain, but those which must be drawn from the very testimony itself of the reporters: and these, though always sufficient with the judicious and knowing, are commonly too fine to fall under the comprehension of the vulgar.

Upon the whole, then, it appears, that no testimony for any kind of miracle has ever amounted to a probability, much less to a proof; and that, even supposing it amounted to a proof, it would be opposed by another proof; derived from the very nature of the fact, which it would endeavour to establish. It is experience only, which gives authority to human testimony; and it is the same experience, which assures us of the laws of nature. When, therefore, these two kinds of experience are contrary, we have nothing to do but substract the one from the other, and embrace an opinion, either on one side or the other, with that assurance which arises from the remainder. But according to the principle here explained, this substraction, with regard to all popular religions, amounts to an entire annihilation; and therefore we may establish it as a maxim, that no human testimony can have such force as to prove a miracle, and make it a just foundation for any such system of religion.

I beg the limitations here made may be remarked, when I say, that a miracle can never be proved, so as to be the foundation of a system of religion. For I own, that otherwise, there may possibly be miracles, or violations of the usual course of nature, of such a kind as to admit of proof from human testimony; though, perhaps, it will be impossible to find any such in all the records of history. Thus, suppose, all authors, in all languages, agree, that, from the first of January 1600, there was a total darkness over the whole earth for eight days: suppose that the tradition of this extraordinary event is still strong and lively among the people: that all travellers, who return from foreign countries, bring us accounts of the same tradition, without the least variation or contradiction: it is evident, that our present philosophers, instead of doubting the fact, ought to receive it as certain, and ought to search for the causes whence it might be derived. The decay, corruption, and dissolution of nature, is an event rendered probable by so many analogies, that any phenomenon, which seems to have a tendency towards that catastrophe, comes within the reach of human testimony, if that testimony be very extensive and uniform.

But suppose, that all the historians who treat of England, should agree, that, on the first of January 1600, Queen Elizabeth died; that both before and after her death she was seen by her physicians and the whole court, as is usual with persons of her rank; that her successor was acknowledged and proclaimed by the parliament; and that, after being interred a month, she again appeared, resumed the throne, and governed England for three years: I must confess that I should be surprised at the concurrence of so many odd circumstances, but should not have the least inclination to believe so miraculous an event. I should not doubt of her pretended death, and of those other public circumstances that followed it: I should only assert it to have been pretended, and that it neither was, nor possibly could be real. You would in vain object to me the difficulty, and almost impossibility of deceiving the world in an affair of such consequence; the wisdom and solid judgement of that renowned queen; with the little or no advantage which she could reap from so poor an artifice: All this might astonish me; but I would still reply, that the knavery and folly of men are such common phenomena, that I should rather believe the most extraordinary events to arise from their concurrence, than admit of so signal a violation of the laws of nature.

But should this miracle be ascribed to any new system of religion; men, in all ages, have been so much imposed on by ridiculous stories of that kind, that this very circumstance would be a full proof of a cheat, and sufficient, with all men of sense, not only to make them reject the fact, but even reject it without farther examination. Though the Being to whom the miracle is ascribed, be, in this case, Almighty, it does not, upon that account, become a whit more probable; since it is impossible for us to know the attributes or actions of such a Being, otherwise than from the experience which we have of his productions, in the usual course of nature. This still reduces us to past observation, and obliges us to compare the instances of the violation of truth in the testimony of men, with those of the violation of the laws of nature by miracles, in order to judge which of them is most likely and probable. As the violations of truth are more common in the testimony concerning religious miracles, than in that concerning any other matter of fact; this must diminish very much the authority of the former testimony, and make us form a general resolution, never to lend any attention to it, with whatever specious pretence it may be covered.

Lord Bacon seems to have embraced the same principles of reasoning. "We ought," says he, "to make a collection or particular history of all monsters and prodigious births or productions, and in a word of every thing new, rare, and extraordinary in nature. But this must be done with the most severe scrutiny, lest we depart from truth. Above all, every relation must be considered as suspicious, which depends in any degree upon religion, as the prodigies of Livy: And no less so, every thing that is to be found in the writers of natural magic or alchimy, or such authors, who seem, all of them, to have an unconquerable appetite for falsehood and fable."[16]

I am the better pleased with the method of reasoning here delivered, as I think it may serve to confound those dangerous friends or disguised enemies to the *Christian Religion*, who have undertaken to defend it by the principles of human reason. Our most holy religion is founded on *Faith*, not on reason; and it is a sure method of exposing it to put it to such a trial as it is, by no means, fitted to endure. To make this more evident, let us examine those miracles, related in scripture; and not to lose ourselves in too wide a field, let us confine ourselves to such as we find in the *Pentateuch*, which we shall examine, according to the principles of these pretended Christians, not as the word or testimony of God himself; but as the production of a mere human writer and historian. Here then we are first to consider a book, presented to us by a barbarous and ignorant people, written in an age when they were still more barbarous, and in all probability long after the facts which it relates, corroborated by no concurring testimony, and resembling those fabulous accounts, which every nation gives of its origin. Upon reading this book, we find it full of prodigies and miracles. It gives an account of a state of the world and of human nature entirely different from the present: Of our fall from that state: Of the age of man, extended to near a thousand years: Of the destruction of the world by a deluge: Of the arbitrary choice of one people, as the favourites of heaven; and that people the countrymen of the author: Of their deliverance from bondage by prodigies the most astonishing imaginable: I desire any one to lay his hand upon his heart, and after a serious consideration declare, whether he thinks that the falsehood of such a book, supported by such a testimony, would be more extraordinary and miraculous than all the miracles it relates; which is, however, necessary to make it be received, according to the measures of probability above established.

What we have said of miracles may be applied, without any variation, to prophecies; and indeed, all prophecies are real miracles, and as such only, can be admitted as proofs of any revelation. If it did not exceed the capacity of human nature to foretell future events, it would be absurd to employ any prophecy as an argument for a divine mission or authority from heaven. So that, upon the whole, we may conclude, that the *Christian Religion* not only was at first attended with miracles, but even at this day cannot be believed by any reasonable person without one. Mere reason is insufficient to convince us of its veracity: And whoever is moved by *Faith* to assent to it, is conscious of a continued miracle in his own person, which subverts all the principles of his understanding, and gives him a determination to believe what is most contrary to custom and experience.

From *Analysis of the Influence of Natural Religion on the Temporal Happiness of Mankind* (1822)

JEREMY BENTHAM AND GEORGE GROTE

[Jeremy Bentham (1748–1832) was a pioneering British philosopher and political theorist. He was the founder of Utilitarianism, a philosophical theory embodied in *Introduction to Principles of Morals and Legislation* (1789) and other works. But Bentham's work ranged widely, from animal rights to law reform. Several of his later works dealt with the intersection of religion with politics and society. *Analysis of the Influence of Natural Religion on the Temporal Happiness of Mankind*, published under a pseudonym in 1822, was a pamphlet condemning the harm that religious belief inflicted on human society; it was written by British historian George Grote (1794–1871)—best known for his *History of Greece* (1846–46)—from notes provided by Bentham. On his own, Bentham wrote *Not Paul but Jesus* (1823), which is a harsh condemnation of St. Paul as a perverter of Jesus' doctrines. In the following section from the *Analysis*, titled "Creating a Particular Class of Persons Incurably Opposed to the Interests of Humanity," Bentham and Grote study the influence of the priestly class and of others who claim to be the interpreters of divine will, as well as the deleterious effects they have on human happiness.]

I have endeavoured in the preceding pages to point out all the different modes in which natural religion acts injuriously upon the temporal happiness of society. One species of injury yet remains to be indicated, and that too of incalculable effect and permanence—partly as it is productive of distinct mischief, independently and on its own account—partly as it subsidizes a standing army for the perpetuation of all the rest.

Those, who believe in the existence and earthly agency of a superhuman being, view all facts which they are unable to interpret, as special interventions of the celestial hand. Incomprehensible phenomena are ascribed naturally to the incomprehensible person above. They call forth of course the deepest horror and astonishment, as being sudden eruptions of the super-aërial volcano, and reminding the spectator of its unsubdued and inexhaustible terrors. When any such events take place, therefore, his mind is extremely embarrassed and unhinged, and in the highest degree unfit for measuring the correctness of any inferences which immediate fear may suggest.

Now incomprehensible phenomena occur very frequently in the persons of different men—that is, certain men are often seen to act in a manner which the spectator is unable to reconcile with the general principles of human action, so far as they are known to him. Incomprehensible men and incomprehensible modes of behaviour, when they do thus happen, are of course subject to the same construction as other unintelligible events, and are supposed to indicate a signal interference of the Deity. When therefore the actions of any man differ strikingly from the ordinary march of human conduct, we naturally imagine him to be under the peculiar impulse and guidance of the divine finger.

Of incomprehensible behaviour the two extremes, though diametrically opposite kinds, are superior wisdom, and extravagant folly. A loftier and better cultivated intelligence attains his ends by means which we cannot fathom—overleaps difficulties which seem to us insurmountable—foresees consequences which we had never dreamt of. His system of action is to us altogether perplexing and inexplicable. There are others again who seem insensible to the ordinary motives of man—whose thoughts, words, and deeds are alike incoherent and inconsequential—whose incapacity disqualifies them from the commonest offices of life. Such is the other species of incomprehensible man, whom we generally term an idiot or madman, according to circumstances. Both the extremes of intelligence and folly thus exhibit phenomena which we are unable to account for, and are each therefore referred to the immediate influence and inspiration of God.[1]

Amongst early societies, where a very limited number of phenomena have yet been treasured up for comparison, and where the established general principles are built upon so narrow an induction, events are perpetually occurring which seem at variance with them. The sum of principles thus established is called *the course of nature* and the exceptions to them, or supernatural inroads, are extremely frequent. Accordingly, men of unaccountable powers and behaviour are easy to be found, where the standard of comparison is so imperfectly known; and the belief in particular persons, as inspired by God, is proportionably prevalent in an early stage of society.

Conformably to the foregoing doctrine, we find that rude nations generally consider madmen and idiots as persons under the impulse of unseen spirits, and view them with peculiar awe and reverence. This however, though a remarkable fact and signally illustrative of the principle, yet leads to no important consequences and may be dismissed without farther comment. But the belief of a divine inspiration and concomitancy in persons of superior intelligence, is productive of great and lasting changes in the structure of the social union; and it is most instructive as well as curious to trace the gradual progress of these alterations. A madman is unable to take advantage of any prejudice existing in his favour among mankind, or to push such a feeling into its most profitable result. It terminates, therefore, in those spontaneous effusions of reverence, which do not extend their effects beyond the actual moment and individual.

In order to lead to any lasting consequence, it is necessary that the performer of incomprehensible acts should possess sufficient acuteness to take advantage of the inference which mankind are disposed to draw from them. He need not indeed be a first-rate intellect—but he must be some degrees above a madman or an idiot.

The inferences which an unenlightened mind is in this case inclined to adopt, are indeed most extensive and important. A man is seen, or believed, to produce some given effect, by means which the spectators did not before know to be adequate to that effect: Astonished at such an unforeseen result, they think they cannot too highly magnify the extent of his power. It has already surpassed their anticipations very much—therefore there is no knowing by how much more it may surpass them—no possibility of conceiving its limits. He is therefore invested for the time with omnipotence, by the supposed momentary descent and co-operation of the unseen Being above. But if the Almighty has condescended to pay such pointed attention to any individual, this must be owing to some very peculiar intimacy between them. The individual must possess extraordinary means of recommending himself to the favour of God, in order to attract the distinction of a supernatural visit, and to be honoured with the temporary loan of a fraction of omnipotence. He must stand high in the estimation of the Deity, and must therefore be well acquainted with his disposition, and with the modes of conciliating or provoking him.

Such are the long train of inferences which the performance of an unaccountable act suggests to the alarmed beholders. It is important to remark the gigantic strides by which the mind is hurried on it knows not where, beyond all power of stoppage or limit, the moment it quits the guidance of observation, and is induced to harbour *extra-experimental* belief. A man is seen to do an incomprehensible deed: The utmost consequence which experience would extract from this, would be, that under circumstances not very dissimilar, the same man could repeat the deed. If a king is seen to remove one man's scrofula by the touch, experience might warrant us in conjecturing, that he might cure the same disease in another: But it would be as ridiculous to infer from this single fact, that he possessed the power of performing any other feats, as it would be to conclude that, because mercury quickened the action of the liver, you might rely upon it for the alleviation of the gout. Such, I say, would be the conclusion of a rational observer. But the mind, when once disengaged from observation, and initiated into extra-experimental belief, rolls about without measure in her newly acquired phrenzy, and glances in a moment from earth to heaven and from heaven to earth. To him that hath, more shall be given:[2] Pursuant to this maxim, we ascribe to the man who astonishes us by one incomprehensible feat, the ability of astonishing us still more by a great many others. Nay, the power, which we are led to conceive as exerted, seems too vast to be ascribed to him alone. We therefore introduce an omnipotent accomplice into the scene, and regard the feat as indicating the intervention of a hand sufficiently mighty to work any imaginable marvel. Such is the prompt and forcible transit whereby the *extra-experimental* believer is hurried on to swell the power which he beholds into a greater, and that still farther into the greatest—until at last an act of legerdemain is magnified into an exhibition of omnipotence.

But however unwarranted the inferences thus stated may appear, their effect is not the less important. The wonder-worker gains credit for possessing an extent of power to which we can assign no limits; we view him as a privileged being, possessed of a general power of attorney from the Almighty to interpret his feelings, to promulgate his will, and to draw for supernatural recompense and punishments at pleasure. In virtue of this extensive deputation, the principal becomes responsible for every thing which his emissary says and does, and is supposed to resign the whole management of earthly affairs in favour of the latter.

A wonder-worker thus, by merely producing an adequate measure of astonishment in the bosoms of mankind, is immediately exalted into a station of supreme necessity and importance. All knowledge of the divine will, all assistance from the divine power, can only be attained through his mediation. The patronage thus ascribed to him is enormous, and is, like all other patronage, readily convertible into every other sort of emolument or desirable object. Every one who seeks the divine favour, will not fail to propitiate the minister by whom his petition must be countersigned—whose blessing or curse determines his future treatment at the hands of the Deity. Knowledge of the divine intentions is another perennial source of influence and lucre to the wonder-worker. Hence he is supposed to foreknow the phenomena of nature, and the ignorant, when in doubt, regulate their behaviour by the results which he prognosticates. His patent too of interpreting the divine decrees, to which no competitor has any access, virtually empowers him to manufacture a decalogue on his own account, and to enforce its mandates by all the terrors of spiritual police and penalties.

Powers of such tremendous magnitude appear amply sufficient to enslave and lay prostrate the whole community. And this they infallibly would do, were the extra-experimental belief steady, equable, and consistent with itself, always applying similar principles on similar occasions; and if it were never over-borne by the more immediate motives and acquisitions of earth. The urgent necessity of providing for temporal exigencies, which are too pressing to await the result of an application to heaven, impels the minds of men in another direction, and models their associations more and more according to the dictates of experience. Having acquired, by their own exertions, the means of satisfying their wants, they have not so great an occasion for aërial aid, and all successive accumulations of knowledge tend to weaken the influence of the divine deputy over them.

My present purpose, however, is to investigate not so much the extent of this influence, as the direction in which it operates. We design to shew, that the performer of prodigies (or this class, if there be more than one) when elevated to the post of interpreter and administrator of the divine will, and exercising an influence built upon these privileges—becomes animated with an interest incurably and in every point hostile to human happiness: That their sway can only be matured and perfected by the entire abasement and dismantling of the human faculties; and that therefore all their energies must be devoted to the accomplishment of this destructive work, by the best means which opportunity presents.

1. They have the strongest interest in the depravation of the human intellect. For the demand for their services as agents for the temporal aid of the Deity, altogether depends upon human ignorance and incapacity, and is exactly proportional to it. Why does a man apply for the divine assistance? Because he does not know how to accomplish his ends without it, or how to procure the requisite apparatus for the purpose. If he knew any physical means of attaining it, he would unquestionably prefer them. Every extension therefore of physical methods in the gratification of our wishes, displaces and throws out of employment by so much the labour of the aërial functionaries. No one prays for the removal of a disease by supernatural aid, when he once knows an appropriate surgical remedy. He therefore who lives by the commission which he charges on the disposal of the former, has a manifest interest in checking the advance and introduction of the latter.

Besides, the accumulation of experimental knowledge excludes the supernatural man from another of his most lucrative employments—that of predicting future events. Those who are the most ignorant of physical connections, and therefore the least qualified to form a judgment as to any particular result, are of course the most frequent in their applications for extra-physical guidance, and the most likely to follow it. This is their sole mode of procuring the most indispensable of all acquisitions. Upon them too it is the most easy to palm a vague and oracular response or decree as to the future, capable of applying to almost any result; and they are the most easily imposed upon by shifts and pretences which veil the incapacity of the respondent. When mankind advance a little in knowledge, and become inquisite,[3] the task of the soothsayer becomes more and more difficult; whereas ignorance and credulity are duped without any great pains. The supernatural agent therefore has a deadly interest against the advance of knowledge, not only as it introduces a better machinery for obtaining acquaintance with the future, and thereby throws, him out of employment as a prophet—but also as it enables mankind to detect the hollow, fictitious, and illusory nature of his own predicting establishment.

2. As he is interested in impeding the progress of knowledge, so he is not the less interested in propagating and cherishing *extra-experimental* belief. Ignorance is his negative ally, cutting off mankind from any other means of satisfying their wants except those which he alone can furnish: *Extra-experimental* belief is the substratum on which all his influence is built. It is this which furnishes to mankind all their evidence of the being, a power and agency of his invisible principal, and also of the posthumous scenes in preparation for us, where these are to be exhibited on a superior and perfect scale. It is this too which supplies mankind with the credentials of his own missions, and makes them impute to him at once, and without cavilling, all that long stretch of aërial dignity and prerogative, the actual proof of which it would have been difficult for him to have gone through. Both the hopes and fears, therefore, which call for his interference, and the selection of him as the person to remove them, rest upon the maintenance of extra-experimental persuasion in the human breast. Were belief closely and inseparably knit with experience, he would never obtain credit for the power of doing any thing else than what mankind really saw him do. His interest accordingly prompts him to disjoin the two—to disjoin them on *every* occasion in his power, if he would ensure their disjunction for his own particular case.

Any one therefore whose power and credit with mankind, rest upon the imputation of supernatural ambassadorship, must be impelled by the most irresistible motives to disunite belief from experience in the bosoms of mankind, as much as he possibly can.

3. Take the same person again, in his capacity of licensed interpreter of the divine will and decrees. What edicts will he be likely to promulgate, as emanating from this consecrated source?

The only circumstance which makes the power of the law-interpreter inferior to that of the legislator, is the accessibility of the text which he professes to explain. Where this is open to the whole public as well as to him, his explanation may be controverted, and recourse will then be had to the production of the original. But if either there exist no original at all, or the interpreter possesses the exclusive custody of it, his power is completely equivalent to that of a legislator.

Now in one of these two alternatives stand the divine decrees. Either there never were any original decrees at all—or if there were, they have been deposited in a spot unknown to any one except the authorised interpreters. And therefore the latter become in fact legislators, issuing whatever edicts they choose in the name and on the behalf of their invisible master—and enforcing them ad libitum by any imaginable measure of punishment or reward, drawn from his inexhaustible magazines.

Now what principle will govern the enactments of an interpreter, or licensed class of interpreters, when thus exercising an unfettered power of legislation? The general principles of human nature suffer us not to hesitate a moment in answering this question. It will be a regard to their own separate interest. Like all other monopolists who possess the exclusive privilege of rendering any particular service—like all other possessors of power independent of, and irresponsible to, the community—they will pursue the natural path of self-preference, and will apply their functions to purposes of aggrandizement and exaction.

Now this separate interest is irreconcileably at variance with that of the society. If any man, or any separate class, are permitted to legislate for their own benefit, they are in effect despots; while the rest of the community are degraded to the level of slaves, and will be treated as such by the legislative system so constructed. Conformable to this system the precepts delivered by the supernatural delegate as enacted by his invisible master, will be such as to subjugate the minds of the community, in the highest practicable degree, to himself and to his brethren, and to appropriate for the benefit of the class as much wealth and power as circumstances will permit. This is a mere statement of the dictates of self-preference.

4. To effect this purpose, he will find it essentially necessary to describe the Deity as capricious, irritable, and vindictive, to the highest extent—as regarding with gloom and jealousy the enjoyments of the human worm, and taking delight in his privations or sufferings—pliable indeed without measure, and yielding up instantaneously all his previous sentiments, when technically and professionally solicited—but requiring the perpetual application of emollients to sooth his wrathful propensities. The more implicitly mankind believe in these appalling attributes, the more essential is he who can stand in the gap and avert the threatened pestilence—the more necessary is it to ensure his activity by feeing and ennobling him. On whatever occasions he can, in the capacity of interpreter to the divine will, persuade them that they are exposed to supernatural wrath—in all such junctures, he will obtain a fee, as mediator or intercessor, for procuring a reprieve.

The more therefore he can multiply the number of offences against God, the greater does his profit become—because on every such act of guilt, the sinner will find it answer to forestall the execution of the sentence by effecting an amicable compromise with the vicegerent of the Almighty. For rendering so important a service, the latter may make his own terms.

But in order to multiply offences, the most efficacious method is to prohibit those acts which there is the most frequent and powerful temptation to commit. Now the temptation to perform any act is of course proportional to the magnitude of the pleasureable, and the smallness of the painful, consequences by which it is attended. Those deeds, therefore, which are the most delightful, and the most innoxious, will meet with the severest prohibitions in the religious code, and be represented as the most deeply offensive to the divine majesty. Because such deeds will be most frequently repeated and will accordingly create the amplest demand for the expiatory formula.

Such therefore will be the code constructed by the supernatural delegate in the name of his unearthly sovereign—including the most rigorous denunciations against human pleasure, and interdicting it the more severely in proportion as it is delicious and harmless. He will enjoin the most gratuitous and unrequited privations, and self-imposed sufferings, as the sole method of conciliating the divine mercy,—inasmuch as the neglect of these mandates must be the most common, and all such remissness will incur a penalty which the transgressor must be compelled to redeem.

5. All the purchase which the interpreter of the divine will has upon the human mind, depends upon the extent of its superhuman apprehensions. It is therefore his decided interest that the dread of these unseen visitations should haunt the bosoms of mankind, like a heavy and perpetual incubus, day and night—that they should live under a constant sense of the suspended arm of God—and thus in a state of such conscious insecurity and helplessness, that all possibility of earthly comfort should be altogether blighted and cast out. The more firmly these undefined terrors can be planted in a man's associations, the more urgent is his need of a mediator with the aërial kingdom to which his apprehensions refer, and the more enormous the sacrifices which he will make in order to purchase such intercession.

6. Again, it will be the decided interest of the inspired legislator, to clothe all his enactments in the most imposing epithets of moral approbation—to describe the Being, by whom he is commissioned, in terms which imply the holiest and most beneficent character, though the proceedings and the system which he attributes to him indicate the very opposite temper—and to make mankind believe that every act of this Being is, and must be, just. By thus perverting their moral sentiments, he tightens and perpetuates the pressure of superhuman apprehensions. There will be less tendency to murmur and revolt at these threats, when men are persuaded that they have justly incurred the anger of an all-beneficent Being.

By this analysis, I think, it appears most demonstratively, that all those whose influence rests on an imputed connection with the Divine Being, cannot fail to be animated by an interest incurably opposed to all human happiness: that the inevitable aim of such persons must be to extend and render irremediable, those evils which natural religion would originate without them, viz, ignorance, extra-experimental belief, appalling conceptions of the Deity, intense dread of his visitations, and a perversion of the terms of praise and censure in his behalf. To this identity of result I have traced them both, although by different and perfectly unconnected roads.

Natural religion is thus provided with an array of human force and fraud for the purpose of enforcing her mandates, and realising her mischievous tendencies. A standing army of ministers is organized in her cause, formed either of men who are themselves believed to be specially gifted from the sky, or of others who pretend not to any immediate inspiration in their own persons, but merely act as the sub-delegates of some heaven-commissioned envoy of aforetime. The interest of both these sorts of persons is precisely identical, nor is it of the smallest importance whether the patent is worked by the original pretender, or by any one else into whose hands it may have subsequently fallen. In either case its fruits are equally deleterious.

In either case, the same conspirators league themselves for the same purposes—that of promulgating and explaining the will of their incomprehensible master, and subjugating to his thraldom the knowledge and the hopes of mankind. And the accession of strength, which religion derives from this special confederation in her favour, is incalculable. They supply many defects, in her means of conquest and influence, which must otherwise have rendered her dominion comparatively narrow.

First, one grand deficiency in unofficered religion, is the absence of any directive rule. Mankind, from their conceptions of the character of the Deity, will doubtless conjecture what sort of conduct will be agreeable to him, and will also fix upon some particular actions belonging to that course as more agreeable than others. But this unguided and promiscuous selection is not likely to be either uniform, earnest, or circumstantial.

When a body of authorised agents is framed, through whom the designs and temper of the Deity can be learnt, this defect is completely supplied. The ceremonial pleasing to him is then officially declared: the acts offensive to him are enumerated and defined, and their greater or less enormity graduated. Doubt and controversy are precluded, or at least exceedingly narrowed, by an appeal to the recognized organ of infallibility. And thus the superhuman terrors are concentrated and particularized, whereby they are brought to act in the most cogent and effective manner which the nature of the case admits.

2. In analysing the efficiency of the religious sanctions, we have already seen that their remoteness and uncertainty will not allow of their producing a steady, equable and unvarying impression upon the mind—although at peculiar moments, these apprehensions become supreme and overwhelming, even

to insanity. For motives thus subject to fluctuation, the constant presence of a standing brotherhood is peculiarly requisite, in order to watch those periods when the mind is most vulnerable to their influence—to multiply and per-petuate, if possible, these temporary liabilities, and to secure the production of some permanent result during the continuance of the fit. The ministers of natural religion, by bringing their most efficient batteries to bear upon the mind at these intervals, frequently succeed in extending the duration of the supernatural fears, and subjugating the whole man for life.

Sickness—mental affliction—approaching death—childhood—all these are periods when the intellect is depressed and feeble, and when the associa-tions are peculiarly liable to the inroads of every species of fear. They are times therefore when the officer of the invisible world exercises the most uncon-trolled despotism over the soul, and bends it whither he will. Were it not for his dexterity in contriving to render the bias permanent, the sick or the despondent would probably relapse, in no long period, into their habitual state, of comparative insensibility to supernatural terrors.

With regard to the dying man, indeed, no ulterior views can be enter-tained; but the immediate effect of the presence and ascendancy of a religious minister, on this occasion is most important. Without his aid, posthumous apprehensions would indeed embitter the hour of death, but this would be productive of no subsequent evil. The minister not only aggravates these terrors to an infinitely higher pitch, but offers to the distracted patient a defi-nite and easy mode by which he may in part alleviate them, and lessen the impending risk. He must make some atonement or satisfaction to God, in return for the offensive acts with which his life has abounded, by transferring a part or the whole of that property which he is at all events about to leave behind. But as he cannot have access in person to the offended principal, this property must be handed over in trust to his accredited agent or minister, for the inaccessible party. By such testamentary donation the sins of the past are in part redeemed.

The religious fears attending upon the hour of death are thus converted into powerful engines for enriching the sacerdotal class, who contrive to extract this lasting profit from an affection of mind which would otherwise have caused nothing beyond momentary pain. The act of mortmain[4] attests the height to which these death-bed commutations have actually been carried: Nor is it extravagant to assert, that had there been no change of the public sentiment and no interposition of the legislature, nearly all the land of England would have become the property of the church.

3. It should by no means be forgotten, that the inefficiency, and the alternation from general indifference to occasional fever, which I have shewn to belong to the religious sanction, constitute the leading source of importance and emolument to the priesthood. Suppose mankind to be perfectly acquainted with all the modifications of the Divine temper, and strictly observant of his commands, the functions of this class would of course become extinct. There would be no necessity for their services either as interpreters, mediators, or intercessors.

It is their decisive interest to multiply offences, as preparations for the lucrative season of repentance, during which their sway is at its zenith, and their most advantageous contracts realized. For each crime a pardon must be obtained through the intercession and agency of the authorized mediator. He must therefore be propitiated by payment both in money and honour, and the profits of the sacerdotal body bear an accurate ratio to the number of offences committed, and of pardons implored.

Thus the nature of the religious sanction, though very ill adapted for the purpose of actually terminating the practices it forbids, is yet calculated in the most precise manner to exalt and enrich the officers busied in enforcing it. This is the end, at which, supposing them like other men, they will be constantly aiming, and they have enjoyed facilities in the attainment of it rarely possessed by mere intermediate agents.

For, first, they have found posthumous terror, from its instability and occasional fierceness, an exquisite preparative of the mind for their dominion. And, secondly, they have united two functions which have placed this feeling entirely under their direction—They are, ex-officio, both framers of the divine law, and venders of the divine pardons for infringements of it. They have named the acts which required forgiveness as well as the price at which forgiveness should be purchased. Suppose only the periodical spring-tides of superhuman fear to reach a certain height, and this machinery for subjugation becomes perfect and irresistible.

If in earthly matters, these two functions were united—if the same person were to become framer of the law, and agent for the sale of licences to elude it—it is manifest, that he would make terrestrial laws inconceivably burdensome and exactive, so that there should be no possibility of observing them. The interest of the sacerdotal class has been completely similar, leading them to require, in the name of the Deity, obedience where obedience is impracticable, and then making men pay for the deficiency. Accordingly they inform us that he is a Being of such an exquisite and irritable temperament—so nicely susceptible and so vehemently impatient of every thing which is not exactly like himself, that we cannot escape his displeasure, except by undergoing a thorough repair and regeneration upon the celestial model. If but the most transient wish for any thing unlike to God, or unholy, shoots across the mind, it constitutes criminality and is deeply abhorrent to the divine perfection. To such a state of entire conformity no human being ever yet attained—and thus, by the invention of an impracticable code, mankind are placed in a constant necessity of discharging expiatory fees, and purchasing licences of evasion.

In this respect, the sacerdotal interest is directly at variance not only with that of the human race, but also with that of the divine Being. He sincerely desires, without doubt, that his edicts should be strictly obeyed, and therefore would be willing to facilitate their execution, so far as is consistent with his own sensitive and exquisite purity. But the middlemen who pretend to serve him have unfortunately an interest in their non-performance, and therefore throw every possible obstacle in the way of obedience.

4. In a former part of this work, I endeavoured to shew, that the real actuating force which gave birth to religious deeds, though so masked as not to be discernible on a superficial view, was *public opinion*. There cannot be a more effectual spur to this popular sentiment, than the formation of a body whose peculiar interest lies in watching its various turns, in kindling it anew, and dexterously diversifying its applications. For this task they possess numerous advantages. The necessity of recurring to their services on many occasions ensures to them a large measure of respect, as well as of wealth, and this re-acts upon the function which they exercise. They labour sedulously to inculcate the deepest reverence in speaking of religious matters, as well as extreme backwardness and timidity of soul in subjecting them to the examination of

reason. They diffuse widely among the community those pious misapplications of moral epithets, which are inseparably annexed to the natural belief
in an omnipotent Being, availing themselves of this confusion of language to
stigmatize as iniquitous every thing which counteracts their own views, and
to extol as virtuous that which favours them.

By thus whipping up and propagating the religious antipathies of
mankind, they generally succeed in organizing that tone of public opinion
which is most conducive to their interest: That is, a sentiment which rigor-
ously enforces a certain measure of religious observance—while it also recognizes in words, as incumbent and necessary duties of piety, a number of other
acts which no one ever performs, and which mankind will allow you to leave
undone, provided you do not question the propriety of doing them. A variance
is thus introduced between the religious feelings and the reigning practice,
and whenever any accident preternaturally kindles the former, such a laxity of
conduct will of course appear pregnant with guilt. Hence that ebb and flow
of mind, and those periodical spasms of repentant alarm, which can only be
charmed away by purchasing comfort at the hands of the spiritual exorcist.
And thus the constitution of the public sentiment becomes a preparation and
medium for the effectual dominion of this class.

5. The fundamental principle, upon which all the superhuman machinery
rests its hold, has been shewn to consist in *extra-experimental* belief. Now in diffusing and strengthening this species of persuasion, the sacerdotal body form
most essential auxiliaries. They are the legitimate and acknowledged interpreters of all incomprehensible events, and any inference which they extract
from thence is universally adopted. This bestows upon them an unlimited
licence of coining and circulating as much *extra-experimental* matter as they
choose, and of distorting the physical links among phenomena by smuggling
in an appeal to the divine intentions. By their constant and well-paid activity,
also, every casual coincidence is magnified into a prodigy—every prediction
accidentally verified, into a proof of their free-right of admission behind the
unexpanded scenes of futurity. Besides, they are continually at hand to spread
abroad those myriads of fictions, which the *extra-experimental* belief has been
shewn to engender. Mendacity itself becomes consecrated, when employed in
behalf of religion; and the infinity of pious frauds, which may be cited from

the pages of history, sufficiently attests the zeal and effect with which the sacerdotal class have laboured in the diffusion of this unreal currency.

From this successive accumulation of particular instances, a large aggregate of *extra-experimental* matter is at last amassed, which lays claim to the title and honours of a separate science. The stories upon which it is founded are so thickly and authoritatively spread abroad—apparently so unconnected one with the other, and relying upon numerous separate attestations—that it seems impossible to discredit the whole, and difficult to know where to draw the line. To fulfil so nice a task, writers arise who compare the different stories together, arrange them into a systematic order, extract meaning and inferences from these collations, and reject those particulars which cannot be reconciled with the theories thus elicited. This aërial matter is distributed into a regular and distinct branch of knowledge, partitioned into various subordinate departments, and the sacerdotal class of course monopolize the guidance and guardianship of this science almost exclusively to themselves. We have only to consult the first book of *Cicero de Divinatione*, in order to observe the minute subdivisions which the imaginary science of augury underwent in those times—the formal array of conclusions which appear to be strictly deduced from its alleged facts, and the various philosophical systems framed to explain and reconcile them.

Accordingly the *extra-experimental* belief, when sufficiently augmented in volume, becomes possessed of a distinct station among the sciences, and reflects upon its practitioners and professors all that credit which is annexed to superiority in any other department. Realities become divided into two separate classes: First, the world of experience, embracing all which we see, feel, hear, taste, or smell, and the various connections among them. Secondly, the world of which we have no experience, consisting of what are called immaterial entities, or of those things which we neither see, nor feel, nor hear, nor taste, nor smell; but which, nevertheless, we are supposed to know without any experience at all. The latter science is always the colleague and correlative of the former—frequently indeed it is more highly esteemed and more assiduously cultivated.

I have endeavoured to trace some of those modes, in which the brotherhood hired and equipped by natural religion have contrived to promote, in so high a degree, the success of the cause inscribed on their banners—and in so much higher a degree, to aggrandize and enrich themselves. My sketch, indeed, has been exceedingly superficial and incomplete; because the facilities which such a standing corps possesses for compassing its ends, are both innumerable and indescribable. We ought not however to forget, that a wealthy and powerful body of this kind not only acts with its own force, but also with that of all who have any thing to hope, or to fear, from it. To become a member of the body constitutes a valuable object of ambition, and all, who have any chance of attaining such a post, will of course conspire vehemently in its support. Besides, there arises a long train of connections and dependants, who diffuse themselves every where through the community, and contribute most materially to spread and enhance the influence of the class.

In addition to these, however, they have yet another ally, more powerful and efficient than all the rest,—the earthly chief, or governing power of the state. He, as well as they, has an interest incurably at variance with that of the community, and all sinister interests have a natural tendency to combine together and to co-operate, inasmuch as the object of each is thereby most completely and most easily secured. But between the particular interest of a governing aristocracy and a sacerdotal class, there seems a very peculiar affinity and coincidence—each wielding the precise engine which the other wants.

The aristocracy, for instance, possess the disposal of a mass of physical force sufficient to crush any partial resistance, and demand only to be secured against any very general or simultaneous opposition on the part of the community. To make this sure, they are obliged to maintain a strong purchase upon the public mind, and to chain it down to the level of submission—to plant within it feelings which may neutralize all hatred of slavery, and facilitate the business of spoliation. For this purpose the sacerdotal class are most precisely and most happily cut out. By their influence over the moral sentiments, they place implicit submission among the first of all human duties. They infuse the deepest reverence for temporal power, by considering the existing authorities as established and consecrated by the immaterial Autocrat above, and as identified with his divine majesty. The duty of mankind towards the earthly government becomes thus the same as duty to God—that is, an unvarying "prostration both of the understanding and will." Besides this direct debasement of the moral faculties for the purpose of assuring non-resistance, the supernatural terrors, and the *extra-experimental* belief, which the priesthood are so industrious in diffusing, all tend to the very same result. They produce that mistrust, alarm, and insecurity, which disposes a man to bless himself in any little fragment of present enjoyment, while it stifles all aspirations for future improvement and even all ideas of its practicability.

Such is the tacit and surreptitious, though incessant and effectual, operation on the public sentiment, by which the priest-hood keep down all disposition on the part of mankind to oppose the inroads of their governors. Their influence is perhaps greater when they preach thus on behalf of the government, than on their own. Because in the former case, the interest which they have in the doctrine is not so obvious, and they appear like impartial counsellors, inculcating a behaviour of which they themselves are first to set the example.

The earthly ruler, on the other hand, amply repays the co-operation which he has thus derived. The mental (or psychagogical[5]) machinery of the priesthood is very excellent; but they are unhappily deficient in physical force. Hence the protection of the earthly potentate is of most essential utility to a class so defectively provided in this main point. The coercion which he supplies is all sanctified by the holy name of religion, in defence of which it is resorted to; and he is extolled, while thus engaged, as the disinterested servant of the invisible Being. He is therefore permitted to employ, in behalf of religion, an extent and disposition of force which would have provoked indignation and revolt, on any other account.

The utmost extent of physical force, which circumstances will permit, is in this manner put forward, to smother any symptom of impiety, or even of dissent from the sacerdotal dogmas: Irreligion and heresy become crimes of the deepest dye, and the class are thus secured, in their task of working on the public mind, from all competition or contest. Under the protection of such powerful artillery, this corps of sappers and miners carries on a tranquil, but effectual, progress in the trenches.

Nor is it merely a negative aid which the earthly governor extends to them. He extorts from the people, in their favour, a large compulsory tribute, in order to maintain them in affluence and in worldly credit; thus securing to them an additional purchase upon the public sentiment, and confirming his own safety from resistance. Under no other pretence could he induce the people to pay taxes, specially for the purpose of quartering throughout the country a standing army of advocates to check and counteract all opinions unfavourable to himself. They may be brought to this sacrifice in behalf of a sacerdotal class, whose interest, by the forced provision thus obtained, becomes still more closely identified with that of the earthly ruler.

One of the most noxious properties therefore, in the profession of men to which natural religion gives birth, is its coincidence and league with the sinister interests of earth—a coincidence so entire, as to secure unity of design on the part of both, without any necessity for special confederation, and therefore more mischievously efficient than it would have proved had the deed of partnership been open and proclaimed. Prostration and plunder of the community is indeed the common end of both. The only point upon which there can be any dissension, is about the partition of the spoil—and quarrels of this nature have occasionally taken place, in cases where the passive state of the people has obviated all apprehension of resistance. In general, however, the necessity of strict amity has been too visible to admit of much discord, and the division of the spoil has been carried on tranquilly, though in different ratios, according to the tone of the public mind.

PART 3

THE AMERICAN ENLIGHTENMENT

Selections

THOMAS JEFFERSON

[Thomas Jefferson (1743–1826), author of the Declaration of Independence and third president of the United States (1801–1809), devoted a lifetime to the study of religion and of its relation to society and government. As a member of the Virginia House of Delegates, he wrote an "Act of Establishing Religious Freedom" (1777); it was not submitted to the House until 1779 and was enacted only in 1786; it guaranteed freedom of thought on religious matters and forbade the state from exacting a tax on citizens to support religious institutions. These concerns led Jefferson and others to insist on the addition of the First Amendment to the US Constitution. In letters, Jefferson frequently declared himself a materialist who rejected the notion of any immaterial or spiritual substances, including an immaterial god. He maintained an admiration for the morals espoused by Jesus but rejected biblical miracles and sought to read the Bible as a historical document no different from the works of the Greek and Roman historians.

In the following extracts, Jefferson expounds the details of his religious views. In *Notes on the State of Virginia* (1782), he argues that without freedom of thought in religion, the state must become a tyranny. In his letter to the Danbury Baptist Association (1802), he calls for a "wall of separation" between church and state. In letters written after his presidency, he tells of how he was accused of being an "infidel" and of his understanding of the historical role of Jesus.]

(1) *NOTES ON THE STATE OF VIRGINIA* (1782)

The first settlers in this country were emigrants from England, of the English church, just at a point of time when it was flushed with complete victory over the religious of all other persuasions. Possessed, as they became, of the powers of making, administering and executing the laws, they shewed equal intolerance in this country with their Presbyterian brethren, who had emigrated to the northern government. The poor Quakers were flying from persecution in England. They cast their eyes on these new countries as asylums of civil and religious freedom; but they found them free only for the reigning sect. Several acts of the Virginia assembly of 1659, 1662, and 1693, had made it penal in parents to refuse to have their children baptized; had prohibited the unlawful assembling of Quakers; had made it penal for any master of a vessel to bring a Quaker into the state; had ordered those already here, and such as should come thereafter, to be imprisoned till they should abjure the country; provided a milder punishment for their first and second return, but death for their third; had inhibited all persons from suffering their meetings in or near their houses, entertaining them individually, or disposing of books which supported their tenets. If no capital execution took place here, as did in New-England, it was not owing to the moderation of the church, or spirit of the legislature, as may be inferred from the law itself; but to historical circumstances which have not been handed down to us. The Anglicans retained full possession of the country about a century. Other opinions began then to creep in, and the great care of the government to support their own church, having begotten an equal degree of indolence in its clergy, two thirds of the people had become dissenters at the commencement of the present revolution. The laws indeed were still oppressive on them, but the spirit of the one party had subsided into moderation, and of the other had risen to a degree of determination which commanded respect.

The present state of our laws on the subject of religion is this. The convention of May 1776, in their declaration of rights, declared it to be a truth, and a natural right, that the exercise of religion should be free; but when they proceeded to form on that declaration the ordinance of government, instead of taking up every principle declared in the bill of rights, and guarding it by legislative sanction, they passed over that which asserted our religious rights, leaving them as they found them. The same convention, however, when they met as a member of the general assembly in October 1776, repealed all *acts of parliament* which had rendered criminal the maintaining any opinions in matters of religion, the forbearing to repair to church, and the exercising any mode of worship; and suspended the laws giving salaries to the clergy, which suspension was made perpetual in October 1779. Statutory oppressions in religion being thus wiped away, we remain at present under those only imposed by the common law, or by our own acts of assembly. At the common law, *heresy* was a capital offence, punishable by burning. Its definition was left to the ecclesiastical judges, before whom the conviction was, till the statute of the 1 El. c. 1.[1] circumscribed it, by declaring that nothing should be deemed heresy but what had been so determined by authority of the canonical scriptures, or by one of the four first general councils, or by some other council having for the grounds of their declaration the express and plain words of the scriptures. Heresy, thus circumscribed, being an offence at the common law, our act of assembly of October 1777, c. 17 gives cognizance of it to the general court, by declaring that the jurisdiction of that court shall be general in all matters at the common law. The execution is by the writ *De haeretico comburendo* [*On Burning Heretics*]. By our own act of assembly of 1705, c. 30, if a person brought up in the christian religion denies the being of a God, or the trinity, or asserts there are more Gods than one, or denies the christian religion to be true, or the scriptures to be of divine authority, he is punishable on the first offence by incapacity to hold any office or employment ecclesiastical, civil, or military; on the second by disability to sue, to take any gift or legacy, to be guardian, executor or administrator, and by three years imprisonment, without bail. A father's right to the custody of his own children being founded in law on his right of guardianship, this being taken away, they may of course be severed from him and put, by the authority of a court, into more orthodox hands. This is a summary view of that religious slavery under which a people have been willing to remain who have lavished their lives and fortunes for the establishment of their civil freedom. The error seems not sufficiently eradicated, that the operations of the mind, as well as the acts of the body, are subject to the coercion of the laws. But our rulers can have authority over such natural rights, only as we have submitted to them. The rights of conscience we never submitted, we could not submit. We are answerable for them to our God. The legitimate powers of government extend to such acts only as are injurious to others. But it does me no injury for my neighbor to say there are twenty gods, or no god. It neither picks my pocket nor breaks my leg. If it be said his testimony in a court of justice cannot be relied on, reject it then, and be the stigma on him. Constraint may make him worse by making him a hypocrite, but it will never make him a truer man. It may fix him obstinately in his errors, but will not cure them. Reason and free inquiry are the only effectual agents against error. Give a loose to them, they will support the true religion by bringing every false one to their tribunal, to the test of their investigation. They are the natural enemies of error, and of error only. Had not the Roman government permitted free inquiry, christianity could never have been introduced. Had not free inquiry been indulged, at the æra of the reformation, the corruptions of christianity could not have been purged away. If it be restrained now, the present corruptions will be protected, and new ones encouraged. Was the government to prescribe to us our medicine and diet, our bodies would be in such keeping as our souls are now. Thus in France the emetic was once forbidden as a medicine, and the potatoe as an article of food. Government is just as infallible, too, when it fixes systems in physics. Galileo was sent to the inquisition for affirming that the earth was a sphere; the government had declared it to be as flat as a trencher, and Galileo was obliged to abjure his error.[2] This error however at length prevailed, the earth became a globe, and Descartes declared it was whirled round its axis by a vortex. The government in which he lived was wise enough to see that this was no question of civil jurisdiction, or we should all have been involved by authority in vortices. In fact the vortices have been exploded, and the Newtonian principle of gravitation is now more firmly established, on the basis of reason, than it would be were the government to step in and to make it an article of necessary faith. Reason and experiment have been indulged, and error has fled before them. It is error alone which needs the support of government. Truth can stand by itself. Subject opinion to coercion: whom will you make your inquisitors? Fallible men; men governed by bad passions, by private as well as public reasons. And why subject it to coercion? To produce uniformity. But is uniformity of opinion desireable? No more than of face and stature. Introduce the bed of Procrustes then, and as there is danger that the large men may beat the small, make us all of a size, by lopping the former and stretching the latter. Difference of opinion is advantageous in religion. The several sects perform the office of a Censor morum[3] over each other. Is uniformity attainable? Millions of innocent men, women and children, since the introduction of Christianity, have been burnt, tortured, fined, imprisoned: yet we have not advanced one inch towards uniformity. What has been the effect of coercion? To make one half the world fools, and the other half hypocrites. To support roguery and error all over the earth. Let us reflect that it is inhabited by a thousand millions of people. That these profess probably a thousand different systems of religion. That ours is but one of that thousand. That if there be but one right, and ours that one, we should wish to see the 999 wandering sects gathered into the fold of truth. But against such a majority we cannot effect this by force. Reason and persuasion are the only practicable instruments. To make way for these, free inquiry must be indulged; and how can we wish others to indulge it while we refuse it ourselves. But every state, says an inquisitor, has established some religion. "No two, say I, have established the same." Is this a proof of the infallibility of establishments? Our sister states of Pennsylvania and New York, however, have long subsisted without any establishment at all. The experiment was new and doubtful when they made it. It has answered beyond conception. They flourish infinitely. Religion is well supported; of various kinds indeed, but all good enough; all sufficient to preserve peace and order: or if a sect arises whose tenets would subvert morals, good sense has fair play, and reasons and laughs it out of doors, without suffering the state to be troubled with it. They do not hang more malefactors than we do. They are not more disturbed with religious dissentions. On the contrary, their harmony is unparalleled, and can be ascribed to nothing but their unbounded tolerance, because there is no other circumstance in which they differ from every nation on earth. They have made the happy discovery, that the way to silence religious disputes, is to take no notice of them. Let us too give this experiment fair play, and get rid, while we may, of those tyrannical laws. It is true we are as yet secured against them by the spirit of the times. I doubt whether the people of this country would suffer an execution for heresy, or a three years imprisonment for not comprehending the mysteries of the trinity. But is the spirit of the people an infallible, a permanent reliance? Is it government? Is this the kind of protection we receive in return for the rights we give up? Besides, the spirit of the times may alter, will alter. Our rulers will become corrupt, our people careless. A single zealot may commence persecutor, and better men be his victims. It can never be too often repeated, that the time for fixing every essential right on a legal basis is while our rulers are honest, and ourselves united. From the conclusion of this war we shall be going down hill. It will not then be necessary to resort every moment to the people for support. They will be forgotten therefore, and their rights disregarded. They will forget themselves, but in the sole faculty of making money, and will never think of uniting to effect a due respect for their rights. The shackles, therefore, which shall not be knocked off at the conclusion of this war, will remain on us long, will be made heavier and heavier, till our rights shall revive or expire in a convulsion.

(2) LETTER TO PETER CARR[4] (AUGUST 10, 1787)

Religion. Your reason is now mature enough to examine this object. In the first place divest yourself of all bias in favour of novelty & singularity of opinion. Indulge them in any other subject rather than that of religion. It is too important, & the consequences of error may be too serious. On the other hand shake off all the fears & servile prejudices under which weak minds are servilely crouched. Fix reason firmly in her seat, and call to her tribunal every fact, every opinion. Question with boldness even the existence of a god; because, if there be one, he must more approve of the homage of reason, than that of blindfolded fear. You will naturally examine first the religion of your own country. Read the bible then, as you would read Livy or Tacitus. The facts which are within the ordinary course of nature you will believe on the authority of the writer, as you do those of the same kind in Livy & Tacitus. The testimony of the writer weighs in their favor in one scale, and their not being against the laws of nature does not weigh against them. But those facts in the bible which contradict the laws of nature, must be examined with more care, and under a variety of faces. Here you must recur to the pretensions of the writer to inspiration from god. Examine upon what evidence his pretensions are founded, and whether that evidence is so strong as that its falsehood would be more improbable than a change in the laws of nature in the case he relates. For example in the book of Joshua we are told the sun stood still several hours. Were we to read that fact in Livy or Tacitus we should class it with their showers of blood, speaking of statues, beasts, &c. But it is said that the writer of that book was inspired. Examine therefore candidly what evidence there is of his having been inspired. The pretension is entitled to your inquiry, because millions believe it. On the other hand you are astronomer enough to know how contrary it is to the law of nature that a body revolving on its axis as the earth does, should have stopped, should not by that sudden stoppage have prostrated animals, trees, buildings, and should after a certain time have resumed its revolution, & that without a second general prostration. Is this arrest of the earth's motion, or the evidence which affirms it, most within the law of probabilities? You will next read the new testament. It is the history of a personage called Jesus. Keep in your eye the opposite pretensions 1. of those who say he was begotten by god, born of a virgin, suspended & reversed the laws of nature at will, & ascended bodily into heaven: and 2. of those who say he was a man of illegitimate birth, of a benevolent heart, enthusiastic mind, who set out without pretensions to divinity, ended in believing them, & was punished capitally for sedition by being gibbeted according to the Roman law which punished the first commission of that offence by whipping, & the second by exile or death *in furcâ* [on the cross]. See this law in the Digest Lib. 48. tit. 19. §. 28. 3. & Lipsius Lib. 2. de cruce. cap. 2. These questions are examined in the books I have mentioned under the head of religion, & several others. They will assist you in your inquiries, but keep your reason firmly on the watch in reading them all. Do not be frightened from this inquiry by any fear of it's consequences. If it ends in a belief that there is no god, you will find incitements to virtue in the comfort & pleasantness you feel in it's exercise, and the love of others which it will procure you. If you find reason to believe there is a god, a consciousness that you are acting under his eye, & that he approves you, will be a vast additional incitement; if that there be a future state, the hope of a happy existence in that increases the appetite to deserve it; if that Jesus was also a god, you will be comforted by a belief of his aid and love. In fine, I repeat that you must lay aside all prejudice on both sides, & neither believe nor reject anything because any other persons, or description of persons have rejected or believed it. Your own reason is the only oracle given you by heaven, and you are answerable not for the rightness but uprightness of the decision.

(3) LETTER TO THE DANBURY BAPTIST ASSOCIATION (JANUARY 1, 1802)[5]

GENTLEMEN

The affectionate sentiments of esteem and approbation which you are so good as to express towards me, on behalf of the Danbury Baptist association, give me the highest satisfaction. My duties dictate a faithful & zealous pursuit of the interests of my constituents, & in proportion as they are persuaded of my fidelity to those duties, the discharge of them becomes more and more pleasing.

Believing with you that religion is a matter which lies solely between Man & his God, that he owes account to none other for his faith or his worship, that the legitimate powers of government reach actions only, & not opinions, I contemplate with sovereign reverence that act of the whole American people which declared that *their* legislature should "make no law respecting an establishment of religion, or prohibiting the free exercise thereof," thus building a wall of separation between Church & State. Adhering to this expression of the supreme will of the nation in behalf of the rights of conscience, I shall see with sincere satisfaction the progress of those sentiments which tend to restore to man all his natural rights, convinced he has no natural right in opposition to his social duties.

(4) LETTER TO MRS. M. MADISON SMITH (AUGUST 6, 1816)

I often call to mind the occasions of knowing your worth, which the societies of Washington furnished; and none more than those derived from your much valued visit to Monticello. I recognize the same motives of goodness in the solicitude you express on the rumor supposed to proceed from a letter of mine to Charles Thomson, on the subject of the Christian religion.[6] It is true that, in writing to the translator of the Bible and Testament, that subject was mentioned; but equally so that no adherence to any particular mode of Christianity was there expressed, nor any change of opinions suggested. A change from what? the priests indeed have heretofore thought proper to ascribe to me religious, or rather anti-religious sentiments, of their own fabric, but such as soothed their resentments against the act of Virginia for establishing religious freedom. They wished him to be thought atheist, deist, or devil, who could advocate freedom from their religious dictations. But I have ever thought religion a concern purely between our God and our consciences, for which we were accountable to him, and not to the priests. I never told my own religion, nor scrutinized that of another. I never attempted to make a convert, nor wished to change another's creed. I have ever judged of the religion of others by their lives, and by this test, my dear Madam, I have been satisfied yours must be an excellent one, to have produced a life of such exemplary virtue and correctness. For it is in our lives, and not from our words, that our religion must be read. By the same test the world must judge me. But this does not satisfy the priesthood. They must have a positive, a declared assent to all their interested absurdities. My opinion is that there would never have been an infidel, if there had never been a priest. The artificial structures they have built on the purest of all moral systems, for the purpose of deriving from it pence and power, revolts those who think for themselves, and who read in that system only what is really there. These, therefore, they brand with such nick-names as their enmity cho[o]ses gratuitously to impute. I have left the world, in silence, to judge of causes from their effects; and I am consoled in this course, my dear friend, when I perceive the candor with which I am judged by your justice and discernment; and that, notwithstanding the slanders of the saints, my fellow citizens have thought me worthy of trusts. The imputations of irreligion having spent their force; they think an imputation of change might now be turned to account as a bolster for their duperies. I shall leave them, as heretofore, to grope on in the dark.

(5) LETTER TO WILLIAM SHORT (AUGUST 4, 1820)

I owe you a letter for your favor of June the 29th, which was received in due time; and there being no subject of the day, of particular interest, I will make this a supplement to mine of April the 13th. My aim in that was, to justify the character of Jesus against the fictions of his pseudo-followers, which have exposed him to the inference of being an impostor. For if we could believe that he really countenanced the follies, the falsehoods, and the charlatanism which his biographers father on him, and admit the misconstructions, interpolations, and theorizations of the fathers of the early, and fanatics of the latter ages, the conclusion would be irresistible by every sound mind, that he was an impostor. I give no credit to their falsifications of his actions and doctrines, and to rescue his character, the postulate in my letter asked only what is granted in reading every other historian. When Livy and Siculus,[7] for example, tell us things which coincide with our experience of the order of nature, we credit them on their word, and place their narrations among the records of credible history. But when they tell us of calves speaking, of statues sweating blood, and other things against the course of nature, we reject these as fables not belonging to history. In like manner, when an historian, speaking of a character well known and established on satisfactory testimony, imputes to it things incompatible with that character, we reject them without hesitation, and assent to that only of which we have better evidence. Had Plutarch informed us that Cæsar and Cicero passed their whole lives in religious exercises, and abstinence from the affairs of the world, we should reject what was so inconsistent with their established characters, still crediting what he relates in conformity with our ideas of them. So again, the superlative wisdom of Socrates is testified by all antiquity, and placed on ground not to be questioned. When, therefore, Plato puts into his mouth such paralogisms, such quibbles on words, and sophisms as a school boy would be ashamed of, we conclude they were the whimsies of Plato's own foggy brain, and acquit Socrates of puerilities so unlike his character. (Speaking of Plato, I will add, that no writer, ancient or modern, has bewildered the world with more *ignes fatui* [foolish fires],[8] than this renowned philosopher, in Ethics, in Politics, and Physics. In the latter, to specify a single example, compare his views of the animal economy, in his

Timaeus, with those of Mrs. Bryan in her Conversations on Chemistry,[9] and weigh the science of the canonized philosopher against the good sense of the unassuming lady. But Plato's visions have furnished a basis for endless systems of mystical theology, and he is therefore all but adopted as a Christian saint. It is surely time for men to think for themselves, and to throw off the authority of names so artificially magnified. But to return from this parenthesis.) I say, that this free exercise of reason is all I ask for the vindication of the character of Jesus. We find in the writings of his biographers matter of two distinct descriptions. First, a groundwork of vulgar ignorance, of things impossible, of superstitions, fanaticisms, and fabrications. Intermixed with these, again, are sublime ideas of the Supreme Being, aphorisms, and precepts of the purest morality and benevolence, sanctioned by a life of humility, innocence and simplicity of manners, neglect of riches, absence of worldly ambition and honors, with an eloquence and persuasiveness which have not been surpassed. These could not be inventions of the grovelling authors who relate them. They are far beyond the powers of their feeble minds. They show that there was a character, the subject of their history, whose splendid conceptions were above all suspicion of being interpolations from their hands. Can we be at a loss in separating such materials, and ascribing each to its genuine author? The difference is obvious to the eye and to the understanding, and we may read as we run to each his part; and I will venture to affirm, that he who, as I have done, will undertake to winnow this grain from the chaff, will find it not to require a moment's consideration. The parts fall asunder of themselves, as would those of an image of metal and clay.

There are, I acknowledge, passages not free from objection, which we may, with probability, ascribe to Jesus himself; but claiming indulgence from the circumstances under which he acted. His object was the reformation of some articles in the religion of the Jews, as taught by Moses. That sect had presented the object of their worship, a being of terrific character, cruel, vindictive, capricious, and unjust. Jesus, taking for his type the best qualities of the human head and heart, wisdom, justice, goodness, and adding to them power, ascribed all of these, but in infinite perfection, to the Supreme Being, and formed him really worthy of their adoration. Moses had either not believed in a future state of existence, or had not thought it essential to be explicitly taught to his people. Jesus inculcated that doctrine with emphasis and precision. Moses had bound the Jews to many idle ceremonies, mummeries, and observances, of no effect towards producing the social utilities which constitute the essence of virtue; Jesus exposed their futility and insignificance. The one instilled into his people the most anti-social spirit toward other nations; the other preached philanthropy and universal charity and benevolence. The office of reformer of the superstitions of a nation, is ever dangerous. Jesus had to walk on the perilous confines of reason and religion; and a step to right or left might place him within the grasp of the priests of the superstition, a blood-thirsty race, as cruel and remorseless as the being whom they represented as the family God of Abraham, of Isaac and of Jacob, and the local God of Israel. They were constantly laying snares, too, to entangle him in the web of the law. He was justifiable, therefore, in avoiding these by evasions, by sophisms, by misconstructions and misapplications of scraps of the prophets, and in defending himself with these their own weapons, as sufficient, *ad homines* [to human beings], at least. That Jesus did not mean to impose himself on mankind as the son of God, physically speaking, I have been convinced by the writings of men more learned than myself in that lore. But that he might conscientiously believe himself inspired from above, is very possible. The whole religion of the Jew, inculcated on him from his infancy, was founded in the belief of divine inspiration. The fumes of the most disordered imaginations were recorded in their religious code, as special communications of the Deity; and as it could not but happen that, in the course of ages, events would now and then turn up to which some of these vague rhapsodies might be accommodated by the aid of allegories, figures, types, and other tricks upon words, they have not only preserved their credit with the Jews of all subsequent times, but are the foundation of much of the religions of those who have schismatised from them. Elevated by the enthusiasm of a warm and pure heart, conscious of the high strains of an eloquence which had not been taught him, he might readily mistake the coruscations of his own fine genius for inspirations of an higher order. This belief carried, therefore, no more personal imputation, than the belief of Socrates, that himself was under the care and admonitions of a guardian Dæmon. And how many of our wisest men still believe in the reality of these inspirations, while perfectly sane on all other subjects. Excusing, therefore, on these considerations, those passages in the gospels which seem to bear marks of weakness in Jesus, ascribing to him what alone is consistent with the great and pure character of which the same writings furnish proofs, and to their proper authors their own trivialities and imbecilities, I think myself authorized to conclude the purity and distinction of his character, in opposition to the impostures which those authors would fix upon him; and that the postulate of my former letter is no more than is granted in all other historical works.

From *Reason, the Only Oracle of Man* (1784)

ETHAN ALLEN

[Ethan Allen (1738–1789) was a leader of the American Revolution. A militia he organized, called the Green Mountain Boys, captured Fort Ticonderoga in 1775. Later that year he was captured by the British after a failed attack on Montreal; he was released in 1778 and continued to serve in the Continental Army. He was also much involved in the political affairs of the newly established state of Vermont. A few years after the American Revolution ended, he published the fiery tract *Reason, the Only Oracle of Man* (1784), which was a harsh denunciation of Christianity. In the following extract from that work, Allen condemns the prophecies in the Old and New Testaments as vague and unsubstantiated, concluding with an attack on the purportedly prophetic dreams of the founder of the Shaker religious sect.]

SECTION I.

The vagueness and unintelligibleness of the Prophecies, render them incapable of proving Revelation.

Prophecy is by some thought to be miraculous, and by others to be supernatural, and there are others, who indulge themselves in an opinion, that they amount to no more than mere political conjectures. Some nations have feigned an intercourse with good spirits by the art of divination; and others with evil ones by the art of magic; and most nations have pretended to an intercourse with the world of spirits both ways.

The Romans trusted much to their sibyline oracles and soothsayers; the Babylonians to their magicians, and astrologers; the Egyptians and Persians to their magicians; and the Jews to their seers or prophets: and all nations and individuals, discover an anxiety for an intercourse with the world of spirits; which lays a foundation for artful and designing men, to impose upon them. But if the foregoing arguments in chapter sixth, respecting the natural impossibility of an intercourse of any unbodied or imperceptible mental beings with mankind, are true, then the foretelling of future events can amount to nothing more than political illusion. For prophecy as well as all other sort of prognostication must be supernaturally inspired, or it could be no more than judging of future events from mere probability or guess-work, as the astronomers ingenuously confess in their calculations, by saying; "Judgment of the weather, &c." So also respecting astrology, provided there is any such thing as futurity to be learned from it, it would be altogether a natural discovery; for neither astronomy or astrology claim any thing of a miraculous or supernatural kind, but their calculations are meant to be predicated on the order and course of nature, with which our senses are conversant, and with which inspiration or the mere co-operation of spirits is not pretended to act a part. So also concerning prophecy, if it be considered to be merely natural, (we will not at present dispute whether it is true or false) upon this position it stands on the footing of probability or mere conjecture and uncertainty. But as to the doctrine of any supernatural agency of the divine mind on ours, which is commonly called inspiration, it has been sufficiently confuted in sixth chapter; which arguments need not be repeated, nor does it concern my system to settle the question, whether prophecy should be denominated miraculous or supernatural, inasmuch as both these doctrines have been confuted; though it is my opinion, that were we to trace the notion of supernatural to its source, it would finally terminate in that which is denominated miraculous; for that which is above or beyond nature, if it has any positive existence, it must be miraculous.

The writings of the prophets are most generally so loose, vague and indeterminate in their meaning, or in the grammar of their present translation, that the prophecies will as well answer to events in one period of time, as in another; and are equally applicable to a variety of events, which have and are still taking place in the world, and are liable to so many different interpretations, that they are incapable of being understood or explained, except upon arbitrary principles, and therefore cannot be admitted as a proof of revelation; *as for instance, "it shall come to pass in the last days, saith God"* [Acts 2:17]. Who can understand the accomplishment of the prophecies, that are expressed after this sort? for every day in its turn has been, and will in its succession be the last day; and if we advert to the express words of the prophecy, to wit, *"the last days,"* there will be an uncertain plurality *"of last days,"* which must be understood to be short of a month, or a year; or it should have been expressed thus, and it shall come to pass in the last months or years, instead of days: and if it had mentioned last years, it would be a just construction to suppose, that it included a less number of years than a century; but as the prophecy mentions *"last days,"* we are at a loss, which among the plurality of them to assign for the fulfilling of the prophecy.

Furthermore, we cannot learn from the prophecy, in what month, year, or any other part of duration those last days belong; so that we can never tell when such vague prophecies are to take place, they therefore remain the arbitrary prerogative of fanatics to prescribe their events in any age or period of time, when their distempered fancies may think most eligible: There are other prophecies still more abstruse; *to wit, "And one said unto the man clothed in linen, which was upon the waters of the river, how long shall it be to the end of these wonders? and I heard the man clothed in linen, which was upon the waters of the river, when he held up his right hand and his left hand unto Heaven, and sware by him that liveth forever, that it should be for a time, times and an half"* [Daniel 12:6–7]. The question in the prophecy is asked *"how long shall it be to the end of these wonders?"* and the answer is given with the solenmity of an oath, *"it shall be for a time, times and a half."* A *time* is an indefinite part of duration, and so are *times*, and the third description of time is as indefinite as either of the former descriptions of it; *to wit, "and an half;"* that is to say, *half a time.* There is no certain term given in any or either of the three descriptions of the end of the wonders alluded to, whereby any or all of them together are capable of computation, as there is no certain period marked out to begin or end a calculation. To compute an indefinite *time* in the single number or quantity of duration is impossible, and to compute an uncertain plurality of such indefinite *times* is equally perplexing and impracticable; and lastly, to define *half a time* by any possible succession of its parts, is a contradiction, for *half a time* includes no time at all; inasmuch as the smallest conception or possible moment or criterion of duration, is a *time*, or otherwise, by the addition of ever so many of those parts together they would not prolong a period; so that there is not, and cannot be such a part of time, as *half a time*, for be it supposed to be ever so momentous, yet if it includes any part of duration, it is a *time*, and not *half a time*. Had the prophet said half a year, half a day, or half a minute, he would have spoken intelligibly; but *half a time* has no existence at all, and consequently no period could ever possibly arrive in the succession or order of time, when there could be an end to the wonders alluded to; and in this sense only, the prophecy is intelligible; to wit, that it will never come to pass.

The revelation of St. John the divine, involves the subject of time, if possible, in still greater inconsistencies, viz. *"and to the woman was given two wings of a great eagle, that she might fly into the wilderness, into her place: Where she is nourished for a time, and times and half a time"* [Rev. 12:14]. *"And the angel which I saw stand upon the sea and upon the earth lifted up his hands to heaven, and sware by him that liveth for ever and ever, who created heaven and the things that therein are, and the earth and the things that therein are, and the sea and the things which are therein, that there should be time no longer"* [Rev. 10:5–6].—Had this tremendous oath been verified there could have been no farther disputations on the calculation of *"time and times and half a time,"* (or about any thing else) for that its succession would have reached its last and final period at that important crisis when time should have been "no longer." The solar system must have ceased its motions, from which we compute the succession of time, and the race of man would have been extinct; for as long as they may be supposed to exist, time must of necessary consequence have existed also; and since the course of nature, including the generation of mankind, has been continued from the time of the positive denunciation of the angel to this day, we may safely conclude, that his interference in the system of nature, was perfectly romantic.

The apostle Peter, at the first christian pentecost, objecting to the accusation of their being drunk with new wine, explains the prophecy of the prophet Joel, who prophesied of the events which were to take place in the last days, as coming to pass at that early period; his words are handed down to us as follows: *"But this is that which is spoken by the prophet Joel, and it shall come to pass*

in the last days, saith God, that I will pour out of my spirit upon all flesh, and your
sons and your daughters shall prophecy, and your young men shall see visions, and your
old men shall dream dreams" [Acts 2:16–17; cf. Joel 2:28].

The history of the out-pouring of the spirit at the pentecost, admitting
it to have been a fact, would have been very inadequate to the prophetical
prediction, *viz. I will pour out my spirit upon all flesh*; the most favourable construction is that the prophet meant human flesh, *i. e.* all human flesh; but
instead of a universal effusion of the spirit, it appears to have been restricted to
a select number, who were collected together at Jerusalem, and the concourse
of spectators thought them to be delirious. It may however be supposed, that
St. Peter was a better judge of the accomplishment of the prophecy than I am:
well then, admitting his application of the prophecy of the last days to take
place at the first pentecost; it being now more than seventeen hundred years
ago, they consequently could not have been the last days.

Still a query arises, whether every of the prophecies, which were predicted
to be fulfilled in the last days, must not have been accomplished at that time; or
whether any of the prophecies thus expressed are still to be completed, by any
events which may in future take place; or by any which have taken place since
those last days called pentecost; or whether any prophecy whatever can be fulfilled more than once; and if so, how many times; or how it is possible for us, out
of the vast variety of events (in which there is so great a similarity) which one
in particular to ascribe to its right prediction among the numerous prophecies.

Furthermore, provided some of the prophecies should point out some particular events, which have since taken place, there might have been previous
grounds of probability, that such or such events would in the ordinary course
of things come to pass; *for instance*, it is no ways extraordinary, that the prophet
Jeremiah should be able to predict that Nebuchadnezzar king of Babylon
should take Jerusalem, when we consider the power of the Babylonish empire
at that time, and the feebleness of the Jews. *"The word, which came to Jeremiah*
from the Lord, when Nebuchadnezzar king of Babylon and all his army, and all the
kingdoms of the earth of his dominion, and all the people fought against Jerusalem, and
against all the cities thereof, saying, thus saith the Lord the God of Israel, go and speak
unto Zedekiah king of Judah, and tell him, thus saith the Lord, behold, I will give
this city Jerusalem into the hand of the king of Babylon" [Jer. 34:1–2]. No politi-

cians could at the time of the prediction be much at a loss respecting the fate of Jerusalem. Nor would it be at all evidential to any candid and ingenious enquirer, that God had any manner of agency in fabricating the prophecies, though some of them should seem to decypher future events, as they might, to human appearance, turn out right, merely from accident or contingency. It is very improbable, or rather incompatible with human nature, that the prophecy of Micah will ever come to pass, who predicts that *'they,'* speaking of mankind, *"shall beat their swords into ploughshares, and their spears into pruning-hooks; nation shall not lift up sword against nation, neither shall they learn war any more"* [Isa. 2:4; Micah 4:3]. Some of the prophecies are so apparently contradictory, that they contain their own confutation; as for instance, the prophecy of Micaiah contained in the book of Chronicles, which probably is as absurd as any thing that is to be met with in story, *"and when he was come unto the king, the king said unto him, Micaiah, shall we go to Ramoth Gilead to battle, or shall I forbear? and he said go ye up and prosper, and they shall be delivered into your hand, and the king said unto him, how many times shall I adjure thee, that thou tell me nothing, but that which is true in the name of the Lord? then he said I did see all Israel scattered upon the mountains, as sheep that have no shepherd, and the Lord said, these have no master, let them return therefore, every man to his house in peace: and the king said unto Jehoshaphat, did not I tell thee, that he would prophecy no good concerning me but evil."* *"Again he said, therefore hear the word of the Lord—I saw the Lord sitting upon his throne, and all the host of Heaven standing on his right hand and on his left, and the Lord said who shall entice Ahab, King of Israel, that he may go up and fall at Ramoth Gilead, and one spake saying after this manner, and another saying after that manner, then there came out a spirit and stood before the Lord, and said I will entice him, and the Lord said unto him wherewith? And he said I will go forth and be a lying spirit in the mouth of all his prophets, and the Lord said thou shalt entice him and thou shalt also prevail, go out and do even so now therefore behold the Lord hath put a lying spirit in the mouth of these thy prophets and the Lord hath spoken evil against thee"* [2 Chron. 18:14–22]. It is observable that the prophet at first predicted the prosperity of Ahab, saying, *"go ye up and prosper, and they shall be delivered into your hand."* But after a little adjurement by the king, he alters his prediction and prophecies diametrically the reverse. What is more certain than that the event of the expedition against Ramoth Gilead must have comported with the one or the other of his prophecies? Certain it was, that Ahab would take it or not take it, he must either prosper or not prosper, as there could be no third way or mean between these two; and it appears that the prophet was determined to be in the right of it by his prophecying both ways. It further appears from his prophecy, that there was a great consultation in Heaven to entice Ahab King of Israel to his destruction, and that a certain lying spirit came and stood before the Lord, and proposed to him to go out and be a lying spirit in the mouth of the king's prophets. But what is the most incredible is, that God should countenance it, and give him positive orders to falsify the truth to the other prophets.—It appears that Micaiah in his first prophecy, viz: *"Go up to Ramoth Gilead and prosper, and they shall be delivered into your hand,"* acted in concert with the lying spirit which stood before the Lord, but afterwards acted the treacherous part by prophecying the truth, which, if we may credit his account, was in direct opposition to the scheme of Heaven.

SECTION II.

The contentions which subsisted between the Prophets respecting their veracity, and their inconsistencies with one another, and with the nature of things, and their omission in teaching the doctrine of immortality, precludes the divinity of their Prophecies.

Whoever examines the writings of the prophets will discover a spirit of strife and contention among them; they would charge each other with fallacy and deception; disputations of this kind are plentifully interspersed through the writings of the prophets; we will transcribe a few of those passages out of many: *"thus saith the Lord[: Woe un]to the foolish prophets that follow their own spirit, and have found nothing, they have seen vanity and lying divination, saying the Lord saith, and the Lord hath not sent them, and they have made others to hope that they would confirm the word"* [Ezek. 13:3, 6]. And in another place, *"I have not sent these prophets yet they ran; I have not spoken unto them yet they prophecy"* [Jer. 23:21]. Again, *"I have heard what the prophets said that prophecy lies in my name, saying, I have dreamed, I have dreamed, yet they are the prophets of the deceit of their own hearts"* [Jer. 23:25–26]. And again, *"Yea they are greedy dogs, which can never have enough, and they are shepherds that cannot understand; they all look to their own way, every one for his gain from his quarter"* [Isa. 56:11].

It being the case that there was such a strife among the prophets to recommend themselves to the people, and every art and dissimulation having been practised by them to gain power and superiority, all which artifice was to be judged of by the great vulgar, or in some instances by the political views of the Jewish Sanhedrim, how could those who were cotemporaries with the several prophets, distinguish the premised true prophets from the false? Much less, how can we, who live more than seventeen hundred years since the last of them, be able to distinguish them apart? And yet, without the knowledge of this distinction, we cannot with propriety give credit to any of them, even admitting there were some true prophets among them. Nor is it possible for us to know but that their very institution was merely a reach of policy of the Israelitish and Judaic governments, the more easily, implicitly and effectually to keep their people in subordination, by inculcating a belief that they were ruled with special directions from heaven, which in fact originated from the Sanhedrim. Many other nations have made use of much the same kind of policy.

In the 22d chapter of Genesis, we have a history of a very extraordinary command from God to Abraham, and of a very unnatural attempt of his to obey it. *"And it came to pass after these things that God did tempt Abraham, and he said unto him Abraham, and he said behold here I am, and he said take now thy only son Isaac, whom thou lovest, and get thee to the land of Moriah, and offer him there for a burnt offering upon one of the mountains which I will tell thee of;"* *"And they came to the place which God had told him of, and Abraham built an altar there, and laid the wood in order, and bound Isaac his son, and laid him on the altar upon the wood; and Abraham stretched forth his hand and took the knife to slay his son"* [Gen. 22:1–2, 9–10]. Shocking attempt! murder is allowed by mankind in general, to be the most capital crime that is possible to be acted among men; it would therefore be incompatible with the divine nature to have enjoined it by a positive command to Abraham to have killed his son; a murder of all others the most unnatural and cruel and attended with the most aggravating circumstances, not merely from a prescribed breach of the ties of parental affection, but from the consideration that the child was to be (if we may credit, the command)

offered to God as a religious sacrifice. What could have been a more complicated wickedness than the obedience of this command would have been? and
what can be more absurd than to suppose that it came from God? It is argued,
in vindication of the injunction to Abraham to kill his son, that it was merely
for a trial of his obedience, and that God never designed to have him do it;
to prevent which an angel from heaven called to him and gave him counter
orders, not to slay his son; but to suppose that God needed such an experiment, or any other, in order to know whether Abraham would be obedient to
his commands, is utterly incompatible with his omniscience, who, without
public exhibitions understands all things; so that had the injunction been in
itself, fit and reasonable, and also from God, the compliance or non-compliance
of Abraham thereto, could not have communicated any new idea to the divine
mind. Every part of the conduct of mankind is a trial of their obedience and
is known to God, as well as the particular conduct of Abraham; besides in the
canonical writings, we read that *"God cannot be tempted with evil, neither tempteth
he any man"* [James 1:13]. How then can it be *"that God did tempt Abraham?"*
a sort of employment which, in scripture, is commonly ascribed to the Devil.
It is a very common thing to hear Abraham extolled for attempting to comply
with the supposed command of sacrificing his son; but it appears to me, that
it had been wiser and more becoming the character of a virtuous man, for
Abraham to have replied in answer to the injunction as follows, *to wit*, that
it could not possibly have come from God; who was the fountain of goodness
and perfection, and unchangeable in his nature, who had endowed him with
reason and understanding, whereby he knew his duty to God, his son, and to
himself, better than to kill his only son, and offer him as a religious sacrifice to
God, for God would never have implanted in his mind such a strong affection
towards him, nor such a conscious sense of duty to provide for, protect and
succour him in all dangers, and to promote his happiness and well being, provided he had designed, that he should have laid violent hands on his life. And
inasmuch as the command was, in itself, morally speaking, unfit, and altogether unworthy of God, he presumed that it never originated from him, but
from some inhuman, cruel and destructive being, who delighted in wo, and
pungent grief; for God could not have been the author of so base an injunction, nor could he be pleased with so inhuman and sinful a sacrifice.

Moses in his last chapter of Deuteronomy crowns his history with the particular account of his own death and burial. *"So Moses, the servant of the Lord died there, in the land of Moab, according to the word of the Lord, and he buried him in a valley, in the land of Moab, over against Bethpeor, but no man knew of his sepulchre unto this day; and Moses was an hundred and twenty years old when he died, his eyes were not dim, nor his natural force abated, and the children of Israel wept for Moses in the plains of Moab thirty days"* [Deut. 34:5–8]. This is the only historian in the circle of my reading, who has ever given the public a particular account of his own death, and how old he was at that decisive period, where he died, who buried him, and where he was buried, and withal of the number of days his friends and acquaintances mourned and wept for him. I must confess I do not expect to be able to advise the public of the term of my life, nor the circumstances of my death and burial, nor of the days of the weeping or laughing of my survivors.

Part of the laws of Moses were arbitrary impositions upon the tribes of Israel, and have no foundation in the reason and fitness of things, particularly that in which he inculcates punishing the children for the iniquities of the father; *"visiting the iniquities of the fathers upon the children, and upon the children's children unto the third and fourth generation"* [Exod. 34:7]. There is no reason to be given, why the iniquity of the father might not as well have involved the fifth, sixth and seventh generations, and so on to the latest posterity in guilt and punishment, as the four first generations; for if it was possible, that the iniquity of the father could be justly visited upon any of his posterity, who were not accomplices with him in the iniquity; or were not some way or other aiding or accessary in it, then the iniquity might as justly be visited upon any one of the succeeding generations as upon another, or upon the generation of any indifferent person: for arbitrary imputations of iniquity are equally absurd in all supposable cases; so that if we once admit the possibility of visiting iniquity, upon any others than the perpetrators, be they who they will, we overturn our natural and scientifical notions of a personal retribution of justice among mankind. It is, in plain English, punishing the innocent for the sin of the guilty. But virtue or vice cannot be thus visited or imputed from the fathers to the unoffending children, or to children's children; or which is the same thing from the guilty to the innocent; for moral good or evil is mental and personal, which cannot be transferred, changed or altered from one person to another, but is inherently connected with its respective personal actors, and constitutes a quality or habit, and is the merit or demerit of the respective agents or proficients in moral good or evil, and is by nature unalienable, *"The righteousness of the righteous shall be upon him, and the wickedness of the wicked shall be upon him"* [Ezek. 18:20]. But as we shall have occasion to argue this matter at large in the twelfth chapter of this treatise, where we shall treat of the imputed sin of Adam to his posterity, and of imputative righteousness, we will discuss the subject of imputation no farther in this place. However, the unjust practice of punishing the children for the iniquity of the father having been an ordinance of Moses, was more or less continued by the Israelites, as in the case of Achan and his children. *"And Joshua and all Israel with him took Achan the son of Zerah, and the silver and the garment, and the wedge of gold, and his sons, and his daughters, and his oxen, and his asses, and his sheep, and his tent, and all that he had, and brought them to the valley of Achor, and all Israel stoned him with stones, and burned them with fire, after that they had stoned them with stones, and they raised over him a great heap of stones unto this day; so the Lord turned from the fierceness of his anger"* [Josh. 7:24–26]. *'Fierce anger'* is incompatible with the divine perfection, nor is the cruel extirpation of the innocent family, and live stock of Achan, to be accounted for on principles of reason. This flagrant injustice of punishing the children for the iniquity of the father had introduced a proverb in Israel, viz. *"The fathers have eaten sour grapes and the children's teeth are set on edge"* [Ezek. 18:2]. But the prophet Ezekiel in the 18th chapter of his prophecies, has confuted Moses's statutes of visiting the iniquities of the father upon the children, and repealed them with the authority of *thus saith the Lord*, which was the manner of expression by which they were promulgated. But the prophet Ezekiel did not repeal those statutes of Moses merely by the authority of *thus saith the Lord*, but over and above gives the reason for it, otherwise he could not have repealed them; for Moses enacted them as he relates, from as high authority as Ezekiel could pretend to in nullifying them; so that had he not produced reason and argument, it would have been *"thus saith the Lord,"* against *"Thus saith the Lord."* But Ezekiel reasons conclusively, viz. *"The word of the Lord came unto me again, saying what mean ye that ye use this proverb concerning the land of Israel, saying, the fathers have eaten sour grapes and the children's teeth are set on edge; as I live saith the Lord God, ye shall not have occasion any more to use this proverb in Israel. Behold all souls are mine, as the soul of the father so* *also the soul of the son is mine; the soul that sinneth it shall die, the son shall not bear* *the iniquity of the father, neither shall the father bear the iniquity of the son, the righ-* *teousness of the righteous shall be upon him, and the wickedness of the wicked shall be* *upon him, therefore, I will judge you O house of Israel, every one according to their ways* *saith the Lord God"* [Ezek. 18:1–4, 20, 30]. It is observable, that the prophet ingeniously says, *"Ye shall not have occasion any more to use this proverb in Israel,"* implicitly acknowledging that the law of Moses had given occasion to that proverb, nor was it possible to remove that proverb or grievance to which the Israelites were liable on account of visiting the iniquities of the fathers upon the children, but by the repeal of the statute of Moses in that case made and provided; which was effectually done by Ezekiel: in consequence whereof the administration of justice became disencumbered of the embarrassments under which it had laboured for many centuries. Thus it appears, that those laws, denominated the laws of God, are not infallible, but have their exceptions and may be dispensed with.

Under the dispensation of the law a breach of the Sabbath was a capital offence, *"And while the children of Israel were in the wilderness, they found a man* *that gathered sticks on the Sabbath day, and the Lord said unto Moses, the man shall* *surely be put to death, and all the congregation shall stone him with stones without* *the camp; and all the congregation brought him without the camp and stoned him with* *stones, and he died, as the Lord commanded Moses"* [Num. 15:32–36]. The very institution of the Sabbath was in itself arbitrary, otherwise it could not have been changed from the last to the first day of the week. For those ordinances which are predicated on the reason and fitness of things can never change: as that which is once morally fit, always remains so, and is immutable, nor could the same crime, in justice, deserve death in Moses's time (as in the instance of the Israelite's gathering sticks) and but a pecuniary fine in ours; as in the instance of the breach of Sabbath in these times.

Furthermore, the order of nature respecting day and night, or the succes-sion of time, is such, as renders it impossible that any identical part of time, which constitutes one day, can do it to all the inhabitants of the globe at the same time, or in the same period. Day is perpetually dawning, and night com-mencing to some or other of the inhabitants of the terraqueous ball without intermission. At the distance of fifteen degrees of longitude to the eastward of us, the day begins an hour sooner than it does with us here in Vermont, and with us an hour sooner than it does fifteen degrees to the westward, and thus it continues its succession round the globe, and night as regularly revolving after it, succeeding each other in their alternate rounds; so that when it is mid-day with us, it is mid-night with our species, denominated the *Periæci*, who live under the same parallel of latitude with us, but under a directly opposite meridian; so likewise, when it is mid-day with them, it is mid-night with us. Thus it appears, that the same identical part of time, which composes our days, compose their nights, and while we are keeping Sunday, they are in their mid-night dreams; nor is it possible in nature, that the same identical part of time, which makes the first day of the week with us, should make the first day of the week with the inhabitants on the opposite side of the globe. The apostle James speaks candidly on this subject, saying, *"Some esteem one day above another, others esteem every day alike, let every one be fully persuaded in his own mind"* [Romans 14:5], and keep the laws of the land. It was unfortunate for the Israelite who was accused of gathering sticks on the Israelitish Sabbath, that he was convicted of it; for though by the law of his people he must have died, yet the act for which he suffered was no breach of the law of nature. Supposing that very delinquent should come to this world again, and gather sticks on Saturday in this country, he might as an hireling receive his wages for it, without being exposed to a similar prosecution of that of Moses; and provided he should gather sticks on our Sunday, his wages would atone for his crime instead of his life, since modern legislators have abated the rigor of the law for which he died.

The barbarous zeal of the prophet Samuel in hewing Agag to pieces, after he was made a prisoner of war by Saul, king of Israel, could not proceed from a good spirit, nor would such cruelty be permitted towards a prisoner in any civilized nation at this day. *"And Samuel hewed Agag to pieces before the Lord in Gilgal"* [1 Sam. 15:33]. The unmanly deed seems to be mentioned with a phiz of religion, viz. that it was done before the Lord; but that cannot alter the nature of the act itself, for every act of mankind, whether good or evil, is done before the Lord, as much as Samuel's hewing Agag to pieces. The orders which Samuel gave unto Saul (as he says by the word of the Lord) to cut off the posterity of the Amalekites, and to destroy them utterly, together with the cause of God's displeasure with them, are unworthy of God as may be seen at large in the 15th chapter of the first Book of Samuel. *"Spare them not, but slay both man and woman, infant and suckling, ox and sheep, camel and ass"* [1 Sam. 15:3]. The ostensible reason for all this, was, because the ancestors of the Amalekites, as long before the days of Samuel as when the children of Israel came out of Egypt, which was near five hundred years, had ambushed and fought against Israel, in their passage from thence to the land which they afterwards inhabited. Although it appears from the history of Moses and Joshua, that Israel was going to dispossess them of their country, which is thought to be a sufficient cause of war in these days. It is true they insinuate that the Lord had given those lands to the children of Israel, yet it appears that they had to fight for it and get it by the hardest notwithstanding, as is the case with nations in these days, and ever has been since the knowledge of history.

But be the old quarrel between Israel and Amalek as it will, it cannot on any principle be supposed, the successors of those Amalekites, in the days of Samuel, could be guilty of any premised transgressions of their predecessors. The sanguinary laws of Moses did not admit of visiting the iniquities of the fathers upon the children in the line of succession, farther than to the fourth generation, but the Amalekites against whom Samuel had denounced the wrath of God, by the hand of Saul, were at a much greater remove from those their progenitors, who were charged with the crime for which they were cut off as a nation. Nor is it compatible with reason to suppose, that God ever directed either Moses or Joshua to extirpate the Canaanitish nations. *"And we took all his cities at that time, and utterly destroyed the men and the women, and the little ones of every city, we left none to remain"* [Deut. 2:34]. There is not more propriety in ascribing these cruelties to God, than those that were perpetrated by the Spaniards against the Mexican and Peruvian Indians or natives of America. Every one who dares to exercise his reason, free from bias, will readily discern, that the inhumanities exercised towards the Canaanites and Amorites, Mexicans and Peruvians, were detestably wicked, and could not be approbated by God, or by rational and good men. Undoubtedly avarice and domination were the causes of those unbounded cruelties, in which religion had as little to do as in the crusades of the holy land (so called).

The writings of the prophets abound with prodigies, strange and unnatural events. The walls of Jericho are represented to have fallen to the ground in consequence of a blast of ram's horns; Balaam's ass to speak to his master, and the prophet Elijah is said to have been carried off bodily into heaven by a chariot, in a whirlwind. Strange stories! But other scriptures tells us, *"Flesh and blood cannot inherit the kingdom of God"* [1 Cor. 15:50]. The history of the affront, which the little children of Bethel gave the prophet Elisha, his cursing them, and their destruction by the bears, has the appearance of a fable. That Elisha should be so exasperated at the children for calling him *bald head*, and telling him to *go up*, was rather a sample of ill breeding: most gentlemen would have laughed at the joke, instead of cursing them, or being instrumental in their destruction, by merciless, wild and voracious beasts. Though the children were saucy, yet a man of any considerable candor, would have made allowance for their non-age, *"for childhood and youth are vanity"* [Eccl. 11:10]. *"And he went up from thence unto Bethel, and as he was going up by the way, there came forth little children out of the city and mocked him, and said unto him, go up thou bald-head, go up thou bald-head, and he turned back and looked on them, and he cursed them in the name of the Lord, and there came forth two she bears out of the wood, and tare forty and two children of them"* [2 Kings 2:23–24]. It seems by the children's address to Elisha, that he was an old bald-headed man, and that they had heard, that his mate, Elijah, had gone up a little before; and as it was an uncommon thing for men to kite away into the air, and leave the world after that sort, it is likely that it excited a curiosity in the children to see Elisha go off with himself in the same manner, which occasioned their particular mode of speech to him, saying, *"go up bald head."* The writings of Solomon, King of Israel must needs have been foisted into the canonical volume by some means or other, for no one passage therein gives the least intimation of inspiration, or that he had any immediate dictation from God in his compositions, but on the contrary, he informs us, that he acquired his knowledge by applying himself to wisdom, *"to seek and to search out concerning all things that are done under the sun, this sore travail,"* says he, *"has God given to the sons of men to be exercised therewith"* [Eccl. 1:13]. And since Solomon never pretended to inspiration, others cannot justly claim his writings to have been any thing more than natural reasonings, for who can, with propriety, stamp his writings with divine authority, when he pretended no such thing, but to the contrary? His song of songs appears to be rather of the amorous kind, and is supposed to have been written at the time he was making love to the daughter of Pharaoh, King of Egypt, who is said to have been a princess of exquisite beauty and exceeding coy, and so captivated his affections that it made him light headed and sing about the *"joints of her thighs,"* and her *"belly"* [Song of Sol. 24:42, 7:2].

The divine legation of Moses and the prophets is rendered questionable from the consideration that they never taught the doctrine of immortality, their rewards and punishments are altogether temporary, terminating at death; they have not so much as exhibited any speculation of surviving the grave; to this is ascribed the unbelief of the Sadducees of the resurrection of the dead, or of an angel or spirit, as they strenuously adhered to the law of Moses, for they could not imagine, but that their great prophet and lawgiver would have apprised them of a state of immortality had it been true; and in this the Sadducees seem to argue with force on their position of the divine legation of Moses. For admitting the reality of man's immortality, it appears incredible to suppose, that God should have specially commissioned Moses, as his prophet and instructor to the tribes of Israel, and not withal to have instructed them in the important doctrine of a future existence.

SECTION III.

> *Dreams or visions uncertain and chimerical channel for the conveyance of Revelation; with remarks on the Communication of the Holy Ghost to the Disciples, by the prayers and laying on of the Apostles hands, with observations on the Divine Dictations of the first Promulgators of the Gospel, and an account of the elect lady, and her new sectary of Shakers.*

It appears from the writings of the prophets and apostles, that part of their revelations were communicated to them by dreams and visions, which have no other existence but in the imagination, and are defined to be "the images which appear to the mind during sleep, figuratively, a chimera, a groundless fancy or conceit, without reason." Our experience agrees with this definition, and evinces that there is no trust to be reposed in them. They are fictitious images of the mind, not under the controul of the understanding, and therefore not regarded at this day except by the credulous and superstitious, who still retain a veneration for them. But that a revelation from God to man, to be continued to the latest posterity as a divine and perfect rule of duty or law, should be communicated through such a fictitious and chimerical channel, carries with it the evident marks of deception itself, or of unintelligibleness, as appears from the vision of St. Paul. *"It is not expedient for me doubtless to glory, I will come to visions and revelations of the Lord: I knew a man in Christ above fourteen years ago, whether in the body I cannot tell, or whether out of the body I cannot tell, God knoweth such an one caught up to the third heavens. And I knew such a man, whether in the body or out of the body I cannot tell, God knoweth, how that he was caught up into Paradise and heard unspeakable words which it is not lawful for a man to utter"* [2 Cor. 12:1–4]. That God knoweth the whole affair, will not be disputed, but that we should understand it is impossible, for the apostle's account of his vision is unintelligible; it appears that he was rather in a delirium or stupor, so that he knew not whether he was in or out of the body: he says he heard *"unspeakable words,"* but this communicates no intelligence of the subject-matter of them to us; and that they *"were not lawful for a man to utter,"* but what they were, or wherein their unlawfulness to be uttered by man consisted, he does not inform us. His revelation from his own story was unspeakable and unlawful, and so he told us nothing what it was, nor does it compose any part of revelation, which is to *make known*. He is explicit as to his being caught up to the third heaven, but how he could understand that is incredible, when at the same time he knew not whether he was in the body or out of the body; and if he was in such a delirium that he did not know so domestic a matter as that, it is not to be supposed that he could be a competent judge whether he was at the first, second, third, or fourth heaven, or whether he was advanced above the surface of the earth, or not.

That the apostles in their ministry were dictated by the Holy Ghost, in the settlement of disputable doctrines, is highly questionable. *"Forasmuch as we have heard that certain, which went out from us have troubled you with words, subverting your souls, saying, ye must be circumcised and keep the law, to whom we gave no such commandment, for it seemed good to the Holy Ghost, and to us; to lay upon you no other burthen than these necessary things."* Acts 15[:24, 28]. And after having given a history of the disputations concerning circumcision, and of keeping the law of Moses, and of the result of the council, the same chapter informs us, that a contention happened so sharp between Paul and Barnabas, *"that they parted asunder the one from the other"* [Acts 15:39]. Had the Holy Ghost been the dictator of the first teachers of christianity, as individuals, there could have been no disputable doctrines or controversies, respecting the religion which they were promulgating in the world or in the manner of doing it, to be referred to a general *"council of the apostles and elders held at Jerusalem"* [Acts 15:2], for had they been directed by the Holy Ghost, there could have been no controversies among them to have referred to the council. And inasmuch as the Holy Ghost neglected them as individuals, why is it not as likely that it neglected to dictate the council held at Jerusalem or elsewhere? It seems that the Holy Ghost no otherwise directed them in their plan of religion, than by the general council of the apostles and elders, the same as all other communities are governed. *"Paul having passed through the upper coasts came to Ephesus, and finding certain disciples he said unto them have ye received the Holy Ghost since ye believed? and they said unto him we have not so much as heard whether there be any Holy Ghost; and when Paul had laid his hands upon them, the Holy Ghost came on them, and they spoke with tongues and prophesied"* [Acts 19:1–2, 6].

The spirit of God is that which constitutes the divine essence, and makes him to be what he is, but that he should be dictated, or his spirit be communicated by any acts or ceremonies of the apostles, is by no means admissible: for such exertions of the apostles, so far as they may be supposed to communicate the holy spirit to their disciples, would have made God passive in the premised act of the gift of the spirit: for it must have been either the immediate act of God or of the apostles, and if it was the immediate act of the one, it could not have been the immediate act of the other.

To suppose that the act of the gift of the spirit was the mere act of God, and at the same time the mere act of the apostles, are propositions diametrically opposed to each other, and cannot both be true. But it may be supposed that the gift of the spirit was partly the act of God and partly the act of the apostles; admitting this to have been the case the consequence would follow, that the act of the gift of the spirit was partly divine and partly human, and therefore the beneficence and glory of the grant of the gift of the spirit unto the disciples, would belong partly to God and partly to the apostles, and in an exact proportion to that which God and they may be supposed to have respectively contributed towards the marvellous act of the gift of the spirit. But that God should act in partnership with man, or share his providence and glory with him, is too absurd to demand argumentative confutation, especially in an act which immediately respects the display or exertion of the divine spirit on the spirits of men.

Such delusions have taken place in every age of the world since history has attained to any considerable degree of intelligence; nor is there at present a nation on earth, but what is more or less infatuated with delusory notions of the immediate influence of good or evil spirits on their minds. A recent instance of it appears in the Elect Lady (as she has seen fit to style herself) and her followers, called Shakers;[1] this pretended holy woman began her religious scheme at Connestaguna, in the Northwestwardly part of the state of New-York, about the year 1769, and has added a new sectary to the religious catalogue. After having instilled her tenets among the Connestagunites, and the adjacent inhabitants, she rambled into several parts of the country, promulgating her religion, and has gained a considerable number of scattering proselytes, not only in the state of New-York, but some in the New-England states. She has so wrought on the minds of her female devotees, respecting the fading nature, vanity and tempting allurements of their ornaments (which by the by are not plenty among her followers) and the deceitfulness of riches, that she has procured from them a considerable number of strings of gold beads and jewels, and amassed a small treasure; and like most sectaries engrosses the kingdom of heaven to herself and her followers, to the seclusion of all others. She gives out that her mission is immediately from heaven, that she travails in pain for her elect, and pretends to talk in seventy two unknown languages, in which she converses with those who have departed this life, and says, that there has not been a true church on earth since the apostles days until she had erected hers. That both the living and the dead must be saved in, by, and through her, and that they must confess their sins unto her and procure her pardon, or cannot be saved. That every of the human race, who have died since the apostle's time, until her church was set up, has been damned, and that they are continually making intercession to her for salvation, which is the occasion of her talking to them in those unknown tongues; and that she gathers her elect from earth and hell. She wholly refuses to give a reason for what she does or says: but says that it is the duty of mankind to believe in her, and receive her instructions, for that they are infallible.

For a time she prohibited her disciples from propagating their species, but soon after gave them ample licence, restricting them, indiscriminately, to the pale of her sanctified church, for that she needed more souls to complete the number of her elect. Among other things, she instructs those who are young and sprightly among her pupils, to practise the most wild, freakish, wanton and romantic gestures, as that of indecently stripping themselves, twirling round, extorting their features, shaking and twitching their bodies and limbs into a variety of odd and unusual ways, and many other extravagancies of external behaviour, in the practice of which they are said to be very alert even to the astonishment of spectators, having by use acquired an uncommon agility in such twirling, freakish and romantic practices. The old Lady having such an ascendancy over them as to make them believe that those extravagant actions were occasioned by the immediate power of God, it serves among them as a proof of the divinity of her doctrines.

A more particular account of this new sectary has been lately published in a pamphlet by a Mr. Rathburn, who, as he relates, was, for a time, one of her deluded disciples, but after a while apostatised from the faith, and has since announced to the world the particulars of their doctrines and conduct.[2]

Probably there never was any people or country, since the era of historical knowledge, who were more confident than they that they are acted upon by the immediate agency of the divine spirit; and as there are facts now existing in a considerable tract of country, and are notoriously known in this part of America, I take the liberty to mention them, as a knowledge of these facts, together with the concurrent testimony of the history of such deceptions in all ages and nations, might induce my countrymen to examine strictly into the claim and reality of ghostly intelligence in general.

A Memorial and Remonstrance against Religious Assessments (1784–85)

JAMES MADISON

[James Madison (1751–1836), fourth president of the United States (1809–17), was long an advocate for religious freedom. It was he who drafted and urged the passage of the First Amendment to the US Constitution and the other nine amendments that constitute the Bill of Rights. Long before that date, he assisted Thomas Jefferson in drafting the Virginia Statute for Religious Freedom, written in 1777 and passed in 1786. This statute disestablished the Church of England and prevented the state from enacting any form of religious compulsion on its citizens. While this bill was being debated, some state legislators sought to secure political support more generally to any "teachers of the Christian religion" by the imposition of a small tax on all citizens of the state. In response, Madison, in 1784–85, wrote *A Memorial and Remonstrance against Religious Assessments*, which argued that such a tax would be the harbinger of tyranny and intolerance. The entire text of the *Memorial* is presented below.]

TO THE HONORABLE THE GENERAL ASSEMBLY OF THE STATE OF VIRGINIA:

We, the subscribers, citizens of the said Commonwealth, having taken into serious consideration a bill printed by order of the last session of the General Assembly, entitled "A bill for establishing a provision for teachers of the Christian religion," and conceiving that the same, if finally armed with the sanctions of a law, will be a dangerous abuse of power, are bound, as faithful members of a free State, to remonstrate against the said bill—

Because we hold it for a "fundamental and undeniable truth," that religion, or the duty which we owe to our Creator, and the manner of discharging it, can be directed only by reason and conviction, not by force or violence. The religion, then, of every man, must be left to the conviction and conscience of every man; and it is the right of every man to exercise it as these may dictate. This right is, in its nature, an unalienable right. It is unalienable, because the opinions of men, depending only on the evidence contemplated in their own minds, cannot follow the dictates of other men: it is unalienable, also, because what is here a right towards men, is a duty towards the Creator. It is the duty of every man to render the Creator such homage, and *such only*, as he believes to be acceptable to him: this duty is precedent, both in order of time and degree of obligation, to the claims of civil society. Before any man can be considered as a member of civil society, he must be considered as a subject of the Governor of the Universe; and if a member of civil society, who enters into any subordinate association, must always do it with a reservation of his duty to the general authority, much more must every man who becomes a member of any particular civil society do it *with the saving his allegiance to the Universal Sovereign*. We maintain, therefore, that in matters of religion, no man's right is abridged by the institution of civil society; and that religion is wholly exempt from its cognizance. True it is, that no other rule exists by which any question which may divide society can be ultimately determined, but the will of the majority; but it is also true that the majority may trespass on the rights of the minority.

Because, if religion be exempt from the authority of the society at large, still less can it be subject to that of the legislative body. The latter are but the creatures and vicegerents of the former. Their jurisdiction is both derivative and limited. It is limited with regard to the co-ordinate departments; more necessarily is it limited with regard to the constituents. The preservation of a free government requires not merely that the metes and bounds which separate each department of power be universally maintained; but more especially, that neither of them be suffered to overleap the great barrier which defends the rights of the people. The rulers who are guilty of such an encroachment, exceed the commission from which they derive their authority, and are tyrants. The people who submit to it are governed by laws made neither by themselves, nor by an authority derived from them, and are slaves.

Because it is proper to take alarm at the first experiment on our liberties. We hold this prudent jealousy to be the first duty of citizens, and one of the noblest characteristics of the late Revolution. The freemen of America did not wait till usurped power had strengthened itself by exercise, and entangled the question in precedents. They saw all the consequences in the principle, and they avoided the consequences by denying the principle. We revere this lesson too much soon to forget it. Who does not see that the same authority which can establish Christianity, in exclusion of all other religions, may establish, with the same ease, any particular sect of Christians, in exclusion of all other sects? That the same authority that can force a citizen to contribute three pence only of his property for the support of only one establishment, may force him to conform to any one establishment, in all cases whatsoever?

Because the bill violates that equality which ought to be the basis of every law, and which is more indispensable in proportion as the validity or expediency of any law is more liable to be impeached. If "all men by nature are equally free and independent," all men are to be considered as entering into society on equal conditions, as relinquishing no more, and therefore retaining no less, one than another, of their rights. Above all, they are to be considered as retaining an "equal right to the free exercise of religion, according to the dictates of conscience." Whilst we assert for ourselves a freedom to embrace, to profess, and to observe, the religion which we believe to be of Divine origin, we cannot deny an equal freedom to those whose minds have not yet yielded to the evidence which has convinced us. If this freedom be abused, it is an offence against God, *not against man*: to God, therefore, *not to men*, must an account of it be rendered. As the bill violates equality by subjecting some to peculiar burdens, so it violates the same principle by granting to others peculiar exemptions. Are the Quakers and Mennonists the only sects who think compulsive support of their religions unnecessary and unwarrantable? Can their piety alone be entrusted with the care of public worship? Ought their religions to be endowed, above all others, with extraordinary privileges, by which proselytes may be enticed from all others? We think too favorably of the justice and good sense of these denominations to believe that they either covet pre-eminence over their fellow citizens, or that they will be seduced by teem from the common opposition to the measure.

Because the bill implies, either that the civil magistrate is a competent judge of truth, or that he may employ religion as an engine of civil policy. The first is an arrogant pretension, falsified by the contradictory opinions of rulers in all ages, and throughout the world; the second is an unhallowed perversion of the means of salvation.

Because the establishment proposed by the bill is not requisite for the support of the Christian religion. To say that it is, is a contradiction to the Christian religion itself; for every page of it disavows a dependence on the powers of this world: it is a contradiction to fact; for it is known that this religion both existed and flourished, not only without the support of human laws, but in spite of every opposition from them; and not only during the period of miraculous aid, but long after it had been left to its own evidence, and the ordinary care of Providence. Nay, it is a contradiction in terms; for a religion not invented by human policy must have pre-existed and been supported before it was established by human policy. It is, moreover, to weaken in those who profess this religion a pious confidence in its innate excellence, and the patronage of its Author; and to foster in those who still reject it, a suspicion that its friends are too conscious of its fallacies to trust it to its own merits.

Because experience witnesseth that ecclesiastical establishments, instead of maintaining the purity and efficacy of religion, have had a contrary operation. During almost fifteen centuries has the legal establishment of Christianity been on trial. What have been its fruits? More or less, in all places, pride and indolence in the clergy; ignorance and servility in the laiety; in both, superstition, bigotry, and persecution. Inquire of the teachers of Christianity for the ages in which it appeared in its greatest lustre; those of every sect point to the ages prior to its incorporation with civil policy. Propose a restoration of this primitive state, in which its teachers depended on the voluntary rewards of their flocks: many of them predict its downfall. On which side ought their testimony to have the greatest weight, when for, or when against their interest?

Because the establishment in question is not necessary for the support of civil government. If it be urged as necessary for the support of civil government only as it is a means of supporting religion, and if it be not necessary for the latter purpose, it cannot be necessary for the former. If religion be not within the cognizance of civil government, how can its legal establishment be said to be necessary to civil government? What influences, in fact, have ecclesiastical establishments had on civil society? In some instances they have been seen to erect a spiritual tyranny on the ruins of civil authority; in many instances they have been seen upholding the thrones of political tyranny; in no instance have they been seen the guardians of the liberties of the People. Rulers who wished to subvert the public liberty may have found an established clergy convenient auxiliaries. A just Government, instituted to secure and perpetuate it, needs them not. Such a Government will be best supported by protecting every citizen in the enjoyment of his religion, with the same equal hand that protects his person and property; by neither invading the equal rights of any sect, nor suffering any sect to invade those of another.

Because the proposed establishment is a departure from that generous policy which, offering an asylum to the persecuted and oppressed of every nation and religion, promised a lustre to our country, and an accession to the number of its citizens. What a melancholy mark is the bill, of sudden degeneracy! Instead of holding forth an asylum to the persecuted, it is itself a signal of persecution. It degrades from the equal rank of citizens all those whose opinions in religion do not bend to those of the legislative authority. Distant as it may be, in its present form, from the Inquisition, it differs only in degree. The one is the *first* step, the other the *last*, in the *career of intolerance*. The magnanimous sufferer under this cruel scourge in foreign regions, must view the bill as a beacon on our coast, warning him to seek some other haven, where liberty and philanthropy, in their due extent, may offer a more certain repose from his troubles.

Because it will have a like tendency to banish our citizens. The allurements presented by other situations are every day thinning their numbers. To superadd a fresh motive to emigration, by revoking the liberty which they now enjoy, would be the same species of folly which has dishonored and depopulated flourishing kingdoms.

Because it will destroy the moderation and harmony which the forbearance of our laws to intermeddle with religion has produced among its several sects. Torrents of blood have been spilt in the world in vain attempts of the secular arm to extinguish religious discord, by proscribing all difference in religious opinions. Time, at length, has revealed the true remedy. Every relaxation of narrow and rigorous policy, wherever it has been tried, has been found to assuage the disease. The American theatre has exhibited proofs, that equal and complete liberty, if it does not wholly eradicate it, sufficiently destroys its malignant influence on the health and prosperity of the State. If, with the salutary effects of this system under our own eyes, we begin to contract the bounds of religious freedom, we know no name that will too severely reproach our folly. At least, let warning be taken at the first fruits of the threatened innovation. The very appearance of the bill has transformed that "Christian forbearance, love, and charity," which of late mutually prevailed, into animosities and jealousies, which may not soon be appeased. What mischiefs may not be dreaded, should this enemy to the public quiet be armed with the force of a law!

Because the policy of the bill is adverse to the diffusion of the light of Christianity. The first wish of those who enjoy this precious gift ought to be, that it may be imparted to the whole race of mankind. Compare the number of those who have as yet received it, with the number still remaining under the dominion of false religions, and how small is the former! Does the policy of the bill tend to lessen the disproportion? No: it at once discourages those who are strangers to the light of Revelation from coming into the region of it: countenances, by example, the nations who continue in darkness, in shutting out those who might convey it to them. Instead of levelling, as far as possible, every obstacle to the victorious progress of truth, the bill, with an ignoble and unchristian timidity, would circumscribe it with a wall of defence against the encroachments of error.

Because attempts to enforce by legal sanctions, acts obnoxious to so great proportion of citizens, tend to enervate the laws in general, and to slacken the bands of society. If it be difficult to execute any law which is not generally deemed necessary or salutary, what must be the case where it is deemed invalid and dangerous? And what may be the effect of so striking an example of impotency in the Government on its general authority?

Because a measure of such general magnitude and delicacy ought not to be imposed, without the clearest evidence that it is called for by a majority of citizens: and no satisfactory method is yet proposed, by which the voice of the majority in this case may be determined, or its influence secured. "The people of the respective counties are, indeed, requested to signify their opinion, respecting the adoption of the bill, to the next session of Assembly;" but the representation must be made equal before the voice either of the representatives or the counties will be that of the people. Our hope is, that neither of the former will, after due consideration, espouse the dangerous principle of the bill. Should the event disappoint us, it will still leave us in full confidence that a fair appeal to the latter will reverse the sentence against our liberties.

Because, finally, "the equal right of every citizen to the free exercise of his religion, according to the dictates of conscience," is held by the same tenure with all our other rights. If we recur to its origin, it is equally the gift of nature; if we weigh its importance, it cannot be less dear to us; if we consult "the declaration of those rights which pertain to the good people of Virginia, as the basis and foundation of Government," it is enumerated with equal solemnity, or rather studied emphasis.

Either then, we must say that the will of the Legislature is the only measure of their authority, and that, in the plenitude of this authority, they may sweep away all our fundamental rights; or, that they are bound to leave this particular right untouched and sacred: either we must say that they may control the freedom of the press, may abolish the trial by jury, may swallow up the Executive and Judiciary powers of the State; nay, that they may despoil us of our right of suffrage, and erect themselves into an independent and hereditary assembly: or, we must say, that they have no authority to enact into law the bill under consideration. We, the subscribers, say that the General Assembly of this Commonwealth have no such authority; and that no effort may be omitted, on our part, against so dangerous an usurpation, we oppose to it this Remonstrance—earnestly praying, as we are in duty bound, that the SUPREME LAWGIVER OF THE UNIVERSE, by illuminating those to whom it is addressed, may, on the one hand, turn their councils from every act which affronts His holy prerogative, or violates the trust committed to them; and, on the other, guide them into every measure that may be worthy of his blessing, may redound to their own praise, and may establish more firmly the liberties of the People, and the prosperity and happiness of the Commonwealth.

From *The Age of Reason* (1794)

THOMAS PAINE

[Thomas Paine (1737–1809) was born in England, the son of a Quaker, but came to the British colonies in 1774. He immediately established himself as a leading propagandist for the American Revolution with the publication of *Common Sense* (1776). Later, on a trip to Europe, he wrote two works that embroiled him in controversy: *The Rights of Man* (1791–92), in which he urged Englishmen to overthrow the monarchy, and *The Age of Reason* (1794–96), which was taken to be the work of an atheist in its scorn of religious revelation and dogma. These works caused him to be socially ostracized upon his return to the United States, and he was denied burial in consecrated ground upon his death. In the "Conclusion" to *The Age of Reason*, presented below, Paine denounces the evils caused by "revealed religion" and makes clear his acceptance of deism.]

In the former part of THE AGE OF REASON I have spoken of the three frauds, *mystery*, *miracle*, and *prophecy*; and as I have seen nothing in any of the answers to that work that in the least affects what I have there said upon those subjects, I shall not encumber this Second Part with additions that are not necessary.

I have spoken also in the same work upon what is called *revelation*, and have shown the absurd misapplication of that term to the books of the Old Testament and the New; for certainly revelation is out of the question in reciting anything of which man has been the actor or the witness. That which man has done or seen needs no revelation to tell him he has done it or seen it; for he knows it already; nor to enable him to tell it or to write it. It is ignorance or imposition to apply the term revelation in such cases; yet the Bible and Testament[1] are classed under this fraudulent description of being all *revelation*.

Revelation, then, so far as the term has relation between God and man, can only be applied to something which God reveals of his *will* to man; but though the power of the Almighty to make such a communication is necessarily admitted, because to that power all things are possible, yet the thing so revealed (if anything ever was revealed, and which, by the bye, it is impossible to prove) is revelation to the person *only to whom it is made*. His account of it to another is not revelation; and whoever puts faith in that account, puts it in the man from whom the account comes; and that man may have been deceived, or may have dreamed it; or he may be an impostor, and may lie. There is no possible criterion whereby to judge of the truth of what he tells; for even the morality of it would be no proof of revelation. In all such cases the proper answer should be, "When it is revealed to me, I will believe it to be revelation; but it is not, and it cannot be incumbent upon me to believe it to be revelation before; neither is it proper that I should take the word of man as the word of God, and put man in the place of God." This is the manner in which I have spoken of revelation in the former part of THE AGE OF REASON, and which, whilst it reverentially admits revelation as a possible thing, because, as before said, to the Almighty all things are possible, it prevents the imposition of one man upon another, and precludes the wicked use of pretended revelation.

But though, speaking for myself, I thus admit the possibility of revelation, I totally disbelieve that the Almighty ever did communicate anything to man by any mode of speech, in any language, or by any kind of vision or appearance, or by any means which our senses are capable of receiving, otherwise than by the universal display of himself in the works of the creation, and by that repugnance we feel in ourselves to bad actions, and disposition to good ones.

The most detestable wickedness, the most horrid cruelties, and the greatest miseries that have afflicted the human race, have had their origin in this thing called revelation or revealed religion. It has been the most dishonorable belief against the character of the divinity, the most destructive to morality and the peace and happiness of man, that ever was propagated since man began to exist. It is better, far better, that we admitted, if it were possible, a thousand devils to roam at large, and to preach publicly the doctrine of devils, if there were any such, than that we permitted one such impostor and monster as Moses, Joshua, Samuel, and the Bible prophets, to come with the pretended word of God in his mouth, and have credit among us.

Whence arose all the horrid assassinations of whole nations of men, women, and infants, with which the Bible is filled, and the bloody persecutions, and tortures unto death, and religious wars, that since that time have laid Europe in blood and ashes; whence arose they but from this impious thing called revealed religion, and this monstrous belief that God has spoken to man? The lies of the Bible have been the cause of the one and the lies of the Testament of the other.

Some Christians pretend that Christianity was not established by the sword; but of what period of time do they speak? It was impossible that twelve men could begin with the sword; they had not the power; but no sooner were the professors of Christianity sufficiently powerful to employ the sword than they did so, and the stake and fagot too; and Mahomet could not do it sooner. By the same spirit that Peter cut off the ear of the high priest's servant (if the story be true) he would have cut off his head, and the head of his master, had he been able. Besides this, Christianity grounds itself originally upon the Bible, and the Bible was established altogether by the sword, and that in the worst use of it; not to terrify, but to extirpate. The Jews made no converts; they butchered all. The Bible is the sire of the Testament, and both are called the *word of God*. The Christians read both books; the ministers preach from both books; and this thing called Christianity is made up of both. It is then false to say that Christianity was not established by the sword.

The only sect that has not persecuted are the Quakers; and the only reason that can be given for it is that they are rather Deists than Christians. They do not believe much about Jesus Christ, and they call the scriptures a dead letter. Had they called them by a worse name, they had been nearer the truth.

It is incumbent on every man who reverences the character of the creator, and who wishes to lessen the catalogue of artificial miseries, and remove the cause that has sown persecution thick among mankind, to expel ideas of revealed religion as a dangerous heresy and an impious fraud. What is it that we have learned from this pretended thing called revealed religion? Nothing that is useful to man, and everything that is dishonorable to his maker. What is it that the Bible teaches us?—rapine, cruelty, and murder. What is it the

Testament teaches us?—to believe that the Almighty committed debauchery with a woman engaged to be married; and the belief of this debauchery is called faith.

As to the fragments of morality that are irregularly and thinly scattered in those books, they make no part of this pretended thing called revealed religion. They are the natural dictates of conscience, and the bonds by which society is held together, and without which it cannot exist; and are nearly the same in all religions and in all societies. The Testament teaches nothing new upon this subject, and where it attempts to exceed, it becomes mean and ridiculous. The doctrine of not retaliating injuries is much better expressed in Proverbs, which is a collection as well from the Gentiles as the Jews, than it is in the Testament. It is there said (Proverbs xxv, 21), "If thine enemy be hungry, give him bread to eat; and if he be thirsty, give him water to drink;"[2] but when it is said, as in the Testament, "If a man smite thee on the right cheek, turn to him the other also" [Matt. 5:39], it is assassinating the dignity of forbearance, and sinking man into a spaniel.

"Loving of enemies" is another dogma of feigned morality, and has besides no meaning. It is incumbent on man, as a moralist, that he does not revenge an injury; and it is equally as good in a political sense, for there is no end to retaliation; each retaliates on the other, and calls it justice; but to love in proportion to the injury, if it could be done, would be to offer a premium for crime. Besides, the word "enemies" is too vague and general to be used in a moral maxim, which ought always to be clear and defined, like a proverb. If a man be the enemy of another from mistake and prejudice, as in the case of religious opinions, and sometimes in politics, that man is different from an enemy at heart with a criminal intention; and it is incumbent upon us, and it contributes also to our own tranquillity, that we put the best construction upon a thing that it will bear. But even this erroneous motive in him makes no motive for love on the other part; and to say that we can love voluntarily, and without a motive, is morally and physically impossible.

Morality is injured by prescribing to it duties that, in the first place, are impossible to be performed, and if they could be would be productive of evil; or, as before said, be premiums for crime. The maxim of *doing as we would be done unto* does not include this strange doctrine of loving enemies; for no man expects to be loved himself for his crime or for his enmity.

Those who preach this doctrine of loving their enemies are in general the greatest persecutors, and they act consistently by so doing; for the doctrine is hypocritical, and it is natural that hypocrisy should act the reverse of what it preaches. For my own part, I disown the doctrine, and consider it as a feigned or fabulous morality; yet the man does not exist that can say I have persecuted him, or any man, or any set of men, either in the American Revolution or in the French Revolution; or that I have in any case returned evil for evil. But it is not incumbent on man to reward a bad action with a good one, or to return good for evil; and wherever it is done, it is a voluntary act, and not a duty. It is also absurd to suppose that such doctrine can make any part of a revealed religion. We imitate the moral character of the Creator by forbearing with each other, for he forbears with all; but this doctrine would imply that he loved man, not in proportion as he was good, but as he was bad.

If we consider the nature of our condition here, we must see there is no occasion for such a thing as *revealed religion*. What is it we want to know? Does not the creation, the universe we behold, preach to us the existence of an almighty power that governs and regulates the whole? And is not the evidence that this creation holds out to our senses infinitely stronger than anything we can read in a book, that any impostor might make and call the word of God? As for morality, the knowledge of it exists in every man's conscience.

Here we are. The existence of an almighty power is sufficiently demonstrated to us, though we cannot conceive, as it is impossible we should, the nature and manner of its existence. We cannot conceive how we came here ourselves, and yet we know for a fact that we are here. We must know also that the power that called us into being can, if he please and when he pleases, call us to account for the manner in which we have lived here; and therefore, without seeking any other motive for the belief, it is rational to believe that he will, for we know beforehand that he can. The probability, or even possibility, of the thing is all that we ought to know; for if we knew it as a fact, we should be the mere slaves of terror; our belief would have no merit, and our best actions no virtue.

Deism then teaches us, without the possibility of being deceived, all that is necessary or proper to be known. The creation is the Bible of the Deist.

He there reads, in the handwriting of the Creator himself, the certainty of his existence, and the immutability of his power, and all other Bibles and Testaments are to him forgeries. The probability that we may be called to account hereafter will, to a reflecting mind, have the influence of belief; for it is not our belief or disbelief that can make or unmake the fact. As this is the state we are in, and which it is proper we should be in, as free agents, it is the fool only, and not the philosopher, nor even the prudent man, that would live as if there were no God.

But the belief of a God is so weakened by being mixed with the strange fable of the Christian creed, and with the wild adventures related in the Bible, and the obscurity and obscene nonsense of the Testament, that the mind of man is bewildered as in a fog. Viewing all these things in a confused mass, he confounds fact with fable; and as he cannot believe all, he feels a disposition to reject all. But the belief of a God is a belief distinct from all other things, and ought not to be confounded with any. The notion of a trinity of gods has enfeebled the belief of one God. A multiplication of beliefs acts as a division of belief; and in proportion as anything is divided it is weakened.

Religion, by such means, becomes a thing of form instead of fact; of notion instead of principle; morality is banished to make room for an imaginary thing called faith, and this faith has its origin in a supposed debauchery; a man is preached instead of God; an execution is an object for gratitude; the preachers daub themselves with the blood, like a troop of assassins, and pretend to admire the brilliancy it gives them; they preach a humdrum sermon on the merits of the execution; then praise Jesus Christ for being executed, and condemn the Jews for doing it.

A man, by hearing all this nonsense lumped and preached together, confounds the God of the creation with the imagined God of the Christians, and lives as if there were none.

Of all the systems of religion that ever were invented, there is none more derogatory to the Almighty, more unedifying to man, more repugnant to reason, and more contradictory in itself, than this thing called Christianity. Too absurd for belief, too impossible to convince, and too inconsistent for practice, it renders the heart torpid or produces only atheists and fanatics. As an engine of power, it serves the purpose of despotism; and as a means of wealth, the avarice of priests; but so far as respects the good of man in general, it leads to nothing here or hereafter.

The only religion that has not been invented, and that has in it every evidence of divine originality, is pure and simple Deism. It must have been the first, and will probably be the last, that man believes. But pure and simple Deism does not answer the purpose of despotic governments. They cannot lay hold of religion as an engine, but by mixing it with human inventions, and making their own authority a part; neither does it answer the avarice of priests but by incorporating themselves and their functions with it, and becoming, like the government, a party in the system. It is this that forms the otherwise mysterious connection of church and state; the church human, and the state tyrannic.

Were man impressed as fully and strongly as he ought to be with the belief of a God, his moral life would be regulated by the force of that belief; he would stand in awe of God and of himself, and would not do the thing that could not be concealed from either. To give this belief the full opportunity of force, it is necessary that it act alone. This is Deism.

But when, according to the Christian trinitarian scheme, one part of God is represented by a dying man, and another part, called the Holy Ghost, by a flying pigeon, it is impossible that belief can attach itself to such wild conceits.[3]

It has been the scheme of the Christian church, and of all the other invented systems of religion, to hold man in ignorance of the Creator, as it is of government to hold him in ignorance of his rights. The systems of the one are as false as those of the other, and are calculated for mutual support. The study of theology, as it stands in Christian churches, is the study of nothing; it is founded on nothing; it rests on no principles; it proceeds by no authorities; it has no data; it can demonstrate nothing, and admits of no conclusion. Not any thing can be studied as a science without our being in possession of the principles upon which it is founded; and as this is not the case with Christian theology, it is therefore the study of nothing.

Instead, then, of studying theology, as is now done, out of the Bible and Testament, the meanings of which books are always controverted, and the authenticity of which is disproved, it is necessary that we refer to the Bible of the creation. The principles we discover there are eternal, and of divine origin; they are the foundation of all the science that exists in the world, and must be the foundation of theology.

We can know God only through his works. We cannot have a conception of any one attribute but by following some principle that leads to it. We have only a confused idea of his powers if we have not the means of comprehending something of its immensity. We can have no idea of his wisdom but by knowing the order and manner in which it acts. The principles of science lead to this knowledge; for the Creator of man is the Creator of science; and it is through that medium that man can see God, as it were, face to face.

Could a man be placed in a situation, and endowed with the power of vision, to behold at one view, and to contemplate deliberately, the structure of the universe; to mark the movements of the several planets, the cause of their varying appearances, the unerring order in which they revolve, even to the remotest comet; their connection and dependence on each other, and to know the system of laws established by the Creator that governs and regulates the whole; he would then conceive, far beyond what any church theology can teach him, the power, the wisdom, the vastness, the munificence of the Creator. He would then see that all the knowledge man has of science, and that all the mechanical arts by which he renders his situation comfortable here, are derived from that source; his mind, exalted by the scene and convinced by the fact, would increase in gratitude as it increased in knowledge; his religion or his worship would become united with his improvement as a man; any employment he followed that had connection with the principles of the creation, as everything of agriculture, of science, and of the mechanical arts has, would teach him more of God and of the gratitude he owes to him than any theological Christian sermon he now hears. Great objects inspire great thoughts; great munificence excites great gratitude; but the groveling tales and doctrines of the Bible and the Testament are fit only to excite contempt.

Though man cannot arrive, at least in this life, at the actual scene I have described, he can demonstrate it because he has a knowledge of the principles upon which the creation is constructed. We know that the greatest works can be represented in model, and that the universe can be represented by the same means. The same principles by which we measure an inch or an acre of ground will measure to millions in extent. A circle of an inch diameter has the same geometrical properties as a circle that would circumscribe the universe. The same properties of a triangle that will demonstrate upon paper the course of a ship, will do it on the ocean, and, when applied to what are called the heavenly bodies, will ascertain to a minute the time of an eclipse, though those bodies are millions of miles distant from us. This knowledge is of divine origin, and it is from the Bible of the creation that man has learned it, and not from the stupid Bible of the church that teacheth man nothing.[4]

All the knowledge man has of science and of machinery, by the aid of which his existence is rendered comfortable upon earth, and without which he would be scarcely distinguishable in appearance and condition from a common animal, comes from the great machine and structure of the universe. The constant and unwearied observations of our ancestors upon the movements and revolutions of the heavenly bodies, in what are supposed to have been the early ages of the world, have brought this knowledge upon earth. It is not Moses and the prophets, nor Jesus Christ, nor his apostles that have done it. The Almighty is the great mechanic of the creation; the first philosopher and original teacher of all science. Let us then learn to reverence our master, and not forget the labor of our ancestors.

Had we, at this day, no knowledge of machinery, and were it possible that man could have a view, as I have before described, of the structure and machinery of the universe, he would soon conceive the idea of constructing some at least of the mechanical works we now have; and the idea so conceived would progressively advance in practice. Or could a model of the universe, such as is called an orrery, be presented before him and put in motion, his mind would arrive at the same idea. Such an object and such a subject would, whilst it improved him in knowledge useful to himself as a man and a member of society, as well as entertaining, afford far better matter for impressing him with a knowledge of and a belief in the Creator, and of the reverence and gratitude that man owes to him, than the stupid texts of the Bible and the Testament, from which, be the talents of the preacher what they may, only stupid sermons can be preached. If man must preach, let him preach something that is edifying, and from the texts that are known to be true.

The Bible of the creation is inexhaustible in texts. Every part of the science, whether connected with the geometry of the universe, with the systems of animal and vegetable life, or with the properties of inanimate matter, is a text as well for devotion as for philosophy—for gratitude as for human improvement. It will perhaps be said that if such a revolution in the system of religion takes place, every preacher ought to be a philosopher. *Most certainly*; and every house of devotion a school of science.

It has been by wandering from the immutable laws of science and the light of reason, and setting up an invented thing called revealed religion, that so many wild and blasphemous conceits have been formed of the Almighty. The Jews have made him the assassin of the human species, to make room for the religion of the Jews. The Christians have made him the murderer of himself, and the founder of a new religion, to supersede and expel the Jewish religion. And to find pretense and admission for these things, they must have supposed his power or his wisdom imperfect, or his will changeable; and the changeableness of the will is the imperfection of the judgment. The philosopher knows that the laws of the Creator have never changed with respect either to the principles of science or the properties of matter. Why, then, is it to be supposed they have changed with respect to man?

I here close the subject. I have shown in all the foregoing parts of this work that the Bible and Testament are impositions and forgeries; and I leave the evidence I have produced in proof of it to be refuted, if anyone can do it; and I leave the ideas that are suggested in the conclusion of the work to rest on the mind of the reader; certain, as I am, that when opinions are free, either in matters of government or religion, truth will finally and powerfully prevail.

NOTES

INTRODUCTION

1. Alexander Pope, "Intended for Sir Isaac Newton, in Westminster Abbey" (1727).

PART 1. THE FRENCH AND GERMAN ENLIGHTENMENTS

Jean Meslier

1. King James II of England was deposed in 1688 by William of Orange, who became William III. James landed in Ireland in March 1689, but he was defeated by William III and fled to France.

Julien Offray de La Mettrie

1. François de Salignac de la Mothe-Fénelon (1651–1715), archbishop of Cambrai and author of numerous works on history and religion. Bernard Nieuwentyt (1654–1718), Dutch mathematician and author of a work attempting to demonstrate the existence of God (*L'Existence de dieu démontrée par des merveilles de la nature*, 1725). Jacques Abbadie (1654–1725), French Protestant theologian and author of the *Traité de la vérité de la religion chrétienne* (1684). William Derham (1657–1735), British theologian and author of numerous works on religion, including *Physico-Theology; or, The Demonstration of the Existence and Attributes of God, by the Works of His Creation* (1713). Jean François Paul de Gondi, cardinal de Retz (1613–1679), a leading French theologian of the period.

2. Marcello Malpighi (1628–1694), Italian physiologist and anatomist, often declared to be the founder of microscopic anatomy.

3. French Cartesian philosopher René Descartes (1596–1650) engaged in some anatomical experiments, embodied in *La Description du corps humaine* (1647). Nicolas

Malebranche (1638–1715) was chiefly known as a rationalist philosopher, but also did some experimental work in anatomy.

4. Lucilio Vanini (1585–1619), Italian freethinker who focused on medicine and astronomy. He was burned at the stake as an atheist and magician. Jacques Vallée Desbarreau (1602–1673), French author accused of being an unbeliever and a skeptic. Nicolas Boindin (1676–1751), French playwright who openly claimed to be an atheist.

5. Abraham Trembley (1700–1784), Swiss naturalist who was the first to study freshwater polyps.

6. The anti-Pyrrhonians were philosophers opposed to Pyrrhonians (skeptics). Accordingly, they believed that the works of nature supported the belief in the existence of God.

7. Bernard Lamy (1640–1715), French author of numerous works on religion, philosophy, and science.

8. Virgil, *Eclogues* 3.108.

Voltaire (François-Marie Arouet)

1. Flavius Josephus (37–100? CE) was a Romano-Jewish historian and author of *The Jewish War* (circa 75; recounting the first Jewish-Roman War of 66–73 CE) and *Jewish Antiquities* (circa 94). The latter work contains two references to Jesus, one of which (20.9.1) is regarded as authentic, the other of which (18.3.3), referring to Jesus' sentencing and execution by Pontius Pilate, is regarded as an interpolation but perhaps based on an actual mention that is now lost.

2. Hilary of Poitiers (300?–368?), bishop of Poitiers and author of an allegorical exegesis of the Gospel of Matthew, among other works.

3. "Getae" is the designation for several tribes in Thracia, in modern Bulgaria and Romania. Voltaire probably got his information from Herodotus, *Histories* 4.93–97.

4. Quoted from Montaigne's "Apology for Raymond Sebond."

5. Amestris was the wife of King Xerxes I of Persia (519–465 BCE). Voltaire's source is again Herodotus, *Histories* 7.114.

6. Luis de Páramo, *De Origine et Progressu Officii Sanctae Inquisitionis* (1598), the first work about the Inquisition. De Páramo was canon of Leon and inquisitor of Sicily from 1584 to 1605. An abstract of his work appeared in French in 1762.

7. Socinians were the followers of Faustus Socinus (1539–1604), who, among other unorthodoxies, denied the doctrine of the Trinity.

8. Clement of Alexandria, *Stromata* 3.16.

9. Voltaire apparently refers to Mark 16:16 ("He that believeth and is baptized shall be saved; but he that believeth not shall be damned"). Most biblical scholars believe that Mark 16:9–20 is a later interpolation.

10. St. Augustine discusses the doctrine of original sin in several texts, most notably in *De Civitate Dei* (413–26 CE; *The City of God*), 16.27.

11. Peter Chrysologus (380?–450?), bishop of Ravenna, did not invent the concept of limbo. It was implicit in the writings of St. Augustine but was not formally adopted by the Catholic Church until around 1300.

12. See John Milton, *Paradise Lost* 3.495–96: "Into a Limbo large and broad, since called / The Paradise of Fools, to few unknown."

Paul-Henri Thiry, Baron d'Holbach

1. See note 1 to La Mettrie's *Man a Machine*.

2. The partisans of the doctrine of the immortality of the soul reason thus: "All men desire to live forever; therefore they will live forever." Suppose the argument retorted on them: "All men naturally desire to be rich; therefore, all men will one day be rich." [Note by d'Holbach]

3. Sir Francis Bacon, "Of Death," *Essays* (1597).

4. Actually, "rehearsal for death." Plato, *Phaedo* 81a.

5. This precise quotation cannot be found in the work of Thomas Hobbes. However, he discusses causality in chapter 9 of *De Corpore* (Latin text, 1655; English text, 1656).

6. Has sufficient attention been paid to the fact that results as a necessary consequence from this reasoning, which on examination will be found to have rendered the first place entirely useless, seeing that by the number and contradiction of these various systems, let man believe whatever he may, let him follow it in the most faithful manner, still he must be ranked as an infidel, as a rebel to the Divinity, because he cannot believe in all; and those from which he dissents, by a consequence of their own creed, condemn him to the prison-house? [Note by d'Holbach]

7. If, as Christians assume, the torments of hell are to be infinite in their duration and intensity, we must conclude that man, who is a finite being, cannot suffer infinitely. God himself, in spite of the efforts he might make to punish eternally for faults that are limited by time, cannot communicate infinity to man. The same may be said of the joys of Paradise, where a finite being will no more comprehend an infinite God than he does in this world. On the other hand, if God perpetuates the existence of the damned, as Christianity teaches, he perpetuates the existence of sin, which is not very consistent with his supposed love of order. [Note by d'Holbach]

8. The idea of Divine Mercy cheers up the wicked and makes him forget Divine Justice. And indeed, these two attributes, supposed to be equally infinite in God, must counterbalance each other in such a manner that neither the one nor the other are able to act. Yet the wicked reckon upon an *immovable* God, or at least flatter themselves to escape from the effects of his justice by means of his mercy. The highwayman, who knows that sooner or later he must perish on the gallows, says that he has nothing to fear, as he will then have an opportunity of making a good end. Every Christian believes that true repentance blots out all their sins. The East Indian attributes the same virtues to the waters of the Ganges. [Note by d'Holbach]

9. It will be said that the fear of another life is a curb useful at least to restrain princes and nobles, who have no other; and that this curb, such as it is, is better than nothing. But it has been sufficiently proved that the belief in a future life does not control the actions of sovereigns. The only way to prevent sovereigns from injuring society is to make them subservient to the laws, and to prevent their ever having the right or power of enslaving and oppressing nations according to the whine or caprice of the moment. Therefore, a good political constitution, founded upon natural rights and a sound education, is the only efficient check to the malpractices of the rulers of nations. [Note by d'Holbach]

Denis Diderot

1. Esprit Flechier (1632–1710), bishop of Nimes (1687–1710) and author of numerous orations, histories, and religious works. The phrase "silence éternel" occurs in his funeral oration for Queen Maria-Theresa of Austria (1683).

2. Pope Urban VIII (1568–1644; pope, 1623–44) was the pope during the trial of Galileo by the Inquisition in 1633, during which Galileo was found guilty of propounding the heresy that the earth revolved around the sun.

3. Joseph-François-Édouard de Coursembleau, sieur de Desmahis (1723–1761), French playwright and colleague of Voltaire.

4. Jean Baptiste Massillon (1663–1742), a leading pulpit orator of his day. He delivered a celebrated sermon on the small number of the elect (based on Matt. 7:14) at the church of St. Eustache, in Paris, around 1700.

5. Louis-Antoine, comte de Bougainville (1729–1811), French explorer who colonized the Falkland Islands (1763–65) and then, in 1766–69, circumnavigated the globe, stopping at Tahiti, Samoa, New Hebrides, and elsewhere.

6. The *Golden Legend* (*Legenda aurea*) is an immensely popular collection of saints' lives written by Jacobus de Voragine around 1260.

7. See Deut. 13:6–11.

8. Maximilien de Béthune, first duke of Sully (1560–1641), Huguenot soldier and superintendent of finances under Henry IV. This precise anecdote cannot be found in Sully's *Mémoires* (1638–42).

9. See Montesquieu, *The Spirit of Laws* (1748), part 5 (books 24–25).

10. The Vaudois (or Waldensians) were a Christian sect emerging in France in the late twelfth century. The sect was declared heretical in 1215 and was vigorously persecuted. The Albigensian Crusade was launched by Pope Innocent III in 1209 to suppress Catharism, a Christian sect in Languedoc. The St. Bartholomew's Day massacre occurred on August 23, 1572, led by a Roman Catholic mob in Paris against the Huguenots. The term *Dragonnades* refers to a French policy initiated by Louis XIV in 1681 to pressure Huguenots into reconverting to Catholicism or leaving the country.

11. Louis Dufour de Longuerue (1652–1733), known as the abbé of Longuerue. Although a clergyman, he developed the reputation of being a freethinker. The comment cited by Diderot is from Longuerue's *Description de France* (1719).

12. More properly, *Os homini sublime dedit.* Ovid, *Metamorphoses* 1.85.

13. Matt. 16:18 (Vulgate).

14. John Craig (1512?–1600), Scottish minister.

15. Louis Bourdaloue (1632–1704), Jesuit and orator. His sermons were published in twelve volumes.

Immanuel Kant

1. See Gottfried Wilhelm Leibniz (1646–1716), *Theodicée* (1710).

2. Albrecht von Haller (1708–1777), Swiss anatomist, naturalist, and poet. Kant refers to his poem "Unvollkommenes Gedichte über die Ewigkeit" (1736; "Imperfect Poem on Eternity").

PART 2. THE BRITISH ENLIGHTENMENT

John Locke

1. Locke refers to Paul's statement (about himself): "I knew a man in Christ above fourteen years ago, (whether in the body, I cannot tell; or whether out of the body, I cannot tell: God knoweth;) such an one caught up to the third heaven" (2 Cor. 12:2).

2. 1. Cor. 2:9. The words *to conceive* are not in the biblical verse.

3. A common misquotation of Tertullian's *De Carne Christi* 5: *Certum est quia impossibile est* ("It is certain because it is impossible"). The point that Tertullian was

trying to make was that the resurrection of Jesus Christ is such an incredible event that it must be true, because otherwise Christians would not cite it as a tool for proselytizing. The fallacy in the argument is that, under this reasoning, any incredible event can be considered true.

Anthony Collins

1. William Chillingworth (1602–1644), author of *The Religion of Protestants* (1637), a defense of the right of the individual conscience to interpret the Bible. The quotation is from "The Answer to the Preface of *Charity Maintained*" (a work that precedes the text of *The Religion of Protestants*), sec. 26.

2. M. Tullius Cicero, *De Divinatione* 2.72. "Tully" was the archaic British name for Cicero, derived from his nomen (Tullius).

3. Horace (Q. Horatius Flaccus), *Epistles* 2.2.205–209.

4. Virgil (P. Vergilius Maro), *Georgics* 2.490–92.

5. The quotation is from *A Perswasive to an Ingenuous Tryal of Opinions in Religion* (1685), by Nicholas Clagett the Younger (1654–1727), a preacher at St. Mary's Church in Bury St. Edmunds and later archdeacon of Sudbury.

6. The Society for Propagating the Gospel in Foreign Parts was founded in 1701 by Thomas Bray.

7. Collins appears to refer to some leading clergymen of the period: Henry Sacheverell (1674–1724), a preacher at St. Saviour's, Southwark, London; Francis Atterbury (1663–1732), dean of Carlisle Cathedral, Christ Church, and Westminster; Philip Stubbs (1665–1738), archdeacon of St. Albans; Francis Higgins (1669–1728), archdeacon of Cashel; Jonathan Swift (1667–1745), dean of St. Patrick's Cathedral, Dublin. M——rns and Sm——ges are unidentified.

8. William Whiston (1667–1752), English theologian and historian. He wrote *A New Theory of the Earth* (1696), a kind of precursor to creationism maintaining that the Noachian flood was caused by a comet, as well as *Primitive Christianity Revived* (1711–12; 5 vols.).

9. Daniel Whitby (1638–1726), Anglican clergyman and author of *Paraphrase and Commentary on the New Testament* (1700).

10. Collins refers to William Carroll, *Remarks upon Mr. Clark's Sermons* (1705) and other works directed at the Anglican clergymen Samuel Clark (1675–1729) and Samuel Bold (1649–1737).

11. The reference is to John Turner (b. 1649?), *A Discourse concerning the Messias* (1685), directed at Ralph Cudworth (1617–1688), *The True Intellectual System of the Universe* (1678), a treatise derived expressly to refute atheism.

12. Samuel Johnson (1649–1703), *Notes on the Phoenix Edition of the Pastoral Letter* (1694), directed against Gilbert Burnet (1643–1715), bishop of Salisbury.

13. Arminians believed that salvation was conditioned rational faith; Calvinists believed that salvation cannot be earned or achieved.

14. Jansenists emphasized original sin and predestination, somewhat in the manner of Calvinists; Jesuits were opposed to them in emphasizing free will. Thomism is the religious philosophy associated with St. Thomas Aquinas. Molinism, named after the Jesuit theologian Luis de Molina (1535–1600), seeks to reconcile free will and divine Providence.

15. John Tillotson (1630–1694), archbishop of Canterbury (1691–94). The quotation is from sermon 130 ("Concerning the Perfection of God").

16. William King (1650–1729), archbishop of Dublin (1703–29). The quotations are from his *Divine Predestination and Fore-knowledge* (1710).

David Hume

1. The term *real presence* refers to the belief that Jesus Christ is actually present in the bread and wine of the Eucharist and is not merely a symbol. For John Tillotson, see note 15 to Anthony Collins's *A Discourse of Free-Thinking*. The reference is to Tillotson's *A Discourse against Transubstantiation* (1722).

2. Hume refers to Cato the Younger (95–46 BCE), a Roman statesman who developed a reputation for strict moral probity. The anecdote is found in Plutarch's *Life of Cato*.

3. No Indian, it is evident, could have experience that water did not freeze in cold climates. This is placing nature in a situation quite unknown to him; and it is impossible for him to tell *a priori* what will result from it. It is making a new experiment, the consequence of which is always uncertain. One may sometimes conjecture from analogy what will follow; but still this is but conjecture. And it must be confessed, that, in the present case of freezing, the event follows contrary to the rules of analogy, and is such as a rational Indian would not look for. The operations of cold upon water are not gradual, according to the degrees of cold; but whenever it comes to the freezing point, the water passes in a moment, from the utmost liquidity to perfect hardness. Such an event, therefore, may be denominated *extraordinary*, and requires a pretty strong testimony, to render it credible to people in a warm climate: But still it is not *miraculous*, nor contrary to uniform experience of the course of nature in cases where all the circumstances are the same. The inhabitants of Sumatra have always seen water fluid in their own climate, and the freezing of their rivers ought to be deemed a prodigy: But they never saw water in Muscovy [i.e., Russia] during the winter; and

therefore they cannot reasonably be positive what would there be the consequence. [Note by Hume]

4. Sometimes an event may not, in *itself*, *seem* to be contrary to the laws of nature, and yet, if it were real, it might, by reason of some circumstances, be denominated a miracle; because, in *fact*, it is contrary to these laws. Thus if a person, claiming a divine authority, should command a sick person to be well, a healthful man to fall down dead, the clouds to pour rain, the winds to blow, in short, should order many natural events, which immediately follow upon his command; these might justly be esteemed miracles, because they are really, in this case, contrary to the laws of nature. For if any suspicion remain, that the event and command concurred by accident, there is no miracle and no transgression of the laws of nature. If this suspicion be removed, there is evidently a miracle, and a transgression of these laws; because nothing can be more contrary to nature than that the voice or command of a man should have such an influence. A miracle may be accurately defined, *a transgression of a law of nature by a particular volition of the Deity, or by the interposition of some invisible agent*. A miracle may either be discoverable by men or not. This alters not its nature and essence. The raising of a house or ship into the air is a visible miracle. The raising of a feather, when the wind wants ever so little of a force requisite for that purpose, is as real a miracle, though not so sensible with regard to us. [Note by Hume]

5. For Tully, see note 2 to Anthony Collins's *A Discourse of Free-Thinking*. Demosthenes (384–322 BCE) was the most renowned orator in classical Greece.

6. The Capuchins (more properly, the Order of Capuchin Friars Minor) were an order of friars of the Roman Catholic Church established in 1520 as an offshoot of the Franciscans.

7. The reference is to Alexander the Paphlagonian (105?–170?), who claimed to be the prophet of a god he had fabricated named Glykon. He was the subject of a satirical attack by the Greek writer Lucian of Samosata (125?–180?), titled *Alexander the False Prophet*. Paphlagonia is a region in north-central Turkey.

8. Archaic English term for Mohammad, the founder of Islam.

9. *Historiae* 4.81. Suetonius gives nearly the same account in the *Life of Vespesian*. [Note by Hume]

10. Tacitus, *Historiae* 4.80.

11. For cardinal de Retz, see note 1 to La Mettrie's *Man a Machine.*.

12. Abbé Paris died in 1727. Hume apparently learned of the various "miracles" occurring around Paris's tomb from an anonymous tract, *Recueil des miracles operés au*

tombeau de monsieur de Paris diacre (1732; *Collection of the Miracles Performed at the Tomb of the Deacon, Monsieur de Paris*).

13. In the Roman civil war, the battle of Pharsalus (48 BCE), between Julius Caesar and Cn. Pompeius Magnus (Pompey), resulted in a decisive victory for Caesar; in the battle of Philippi (42 BCE), Caesar defeated Pompey's successors to gain control of the Roman Republic.

14. Apparently a reference to Juan de Mariana (1536–1624), a Spanish Jesuit priest and author of *Historiae de rebus Hispaniae* (1592; *History of Spain*).

15. More properly, *omne / humanum genus est avidum nimis auricularum* ("The entire human race is too eager for gossip" [literally, "has itching ears"]). Lucretius, *De Rerum Natura* (*On the Nature of Things*) 4.593–94.

16. Sir Francis Bacon, *Novum Organum* (1620), book 2, aphorism 29.

Jeremy Bentham and George Grote

1. In a former part of this volume, I have assimilated the God of natural religion, on the ground of his attribute of incomprehensibility, to a madman. But as this property is here asserted to belong to the superior intelligence also, it may be asked why I did not compare the divine being to him, instead of choosing a simile apparently so inappropriate. In reply to this, I must introduce a concise but satisfactory distinction.

The madman is one, incomprehensible both in the ends which he seeks and in the means which he takes to attain them—one whose desires and schemes are alike inconsistent and unfathomable. The superior genius is one, whose ends we can understand and assign perfectly, but whose means for attaining them are inexplicable—inasmuch as his fertility of invention, and originality of thought, has enabled him to combine his operations in a manner never previously witnessed.

Now both the ends which the Deity proposes, and the means by which he pursues them, are alike above the comprehension of our finite intellects. And this suffices to vindicate the propriety of my original comparison. [Note by Bentham and Grote]

2. A paraphrase of Matt. 13:12: "For whosoever hath, to him shall be given, and he shall have more abundance."

3. Archaic variant of *inquisitive*.

4. In this sense, *mortmain* refers to the inalienable possession of property by religious institutions.

5. An archaic term meaning "influencing or leading the mind or soul."

PART 3. THE AMERICAN ENLIGHTENMENT

Thomas Jefferson

1. A reference to a statute passed in the first year of the reign of Elizabeth I, Queen of England (r. 1558–1603). Future mentions of "c." in this section refer to a specific chapter with the chapter number following the abbreviation.

2. Jefferson is in error. See note 2 to Diderot's "Conversation between the Abbé Barthélemy and Diderot" (1772–73).

3. A censor of morals.

4. Peter Carr was Jefferson's nephew.

5. Jefferson admitted that this letter was written not only to emphasize the separation of church and state but also to explain "why I do not proclaim fastings and thanksgivings, as my predecessors did." Letter to Attorney General Levi Lincoln (January 1, 1802).

6. Charles Thomson (1729–1824) was secretary of the Continental Congress (1774–89) and a longtime friend of Jefferson. Thomson also prepared a new translation of the Bible from the Greek text (1808). The letter referred to may have been that of January 9, 1816, in which Jefferson states that he has made a "wee little book . . . which I call the Philosophy of Jesus" by cutting out portions of the Synoptic Gospels and pasting them in a blank book. This document is now called the *Jefferson Bible*.

7. Diodorus Siculus (1st century BCE), Greek author of a universal history treating the Egyptians, Mesopotamians, Greeks, Romans, and other peoples.

8. This is a literal translation—the light that rises from a swamp at night, probably caused by rotting organic matter; more generally, the phrase (more often in the singular, *ignis fatuus*) means "a delusion."

9. *Conversations on Chemistry* (1806), initially published anonymously but thought to be the work of either Margaret Bryan or Jane Haldimand Marcet.

Ethan Allen

1. The Shakers (a slang term for a group that calls itself the United Society of Believers in Christ's Second Appearing) are a religious sect based around the teachings of Ann Lee (1736–1784), an English-born woman who joined a group called the Shaking Quakers in 1758. She came to the British colonies in 1774 and continued to gather converts in the final decade of her life. The sect has continued to the present day, although in diminished numbers.

2. See Valentine Rathbun, *Some Brief Hints of a Religious Scheme* (Hartford, CT, 1781).

Thomas Paine

1. Paine uses the term *Bible* as a reference to the Old Testament and the term *Testament* as a reference to the New Testament.

2. According to what is called Christ's Sermon on the Mount, in the book of Matthew, where, among some good things, a great deal of this feigned morality is introduced, it is there expressly said that the doctrine of forbearance, or of not retaliating injuries, *was not any part of the doctrine of the Jews*; but as this doctrine is found in Proverbs it must, according to that statement, have been copied from the Gentiles, from whom Christ had learned it. Those men whom Jewish and Christian idolaters have abusively called heathens had much better and clearer ideas of justice and morality than are to be found in the Old Testament, so far as it is Jewish, or in the New. The answer of Solon on the question, "Which is the most perfect popular government?" has never been exceeded by any man since his time, as containing a maxim of political morality. "That," says he, "*where the least injury done to the meanest individual is considered as an insult on the whole constitution*." Solon lived about 500 B. C. [Note by Paine]

3. The book called the book of Matthew says (iii, 16) that *the Holy Ghost descended in the shape of a dove*. It might as well have said a goose; the creatures are equally harmless, and the one is as much a nonsensical lie as the other. Acts ii, 2, 3, says that it descended in a mighty *rushing wind*, in the shape of *cloven tongues*; perhaps it was cloven feet. Such absurd stuff is only fit for tales of witches and wizards. [Note by Paine]

4. The Bible-makers have undertaken to give us, in the first chapter of Genesis, an account of the creation; and in doing this they have demonstrated nothing but their ignorance. They make there to have been three days and three nights, evenings and mornings, before there was any sun; when it is the presence or absence of the sun that is the cause of day and night—and what is called his rising and setting, that of morning and evening. Besides, it is a puerile and pitiful idea to suppose the Almighty to say, "Let there be light." It is the imperative manner of speaking that a conjuror uses when he says to his cups and balls, "Presto! be gone" and most probably has been taken from it, as Moses and his rod are a conjuror and his wand. Longinus calls this expression the sublime; and by the same rule the conjuror is sublime too; for the manner of speaking is expressively and grammatically the same. When authors and critics talk of the sublime, they see not how nearly it borders on the ridiculous. The sublime of the critics, like some parts of Edmund Burke's sublime and beautiful, is like a windmill just visible in a fog, which imagination might distort into a flying mountain, or an archangel, or a flock of wild geese. [Note by Paine]

SOURCES

PART 1. THE FRENCH AND GERMAN ENLIGHTENMENTS

Jean Meslier

Meslier, Jean [and others]. *Superstition in All Ages*. Translated by Anna Knoop. New
York: Anna Knoop, 1878, pp. 316–39.

Julien Offray de La Mettrie

La Mettrie, Julien Offray de. *Man a Machine*. Translated by Gertrude Carman Bussey.
La Salle, IL: Open Court Publishing, 1912, pp. 122–28.

Étienne Bonnot de Condillac

Condillac, Étienne Bonnot de. *Oeuvres de Condillac, Volume 2: Traité des systèmes*. Paris:
Ch. Houel, 1798, pp. 57–85. [This selection translated by S. T. Joshi]

Voltaire (François-Marie Arouet)

Voltaire. *The Works of Voltaire*. Translated by Tobias Smollett. Revised by William
F. Fleming. Akron, OH: Werner, 1906, 6:105–10; 7:70–72, 75, 329–31; 8:5,
8–12; 9:219–27; 11:118–25.

Paul-Henri Thiry, Baron d'Holbach

d'Holbach, Baron, Paul-Henri Thiry. *The System of Nature*. Translated by H. D.
Robinson. 1835. Reprint, Boston: J. P. Mendum, 1868, pp. 116–29.

Denis Diderot

Diderot, Denis. *Diderot: Interpreter of Nature*. Translated by Jean Stewart and Jonathan
Kemp. New York: International Publishers, 1938, pp. 192–213.

Immanuel Kant

Kant, Immanuel. *Critique of Pure Reason*. Translated by J. M. D. Meiklejohn. London: George Bell, 1901, pp. 327–53.

PART 2. THE BRITISH ENLIGHTENMENT

John Locke

Locke, John. *An Essay concerning Human Understanding*. Edited by Alexander Campbell Fraser. Oxford: Clarendon Press, 1894, 2:415–27.

Anthony Collins

Collins, Anthony. *A Discourse of Free-Thinking*. London, 1713, pp. 32–52, 54, 55, 97–99.

David Hume

Hume, David. *An Enquiry concerning Human Understanding*. Edited by L. A. Selby-Bigge. Oxford: Clarendon Press, 1902, pp. 109–31.

Jeremy Bentham and George Grote

"Beauchamp, Philip" [i.e., Jeremy Bentham and George Grote]. *Analysis of the Influence of Natural Religion upon the Temporal Happiness of Mankind*. London: R. Carlisle, 1822, pp. 116–40.

PART 3. THE AMERICAN ENLIGHTENMENT

Thomas Jefferson

(1 & 2) *The Works of Thomas Jefferson*. Edited by Paul Leicester Ford. New York: G. P. Putnam's Sons, 1904, 4:74–82; 5:324–27.

(3, . . .) *The Writings of Thomas Jefferson*. Edited by H. A. Washington. New York: J. C. Riker, 1856, 8:113–14; 7:28–29, 164–68.

Ethan Allen

[Allen, Ethan]. *Reason, the Only Oracle of Man*. Philadelphia: Wm. Sinclair, 1784, pp. 51–68.

James Madison

Madison, James. *A Memorial and Remonstrance on the Religious Rights of Man.* Washington, DC: S. C. Ustick, 1828, pp. 3–12.

Thomas Paine

Paine, Thomas. *The Age of Reason.* New York: Truth Seeker, 1898, pp. 168–80.

BIBLIOGRAPHY

A. GENERAL WORKS

Barnett, S. J. *The Enlightenment and Religion: The Myths of Modernity*. Manchester, UK: Manchester University Press, 2003.

Byrne, James M. *Religion and the Enlightenment: From Descartes to Kant*. Louisville, KY: Westminster John Knox Press, 1997.

Curran, Mark. *Atheism, Religion and Enlightenment in Pre-Revolutionary Europe*. Woodbridge, UK: Boydell Press, 2012.

Gay, Peter. *The Enlightenment: An Interpretation*. 2 vols. New York: Knopf, 1967–69.

Haakonssen, Knut, ed. *Enlightenment and Religion: Rational Dissent in Eighteenth-Century Britain*. Cambridge: Cambridge University Press, 1996.

Holmes, David L. *The Faiths of the Founding Fathers*. Oxford: Oxford University Press, 2006.

Kors, Alan Charles, ed. *Encyclopedia of the Enlightenment*. New York: Oxford University Press, 2003.

Manuel, Frank Edward. *The Eighteenth Century Confronts the Gods*. Cambridge, MA: Harvard University Press, 1959.

Palmer, R. R. *Catholics and Unbelievers in Eighteenth Century France*. Princeton, NJ: Princeton University Press, 1939.

Savage, Ruth, ed. *Philosophy and Religion in Enlightenment Britain: New Case Studies*. Oxford: Oxford University Press, 2012.

Thomson, Ann. *Bodies of Thought: Science, Religion, and the Soul in the Early Enlightenment*. Oxford: Oxford University Press, 2008.

Young, B. W. *Religion and Enlightenment in Eighteenth-Century England: Theological Debate from Locke to Burke*. Oxford: Clarendon Press, 1998.

B. WORKS ON SPECIFIC AUTHORS

a. Jean Meslier

Meslier, Jean. *Oeuvres complètes*. Edited by Roland Desné et al. 3 vols. Paris: Éditions Anthropos, 1970–72.

————. *Testament*. Translated by Michael Shreve. Amherst, NY: Prometheus Books, 2009. [First complete English translation]

Morehouse, Andrew R. *Voltaire and Jean Meslier*. New Haven, CT: Yale University Press, 1936. Reprint, New York: AMS Press, 1973.

b. Julien Offray de La Mettrie

Thomson, Ann. *Materialism and Philosophy in the Mid-Eighteenth Century: La Mettrie's Discours préliminaire*. Geneva, Swit.: Droz, 1981.

Vartanian, Aram. *Science and Humanism in the French Enlightenment*. Charlottesville, VA: Rookwood Press, 1999.

Wellman, Kathleen Anne. *La Mettrie: Medicine, Philosophy, and Enlightenment*. Durham, NC: Duke University Press, 1992.

c. Étienne Bonnot de Condillac

Knight, Isabel F. *The Geometric Spirit: The Abbé de Condillac and the French Enlightenment*. New Haven, CT: Yale University Press, 1968.

McNiven, Ellen. *A Critical Study of Condillac's* Traité des systèmes. The Hague: Martinus Nijhoff, 1979.

d. Voltaire (François-Marie Arouet)

Florida, R. E. *Voltaire and the Socinians*. Banbury, UK: Voltaire Foundation, 1974.

Gargett, Graham. *Voltaire and Protestantism*. Oxford: Voltaire Foundation, 1980.

Schwarzbach, Bertram Eugene. *Voltaire's Old Testament Criticism*. Geneva, Swit.: Droz, 1971.

Trapnell, William H. *Voltaire and the Eucharist*. Oxford: Voltaire Foundation, 1981.

e. Paul-Henri Thiry, Baron d'Holbach

Belgrado, Anna Minerbi. *Paura e ignoranza: Studio sulla teoria della religione in d'Holbach*. Florence: L. S. Olschki, 1983.

Kors, Alan Charles. *D'Holbach's Coterie: An Enlightenment in Paris*. Princeton, NJ: Princeton University Press, 1976.

Topazio, Virgil W. *D'Holbach's Moral Philosophy: Its Background and Development.* Geneva, Swit.: Institut et Musée Voltaire, 1956.

f. Denis Diderot

Anderson, Wilda C. *Diderot's Dream.* Baltimore: Johns Hopkins University Press, 1990.

Fowler, James, ed. *New Essays on Diderot.* Cambridge: Cambridge University Press, 2011.

France, Peter. *Diderot.* Oxford: Oxford University Press, 1983.

Hobson, Marian. *Diderot and Rousseau: Networks of Enlightenment.* Oxford: Voltaire Foundation, 2011.

Schwartz, Leon. *Diderot and the Jews.* Rutherford, NJ: Fairleigh Dickinson University Press, 1980.

g. Immanuel Kant

Anderson, Pamela Sue. *Kant and Theology.* London: T. and T. Clark, 2010.

DiCenso, James. *Kant, Religion, and Politics.* Cambridge: Cambridge University Press, 2011.

Firestone, Chris L. *Kant and Theology at the Boundaries of Reason.* Farnham, UK: Ashgate, 2009.

Michalson, Gordon E. *The Historical Dimensions of a Rational Faith: The Role of History in Kant's Religious Thought.* Washington, DC: University Press of America, 1977.

———. *Kant and the Problem of God.* Oxford: Blackwell, 1999.

Palmquist, Stephen. *Kant's Critical Religion.* Aldershot, UK: Ashgate, 2000.

Ray, Matthew Alun. *Subjectivity and Irreligion: Atheism and Agnosticism in Kant, Schopenhauer and Nietzsche.* Aldershot, UK: Ashgate, 2003.

Rossi, Philip J., and Michael Wreen, eds. *Kant's Philosophy of Religion Reconsidered.* Bloomington: Indiana University Press, 1991.

h. John Locke

Marshall, John. *John Locke: Resistance, Religion, and Responsibility.* Cambridge: Cambridge University Press, 1994.

Nuovo, Victor. *Christianity, Antiquity, and Enlightenment: Interpretations of Locke.* Heidelberg, Ger.: Springer, 2011.

Rogers, G. A. J. *Locke's Enlightenment: Aspects of the Origin, Nature and Impact of His Philosophy.* Hildesheim, Ger.: G. Olms, 1998.

Wolterstorff, Nicholas. *John Locke and the Ethics of Belief.* Cambridge: Cambridge University Press, 1996.

Yolton, John W. *Locke and French Materialism*. Oxford: Clarendon Press, 1991.

i. Anthony Collins

Berman, David. "Anthony Collins and the Question of Atheism in the Early Part of the Eighteenth Century." *Proceedings of the Royal Irish Academy* 75 (1975): 85–102.

O'Higgins, James. *Anthony Collins: The Man and His Works*. The Hague: Martinus Nijhoff, 1970.

j. David Hume

Earlman, John. *Hume's Abject Failure: The Argument against Miracles*. Oxford: Oxford University Press, 2000.

Gaskin, G. C. A. *Hume's Philosophy of Religion*. Houndmills, UK: Macmillan Press, 1988.

Herdt, Jennifer A. *Religion and Faction in Hume's Moral Philosophy*. Cambridge: Cambridge University Press, 1997.

Johnson, David. *Hume, Holism, and Miracles*. Ithaca, NY: Cornell University Press, 1999.

Mounce, H. O. *Hume's Naturalism*. London: Routledge, 1999.

Owen, David. *Hume's Reason*. Oxford: Oxford University Press, 1999.

Phillips, D. Z., and Timothy Tessin, eds. *Religion and Hume's Legacy*. Houndmills, UK: Macmillan Press, 1999.

Reich, Lou. *Hume's Religious Naturalism*. Lanham, MD: University Press of America, 1998.

Tweyman, Stanley, ed. *Hume on Natural Religion*. Bristol, UK: Thoemmes Press, 1996.

Yandell, Keith E. *Hume's "Inexplicable Mystery": His Views on Religion*. Philadelphia: Temple University Press, 1990.

Yoder, Timothy S. *Hume on God: Irony, Deism and Genuine Theism*. New York: Continuum, 2008.

k. Jeremy Bentham

Blake, Kathleen. *The Pleasures of Benthamism*. Oxford: Oxford University Press, 2009.

Crimmins, James E. *Secular Utilitarianism: Social Science and the Critique of Religion in the Thought of Jeremy Bentham*. Oxford: Clarendon Press, 1990.

McKown, Delos Banning. *Behold the Antichrist: Bentham on Religion*. Amherst, NY: Prometheus Books, 2004.

l. Thomas Jefferson

Brenner, Lenni, ed. *Jefferson and Madison on Separation of Church and State*. Fort Lee, NJ: Barricade, 2004.

Foote, Henry Wilder. *The Religion of Thomas Jefferson*. Boston: Beacon Press, 1960.

Gaustad, Edwin E. *Sworn on the Altar of God: A Religious Biography of Thomas Jefferson*. Grand Rapids, MI: W. B. Eerdmans, 1996.

Sanford, Charles B. *The Religious Life of Thomas Jefferson*. Charlottesville: University Press of Virginia, 1984.

m. Ethan Allen

Jellison, Charles A. *Ethan Allen: Frontier Rebel*. Syracuse, NY: Syracuse University Press, 1969.

Randall, Willard Sterne. *Ethan Allen: His Life and Times*. New York: W. W. Norton, 2011.

n. James Madison

Brenner, Lenni, ed. *Jefferson and Madison on Separation of Church and State*. Fort Lee, NJ: Barricade, 2004.

Brookhiser, Richard. *James Madison*. New York: Basic Books, 2011.

Labunski, Richard E. *James Madison and the Struggle for the Bill of Rights*. Oxford: Oxford University Press, 2006.

Madison, James. *James Madison on Religious Liberty*. Edited by Robert S. Alley. Amherst, NY: Prometheus Books, 1985.

Willis, Garry. *James Madison*. New York: Times Books, 2002.

o. Thomas Paine

Davidson, Edward H. *Paine, Scripture, and Authority:* The Age of Reason *as Religious and Political Ideal*. Bethlehem, PA: Lehigh University Press, 1994.

Kaye, Harvey J. *Thomas Paine and the Promise of America*. New York: Hill and Wang, 2005.

INDEX